HOW *to* USE

Adobe®
Photoshop® 7

que®

201 W. 103rd Street
Indianapolis, Indiana 46290

Daniel Giordan

Feb. 17, 2004

Visually in **Full Color**

How to Use Adobe® Photoshop® 7

Copyright © 2002 by Que Publishing

International Standard Book Number: 0-7897-2770-6

Library of Congress Catalog Card Number: 2002103159

Printed in the United States of America

First Printing: May 2002

05   04   03   02   4   3   2   1

Trademarks

All terms mentioned in this book that are known to be trademarks or service marks have been appropriately capitalized. Que cannot attest to the accuracy of this information. Use of a term in this book should not be regarded as affecting the validity of any trademark or service mark.

Warning and Disclaimer

Every effort has been made to make this book as complete and as accurate as possible, but no warranty or fitness is implied. The information provided is on an "as is" basis. The author and the publisher shall have neither liability nor responsibility to any person or entity with respect to any loss or damages arising from the information contained in this book.

Acquisitions Editor
Betsy Brown

Development Editor
Alice Martina Smith

Managing Editor
Charlotte Clapp

Project Editor
Elizabeth Finney

Indexer
Chris Barrick

Proofreader
Matt Wynalda

Technical Editor
Alan Hamill

Team Coordinator
Amy Patton

Interior Designer
Nathan Clement

Cover Designers
Nathan Clement
Aren Howell

Contents at a Glance

Contents

About the Author

Daniel Giordan is an artist and designer who works as the Design Director for AOL Web Properties, coordinating the publishing designs for online properties such as Netscape, CompuServe, Mapquest, AIM, ICQ, and others. In addition to this book, he has authored three other books on Photoshop, including *Using Photoshop* and *Dynamic Photoshop*. He has written other books addressing subjects such as Dreamweaver, Kai's PowerTools, and general design subjects. Dan writes a monthly column, "Giordan on Photoshop," for *Digital Camera* magazine and is a frequent contributor to *Adobe Magazine*.

With a master's degree in fine arts, Dan also paints and works with photography while indulging an excessive interest in capturing every moment of his son's life on film.

Acknowledgments

Where do I start here? So many thanks, so little time....

Let me start by thanking everyone at Adobe for building the software application most responsible for the ongoing evolution and refinement in computer graphics. Photoshop is the world's most popular design program, nothing else even comes close.

I also want to thank Alice Martina Smith, Betsy Brown, Elizabeth Finney, and the whole team of editors and designers at Sams and Que Publishing. When I start feeling like my part of the project is overwhelming, I think about these people who are juggling details and deadlines for up to 12 different titles at a time—and all I have to worry about is what's on page 56.

Finally, I must thank God and my family for all their support. Writing this book was a huge task that consumed the overwhelming majority of my time and attention. Even when I wasn't writing, I was thinking about content, solutions, and upcoming deadlines. Although I've made every effort to keep Barb and Josh in my sights, I'm sure that my attention has slipped over the past few weeks. Thank you, Barb, for putting up with the schedule, my moods, and my absence. I thank God every day for you and Josh, and I thank Him for what He's done for all of us.

Dedication

This book is for Barb and Josh.

Tell Us What You Think!

As the reader of this book, *you* are our most important critic and commentator. We value your opinion and want to know what we're doing right, what we could do better, what areas you'd like to see us publish in, and any other words of wisdom you're willing to pass our way.

I welcome your comments. You can email or write me directly to let me know what you did or didn't like about this book—as well as what we can do to make our books stronger.

Please note that I cannot help you with technical problems related to the topic of this book, and that because of the high volume of mail I receive, I might not be able to reply to every message.

When you write, please be sure to include this book's title and author, as well as your name and phone or fax number. I will carefully review your comments and share them with the author and editors who worked on the book.

Email: **feedback@quepublishing.com**

Mail: Greg Wiegand
         Que Publishing
         201 West 103rd Street
         Indianapolis, IN 46290 USA

How to Use This Book

The Complete Visual Reference

Each part of this book consists of a series of short instructional tasks designed to help you understand the information you need to get the most out of Photoshop.

 **Click:** Click the left mouse button once.

 **Double-click:** Click the left mouse button twice in rapid succession.

 **Right-click:** Click the right mouse button once.

Selection: This circle highlights the area that is discussed in the step.

 **Keyboard:** Type information or data into the indicated location.

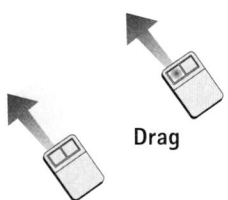
Drag
Drop

Drag & Drop: Position the mouse pointer over the object, click and hold the left mouse button, drag the object to its new location, and release the mouse button.

Each task includes a series of easy-to-understand steps designed to guide you through the procedure.

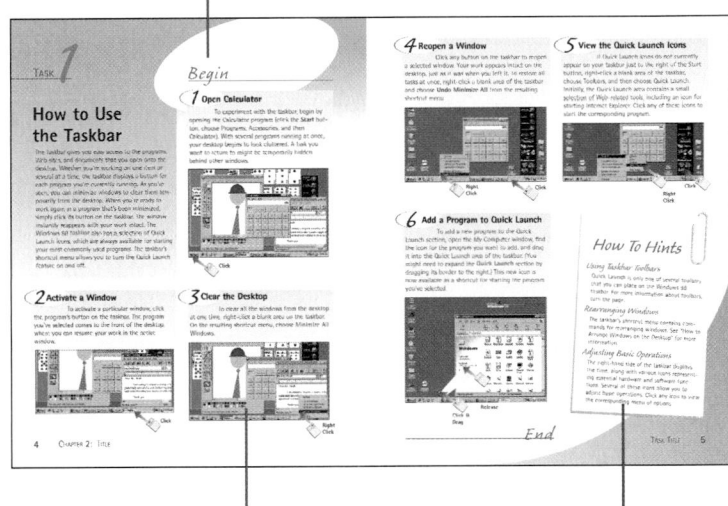

Each step is fully illustrated to show you how it looks onscreen.

Extra hints that tell you how to accomplish a goal are provided in most tasks.

Screen elements (such as menus, icons, windows, and so on), as well as things you enter or select, appear in **boldface** type.

Continues

If you see this symbol, it means that the task you're in continues on the next page.

Introduction

The history of image-editing applications should be divided into two categories: BP and AP (Before Photoshop and After Photoshop). Before Photoshop, there were various bitmap applications available, some of which were very good. There was Pixel Paint Pro, Studio 8, Digital Darkroom, and, of course, MacPaint. Like dinosaurs facing extinction, all these applications faded away after the comet called Photoshop fell to earth in the late 1980s.

I am told that Photoshop got its start as a file-conversion program at Industrial Light and Magic, the special-effects studio started by George Lucas. This was the mid-1980s, when graphics file formats were all over the map and PostScript was nonexistent. Photoshop began as an application that converted one format to another. One look at the extensive list of Photoshop's **Save As** file options, and this begins to make some sense.

One could argue that Photoshop is the most influential facilitator for the growth of digital graphics since the Macintosh. And although the Mac got us started in the mid-80s, Adobe has kept things moving forward with interface standards and cross-platform compatibility that make graphics accessible to just about every computer in the world. This universality has made Photoshop the core application driving new advances in the computer graphics world. Photoshop combines with After Effects for professional video editing, with Quark and InDesign for industry-standard page layout, and with Illustrator and FreeHand for desktop illustration. In all these instances, Photoshop sits right in the middle. Photoshop also drives the advancement of digital photography and professional Web design.

It was the boom in Web design books in the early 1990s that prompted Adobe to launch a complementary application to Photoshop called ImageReady. Although Photoshop was the creative powerhouse, ImageReady excelled in prepping images for the Web; compressing file sizes; converting colors; and building clean, concise animations. ImageReady also featured a bare-bones set of image-editing tools for basic image editing.

Because this book covers Photoshop 7, it also addresses how ImageReady 7 supports graphic design workflow and integration with Photoshop, especially where Web design is concerned. Therefore, you will see ImageReady written into some of the task instructions—and even featured in a few standalone tasks. Because of the redundant feature set created when they were separate programs, many of the tasks described for Photoshop can be executed in virtually the same way in ImageReady.

And another thing...because Adobe does such an excellent job of building cross-platform applications, you should not be concerned that all the screen shots in the book are Mac-based. Everything works the same in Windows (except for the keystrokes, which I've identified for both systems).

Whether you're working with ImageReady or Photoshop, this book is designed to get you up and running quickly, with straightforward solutions to your questions. The challenge comes from the fact that Photoshop's complexity cannot always be clearly addressed in seven steps or less. I've tried to address the details as much as I can, expounding in the How-To Hints sections and task and part openers. Although the format of this book resists long narratives and detailed explanations, a ton of solid information is still packed into the tasks that follow. I was very pleased that we were able to drill a bit deeper into some of the advanced features in this book, and I hope it helps you push things further and get the most out of Photoshop.

Task

Getting Started with Photoshop

ost people look at Photoshop as a program that has many levels of complexity. They say things such as "I probably don't use 10 percent of the program," or "I just use it to open my digital camera images." Although it's true that Photoshop has a deep level of complexity, it's also true that the program is easy for the beginner to use. This is one of the features that has made Photoshop so popular: It's easy to jump in and get started and, as your needs grow, the program grows right along with you.

The first step in getting started is to set up Photoshop to work the way you want it to work. How do you set the preferences? What about customizing the desktop or setting ruler increments? You should consider a few customizable features, as well as specific tools built into the program that can come in handy with just about any file on which you might be working.

Because Adobe is shipping ImageReady along with Photoshop 7, you also should consider how to optimize ImageReady for the way you work and familiarize yourself with how ImageReady integrates with Photoshop. ●

Welcome to Photoshop and ImageReady

This task is a basic introduction to Photoshop and ImageReady. In this task, you launch each program and evaluate the general workspace.

2 The Basic Photoshop Screen Areas

After closing the wizard, you'll see the full range of Photoshop controls arranged on your screen. The **toolbox** is on the left side of the screen and contains all the Photoshop tools. All the Photoshop **palettes** appear on the right side of the screen, and the **menu bar** appears across the top of the screen. The **Options** bar runs under the menu bar and contains the modifiers for each tool you select.

Options bar   Menu bar

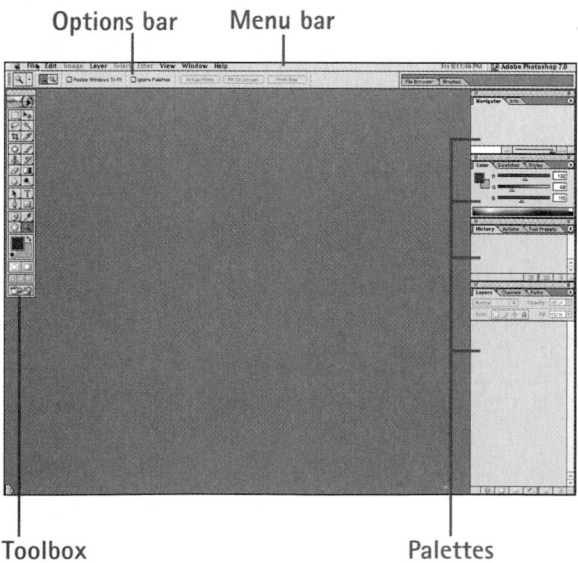

Toolbox   Palettes

Begin

1 Launch Photoshop

To launch Photoshop in Windows, click the **Start** button and choose **Programs, Adobe, Photoshop 7.0, Adobe Photoshop 7.0.** To launch Photoshop on a Mac, open the folder labeled **Adobe Photoshop 7.0** and double-click the **Adobe Photoshop 7.0** icon.

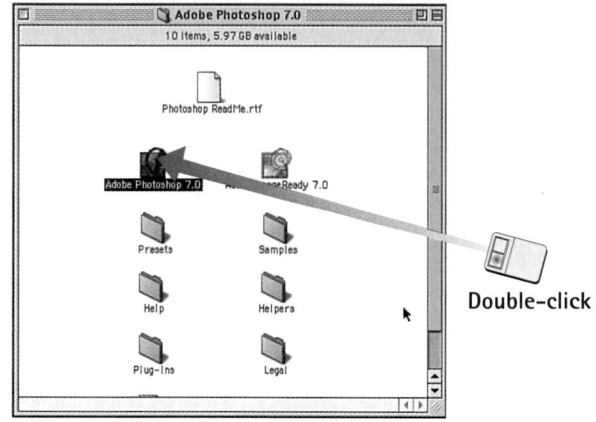

Double-click

3 Launch ImageReady

To launch ImageReady in Windows, click the **Start** button and choose **Programs, Adobe, Photoshop 7.0, Adobe ImageReady.** To launch ImageReady on a Mac, open the folder labeled **Adobe Photoshop 7.0** and double-click the **Adobe ImageReady** icon.

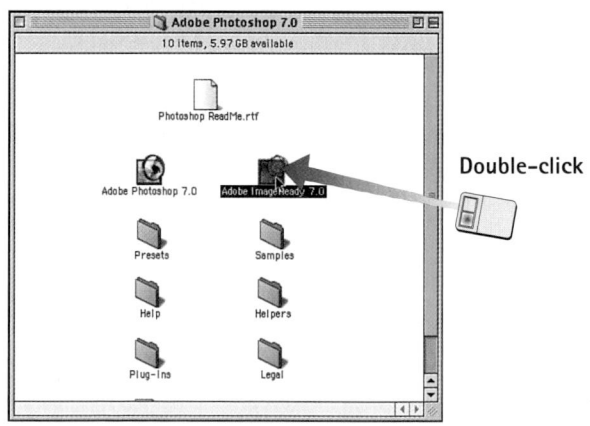

Double-click

4 The Basic ImageReady Screen Areas

You will find that the ImageReady desktop looks very similar to the Photoshop desktop. Closer examination reveals that some of the tool icons and palettes are different, and that the **Animation, Rollover, Image Map,** and **Style** palettes appear in the lower-left corner of the screen.

Options bar   Menu bar

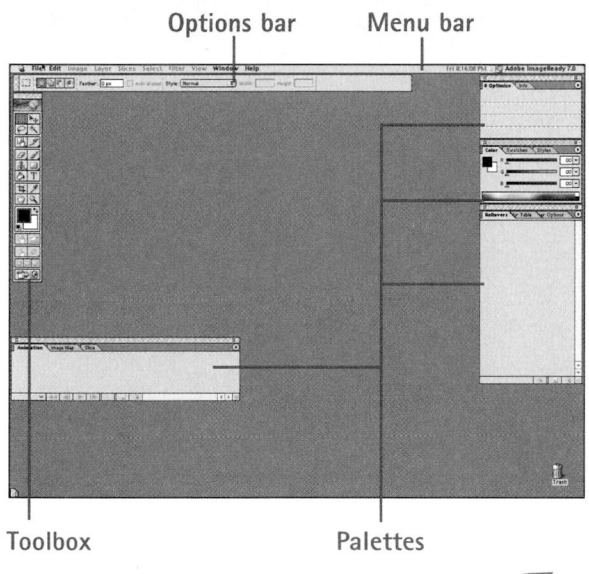

Toolbox   Palettes

End

How-To Hints

Photoshop or ImageReady?

Because the desktops for Photoshop and ImageReady look so similar, you sometimes may wonder which application you're in. A quick way to verify your location is to look at the top of the toolbox. In Photoshop, the toolbox has a graphic featuring an eye; in ImageReady, the toolbox has a compass.

Jumping from Photoshop to ImageReady

Switching from Photoshop to ImageReady is as easy as clicking the **Jump To** button at the bottom of the toolbox. If you are in Photoshop when you click this button, ImageReady opens (if you haven't already launched ImageReady, clicking the **Jump To** button does that for you). If you're in ImageReady when you click **Jump To,** Photoshop opens (and launches, if necessary). On the Mac, press ⌘+Shift+M to jump from one application to the other; in Windows, press **Ctrl+Shift+M**.

How to Use the Toolbox

Each time you launch Photoshop, the toolbox appears on the screen, usually in the upper-left corner. In the process of editing an image, you will go to the toolbox frequently to choose various selection, painting, and specialty tools. This task outlines what you'll find in the toolbox and how to access it.

Begin

1 Open the Photoshop Toolbox

The toolbox should appear automatically on the desktop, but it can be closed, which means you'll have to reopen it. To open the toolbox, choose **Window, Tools.**

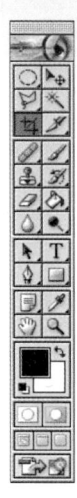

2 Select a Photoshop Tool

Click a tool to select it. If the tool button contains a small triangle in the lower-right corner, that tool offers additional tool options in a pop-out menu. Click and hold the tool button to view the pop-out menu and drag through the pop-out menu to select one of the additional tools.

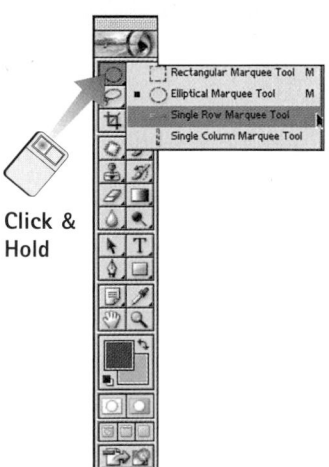

Click & Hold

3 Open the ImageReady Toolbox

The ImageReady toolbox should appear on the desktop as soon as ImageReady opens. Like its Photoshop counterpart, the ImageReady toolbox also can be closed, requiring you to reopen it. To open the toolbox in ImageReady, choose **Window, Tools.**

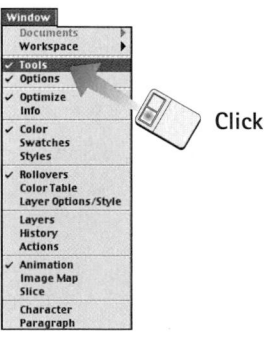

Click

4 Select an ImageReady Tool

Click a tool to select it. If the tool button contains a small triangle in the lower-right corner, that tool offers additional tool options in a pop-out menu. Click and hold the tool button to view the pop-out menu and drag through the pop-out menu to select one of the additional tools.

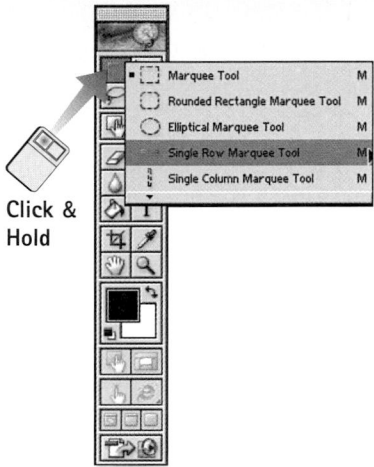

Click & Hold

5 Jump Between ImageReady and Photoshop

Click the **Jump To** button at the bottom of either the Photoshop or the ImageReady toolbox to move between Photoshop and ImageReady. This technique is especially useful when you have a file open and want to use features from both applications. You can also perform this command from a menu by selecting **File, Jump to, Photoshop/ImageReady** or by pressing ⌘**+Shift+M** (Mac users) or **Ctrl+Shift+M** (Windows users).

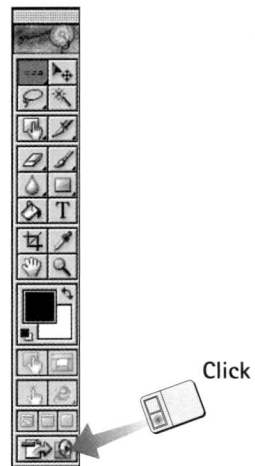

Click

End

How-To Hints

Path to Adobe Online

Click the **Adobe Online** button at the top of the toolbox (the eye icon in Photoshop or the compass icon in ImageReady) to access the **Adobe.com** Web site. Alternatively, select **Help, Adobe Online** from the menu bar.

Configuring the Jump To Button

By default, you can jump to Photoshop or ImageReady by clicking the **Jump To** button. You can access alternative graphics editors as well as HTML editors by creating a shortcut or alias to a desired application and dragging it to the following location on the Mac: **Adobe\Photoshop 7.0\Helpers\Jump To Graphics Editor**. In Windows, create the shortcut to the desired application by opening Windows Explorer, right-clicking the application's filename, and selecting **Create Shortcut** from the context menu. Then drag the shortcut to the following location: **Program Files\Adobe\Photoshop 7.0\Helpers\Jump To Graphics Editor.**

How to Use the Menu Bars

The menu bars in Photoshop and ImageReady operate like the menu bars in any other application. Click the menu name so that the menu drops down. Choose an option that has a solid right-facing arrowhead, and a submenu pops out. Choose an option that has a three-dot ellipsis (...) following it, and a dialog box opens. Click *any* option to choose it. This task looks at the grouping of the different menus to help you understand the functionality associated with each menu.

Begin

1 The Photoshop File Menu

You use the Photoshop **File** menu to address the basic opening, closing, and saving of files. This menu covers the import/export of files, workflow management and automated tasks, preferences, and color settings for the overall application as well. It also contains the **Quit** command (**Exit** in Windows) for closing down the application.

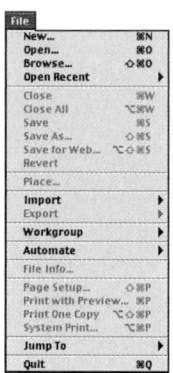

2 The Photoshop Edit and Image Menus

You use the Photoshop **Edit** and **Image** menus to specify most of the standard global changes to an open image. You'll find controls for cut and paste, as well as transformations, fill, stroke, and pattern on the **Edit** menu. On the **Image** menu, you'll find options for color mode, canvas and image size, and global color adjustments.

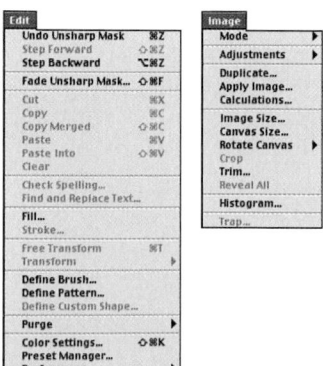

3 The Photoshop Layer Menu

The Photoshop **Layer** menu covers all your layer options—creating and deleting layers, merging, applying layer effects, and grouping. You can find most of these same controls on the **Layers** *palette menu.*

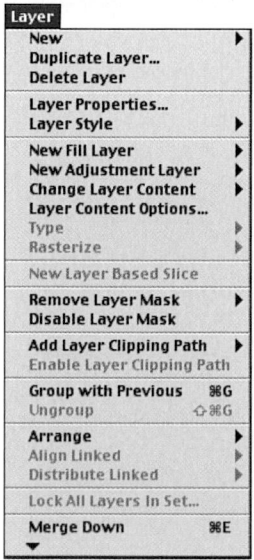

4 The Photoshop Select Menu

You use the Photoshop **Select** menu to control selection options within the program. These options include inverting selections, feathering, selection modifiers, and saving and loading selections.

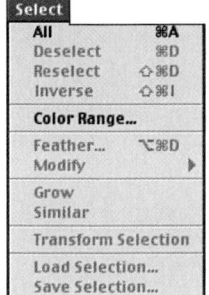

5 The Photoshop Filter Menu

Simply put, the Photoshop **Filter** menu contains all 101 of the native Photoshop filters, divided into 14 subheadings. The **Filter** menu also can include any third-party filters you may have loaded in the Photoshop plug-ins folder.

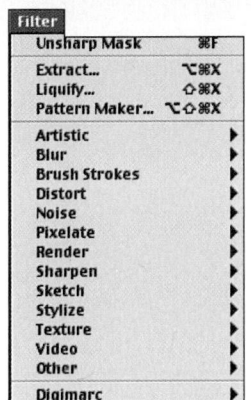

6 The Photoshop View and Window Menus

You use the **View** menu to control zooming and previews, as well as the visibility of rulers and guides. The **Window** menu lets you launch and close any of the 17 palettes. In addition, the **Window** menu lists all open file windows so that you can move a file to the front of the screen simply by choosing it from this menu.

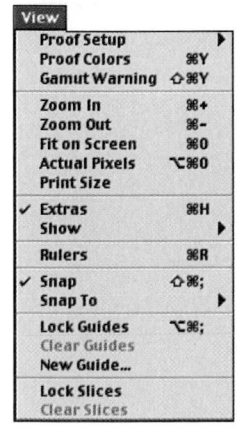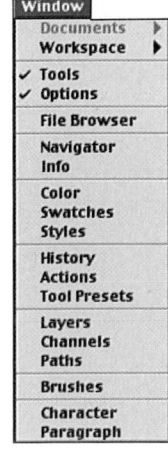

7 The Photoshop and ImageReady Help Menus

The ImageReady and Photoshop **Help** menus enable you to turn balloon help on and off (for the Macintosh), as well as to access help by topic. The Windows version of the **Help** menu offers two **About** options, which provide version information about Photoshop and plug-ins.

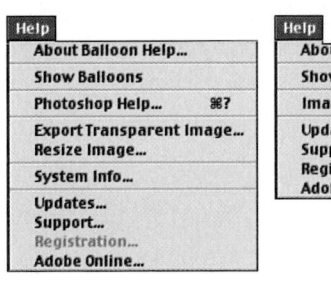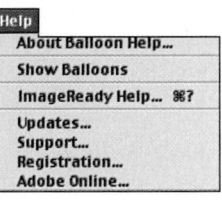

Photoshop Help
menu

ImageReady
Help menu

Continues

8 The ImageReady File Menu

You use the ImageReady **File** menu to open, close, and save files, as well as to save files optimized as GIFs or JPEGs. This menu also covers the import and export of files, HTML browser previews, and recent files. The **File** menu also contains the **Quit** command (**Exit** in Windows) for closing down the application.

9 The ImageReady Edit and Image Menus

You use the ImageReady **Edit** and **Image** menus to control most of the standard global changes to an open image. Controls for cutting and pasting image data and HTML, as well as options for transformations, fill, stroke, pattern, and setting preferences are located on the **Edit** menu. The **Image** menu is more limited than its Photoshop counterpart; it offers canvas and image size controls, as well as a few global color adjustments.

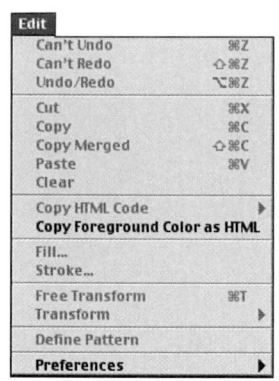
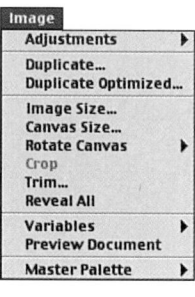

10 The ImageReady Layer Menu

The ImageReady **Layer** menu covers all your layer options—creating and deleting layers, merging, applying layer styles, and grouping. It also offers control over layer-to-imagemap conversion (from the **Layer Options** selection), slice and image-map layer creation, and precise layer placement and locking. You can find many of these same controls in the **Layers** *palette menu*.

11 The ImageReady Slices Menu

The **Slices** menu specifies the handling of image slices. A *slice* is the portion of the image when ImageReady divides an image into smaller pieces for optimization and display in an HTML table. This menu specifies how image slices are created, modified, linked, and deleted. You can also preview JavaScript rollovers and link slices and slice selections. If it has to do with slices, you'll find that option on this menu.

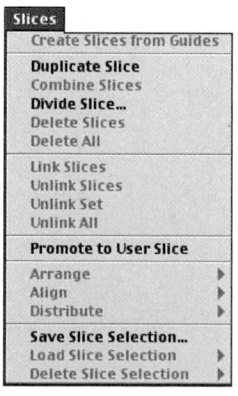

12 The ImageReady Select Menu

You use the ImageReady **Select** menu to control selection options within the program. These options include inverting selections, feathering, selection modifiers, and saving and loading selections.

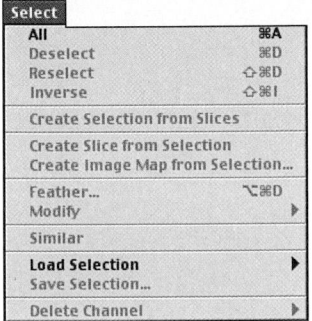

13 The ImageReady Filter Menu

The ImageReady **Filter** menu contains 81 ImageReady filters divided into 13 subheadings. This menu also includes any third-party filters you may have loaded into the plug-ins folder.

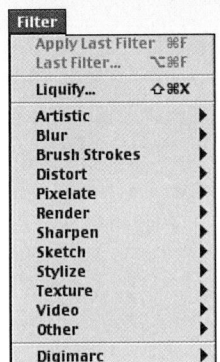

14 The ImageReady View and Window Menus

You use the **View** menu to control zooming and previews as well as the visibility of rulers and guides. The **Window** menu lets you launch and close any of the 18 ImageReady palettes. In addition, it also lists all open file windows and all the window-arrangement commands.

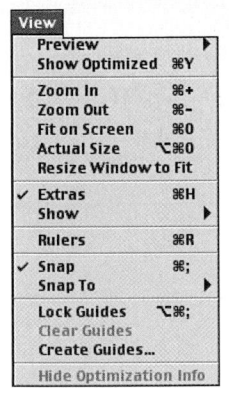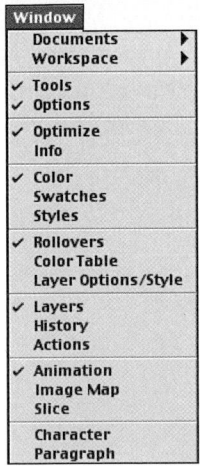

How-To Hints

Why Menus Are Grayed Out

Menu commands are *context sensitive*, meaning that they are accessible only if they can actually be used. For this reason, if a command is grayed out and unresponsive, that means you cannot use it in the given situation.

Keeping up with Photoshop Tech Support News

Adobe has made it easy to stay abreast of news, trends, and technical issues with links available from within Photoshop itself. To view the current Photoshop tech notes, select **Help, Support.** This action accesses the Adobe Web site using your modem, downloads and launches an Acrobat PDF file that contains Adobe database tech notes questions. If you have downloaded this file already, selecting the command simply opens the file from your desktop.

End

How to Use Photoshop and ImageReady Palettes

Photoshop and ImageReady use a floating palette system to group items and controls such as brushes and tool options. ImageReady uses 18 palettes; Photoshop uses 17. You can open and close palettes on demand and easily compress or expand them to optimize your workspace.

Begin

1 Examine a Group of Palettes

To open a palette in ImageReady or Photoshop, click the **Window** menu; while still holding the mouse button, choose the command related to the desired palette. To optimize your workspace, the application groups multiple palettes in a single window and separates them with tabs. If the palette you want is hidden, click its tab to bring it to the front of the window.

Multiple palettes in a single window

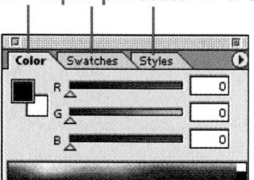

2 Collapse and Expand a Palette

To collapse or expand a palette, click the **Minimize/Maximize** button (in Windows) or the **Resize** button (on a Mac).

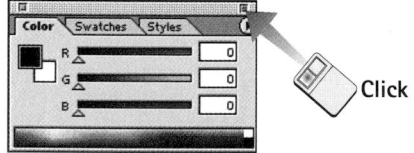
Click

3 Resize a Palette

To resize most palettes (some cannot be resized), click and drag the lower-right corner of the window. To return a palette to its default size, click the **Minimize/Maximize** button (in Windows) or the **Resize** button (on a Mac).

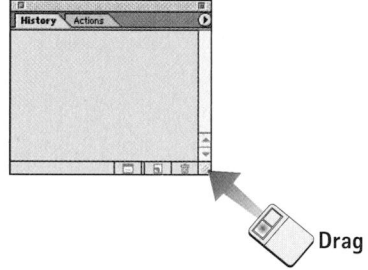
Drag

4 Tools and the Options Bar

The **Options** bar in ImageReady and Photoshop is unique in that its content varies depending on the tool selected in the toolbox. By default, the **Options** bar runs across the top of the screen, docked just below the menu bar. Should you close it, you can reopen it by choosing **Window, Options** or by double-clicking a tool in the toolbox.

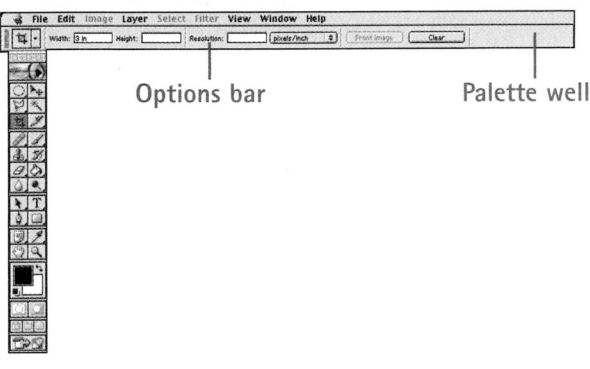

Options bar   Palette well

5 The Palette Menu

A **palette menu** lists options related to the functionality of the associated palette. To open any palette menu, click the black triangle in the upper-right corner of the palette; click again to make a selection from the list of options.

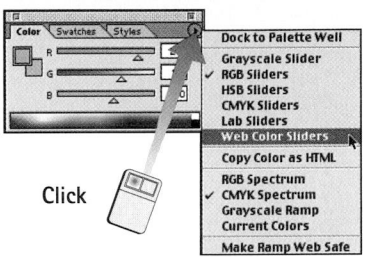

Click

6 Use the Palette Shortcut Buttons

At the bottom of some palettes are shortcut buttons for easy access to common tasks. To find out what each button does, first make sure that the **Show Tool Tips** option is selected in the **Options** section of the **General Preferences** box (choose **Edit, Preferences, General**), and then position your mouse pointer over the button to read the description. Refer to Task 9, "How to Set Photoshop Preferences," for more information.

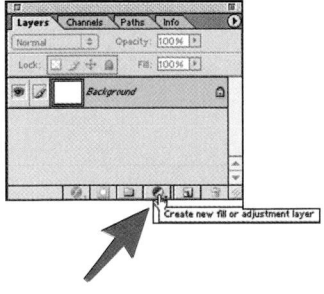

How-To Hints

Grouping Palettes

To move a palette into another palette group, click and hold the palette's tab and drag it to the target palette window. To separate a palette as a standalone window, click the tab and drag it to an empty area on the desktop. Note that the **Options** bar includes a *palette well* (the gray rectangle to the right of the bar; it is not shown in many figures in this book) that holds palettes and keeps their title tabs visible for easy access. Drag a palette to the well to add it, click once on its tab to expand or collapse it.

Palette Placement

As you open and reposition palettes, Photoshop remembers their size and where you used them last. To reset the palettes to their defaults each time you open them, choose **Edit, Preferences, General;** the **General Preferences** box opens. Disable the **Save Palette Locations** option. You must restart Photoshop before the changes take effect.

End

How to Use the Photoshop Color Picker

The Photoshop **Color Picker** is the standard Photoshop interface for selecting a color. It allows fast and intuitive color selection from millions of colors. The **Color Picker** also offers Pantone color matching and Web-safe color choices.

Begin

1 Set Color Picker Preferences

Choose **Edit, Preferences, General** to open the **Preferences** box to the **General** page. Select **Adobe** from the **Color Picker** drop-down list. Although you could select the Windows or Apple color picker, the Adobe version is the recommended choice. Click **OK** to close the dialog box.

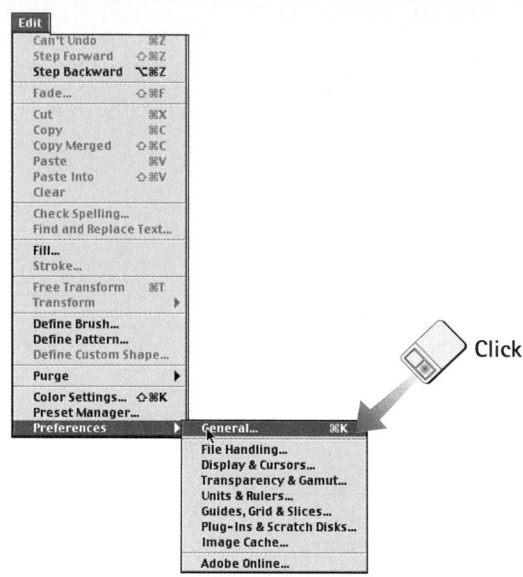

Click

2 Launch the Color Picker

In the toolbox, click the **Foreground** color swatch to launch the **Color Picker** dialog box.

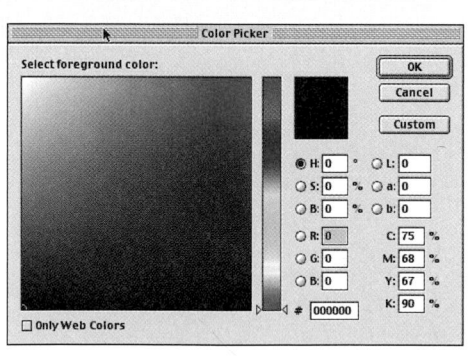

Click

3 Set the Hue

Click and drag the white triangles on the **Hue** slider to select the desired hue. As you drag, notice that the range of colors displayed in the large **Select foreground color** window changes.

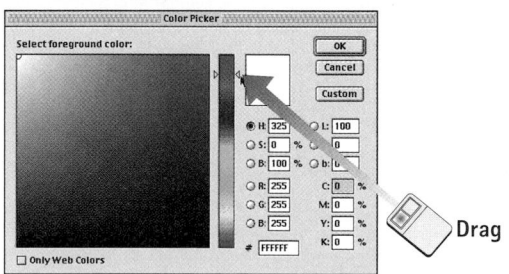

Drag

4 Select a Value

Move the cursor into the **Select foreground color** window. Notice that the cursor changes into a sample dot as you do so. Click in the color window to select a color; that color selection is reflected in the color swatch at the top right of the dialog box.

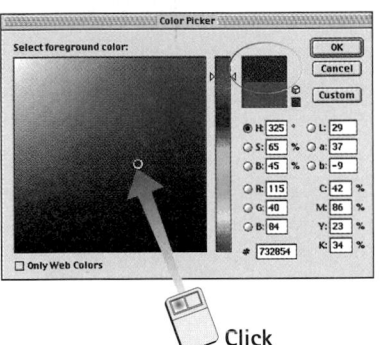

Click

5 Check the Gamut Warnings

If the color you selected falls outside the printable CMYK color gamut, a triangle with an exclamation point appears next to the selected color. The small color box that appears below the triangle indicates which color will print based on the current conversion settings. If the color you selected does not fall within the browser-safe color palette, a cube appears just below the triangle, along with another small color box that indicates the corresponding Web-safe color.

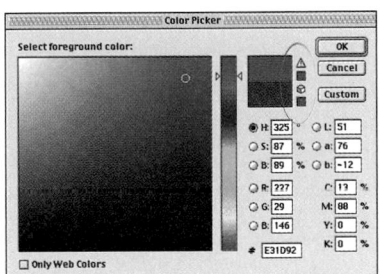

6 Select Pantone-Type Colors

In the **Color Picker,** click the **Custom** button to open the **Custom Colors** dialog box. Select a color-matching system from the **Book** drop-down list and type the color number (if you know it) or click in the color spectrum slider to select a color. Click the **Picker** button to go back to the Photoshop **Color Picker,** or click **OK** to select the color and close the color-selection dialog boxes.

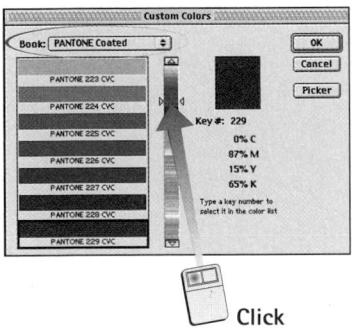

Click

End

How-To Hints

Comparing Relative Values

By default, the **Select foreground color** window in the **Color Picker** is based on a color's hue. Click in any of the other boxes (which represent Brightness, Saturation, RGB, CMYK, or Lab) to change the way color is displayed in the window. You also can enter a numerical value in any of these fields to change the current color value numerically.

Entering a Hexadecimal Color or Checking Only Web Colors

To select Web colors (colors that will display in most Web browsers), type a hexadecimal value in the **#** box at the bottom of the **Color Picker.** You also can enable the **Only Web Colors** check box, which forces the **Select foreground color** window to display only a Web-safe color range.

TASK *6*

How to Select a Color

Task 5 explained how to use the **Color Picker** to select a color. This task looks at the different ways you can specify a color in Photoshop. The methods described in this task use a combination of working with the **Color Picker,** sampling colors from images, and using preset swatches. Use the method that best suits the task at hand.

1 Select a Foreground Color

Click the **Foreground** color swatch in the toolbox to launch the **Color Picker.** Follow the steps in Task 5, "How to Use the Photoshop Color Picker," to select a color.

Click

2 Select a Background Color

Click the **Background** color swatch in the toolbox to launch the **Color Picker.** Follow the steps in Task 5 to select a color.

 Click

3 Sample a Color

Click the **Eyedropper** tool in the toolbox. Move the tool in the image over the color you want to sample and click to select the desired color. The color you select becomes the foreground color (check the color swatch in the toolbox).

Click

4 Use the Color Palette

Choose **Window, Color** to open the **Color** palette. Move the RGB sliders as necessary to "mix" the desired color; watch the color you are creating in the swatch on the left side of the palette or in the toolbox. You also can select additional color models and options from the **Color** palette menu.

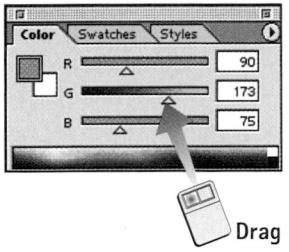

Drag

5 Use the Color Swatches

Choose **Window, Swatches** to open the **Swatches** palette, which contains an array of preset color swatches. Click the desired color to select it (it becomes the foreground color in the toolbox). To add the current foreground color as a swatch on this palette, move the pointer to an empty space on the palette until the pointer changes to the **Paint Bucket**; click to add the color as a swatch on the palette.

Click

End

How-To Hints

Color Switcher

To switch the foreground and background colors, click the **Switch Colors** button (the double-headed, curved arrow to the right of the **Foreground** color swatch in the toolbox). Alternatively, press the **X** key to switch the foreground and background colors.

Reverting to Black and White

Click the **Default Colors** button in the toolbox (the black square on top of the white square to the left of the **Background** color swatch) to reset the foreground and background colors to black and white. Alternatively, press the **D** key to set the foreground and background colors to black and white.

How to Use Rulers, Grids, and Guides

The importance of rulers and guides has grown considerably in the last few revisions of Photoshop. *Guides* are user-defined alignment lines. The *grid* is an underlying matrix of lines you can use for general alignment of all items on the page. The enhanced type features have made text-alignment issues much easier to address. In addition, designers are creating complete Web pages in Photoshop and ImageReady, which necessitates using guides and grids to maintain spacing and alignment.

Begin

1 Set Rulers Preferences

Choose **Edit, Preferences, Units & Rulers** to open the **Preferences** box to the **Units & Rulers** page. From the **Units** drop-down list, choose the desired unit of measurement and click **OK**. In this instance, you do not have to restart Photoshop for the preference change to take effect.

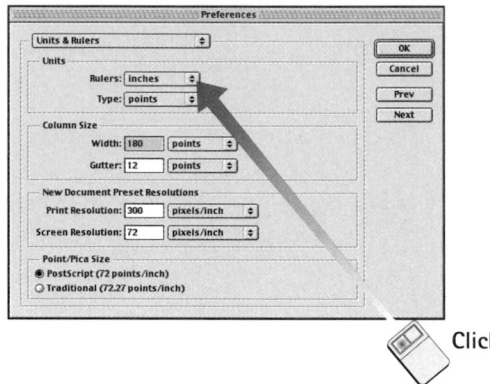

Click

2 Activate Rulers

Choose **View, Rulers** to make the rulers visible around the top and left edges of the image area.

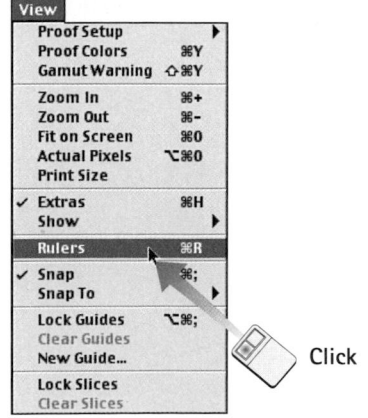

Click

3 Set Guides Preferences

Choose **Edit, Preferences, Guides, Grid & Slices** to open the **Preferences** box to the **Guides, Grid & Slices** page. Here you can specify the color and format of the guide and gridlines, as well as the spacing for the grid. Click the color swatches to select a custom color, or use the **Color** drop-down lists to select from preset colors. You can also select slice colors and toggle slice numbers on and off.

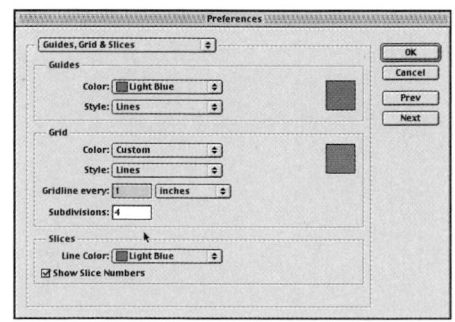

4 Create and Activate Guides

To create a guide, click the **Move** tool in the toolbox. Click in the ruler area and drag into the image area. A vertical or horizontal guide will follow the tool, depending on which ruler you started with. You can drag out as many guides as you need. You can also place a guide in a specific place by selecting **View, New Guide** and entering the orientation and pixel position in the dialog box that appears.

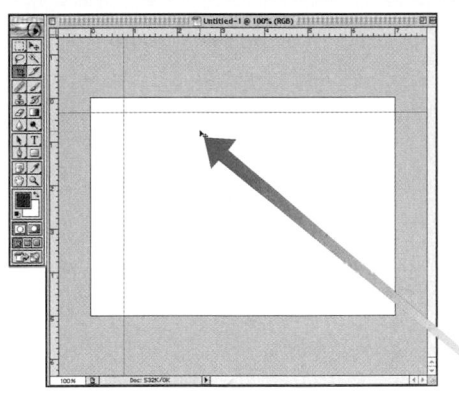

Drag

5 Set Snap-To Parameters

To precisely align elements to guides and grids as you drag the elements, choose **View, Snap To, Guides** or **View, Snap To, Grid.** Choose these commands again to turn them off.

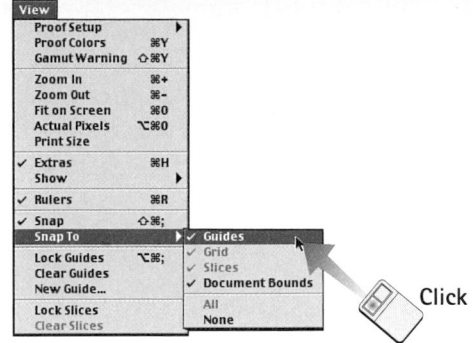

Click

6 Lock Guides as Needed

To lock the guides in place, choose **View, Lock Guides.** When you lock the guide lines, you prevent them from moving accidentally, especially when you are using numerous guides.

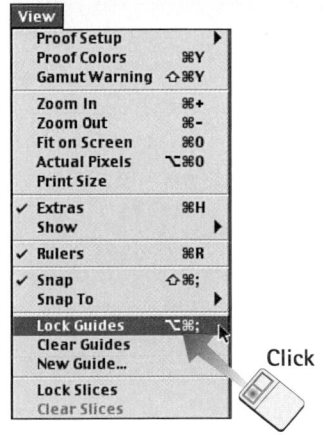

Click

End

How-To Hints

Web Measurements

When working with a Web design, set the ruler increments to pixels on the **Units & Rulers** page of the **Preferences** box. Then scroll the image against the rulers to take rough measurements of page elements. An alternative way to make quick measurements is to use the **Measure** tool to measure areas within your images.

Using Guides for Precise Text Alignment

When positioning multiple text elements or multiple lines of type, use the guides feature to ensure precise alignment.

How to Specify Photoshop Color Models

It is very important to specify how Photoshop is going to handle the color characteristics for each image file you open. These characteristics are divided between *RGB color models* (for screen viewing), *CMYK color models* (for offset printing), and *grayscale* conversions. Each model allows for a different range of color, which can dramatically impact the final design.

Choose **Edit, Color Settings** to open the **Color Settings** dialog box. You use this dialog box to set the default color spaces and color management options for all the files you open in Photoshop.

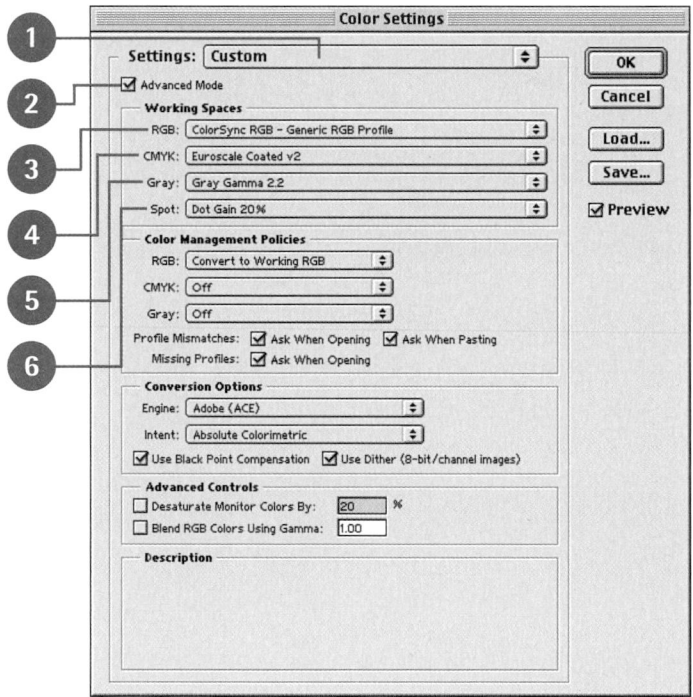

1 **Settings pop-up menu:** Click the arrow to display a list of color management presets designed for specific tasks. Use the settings presets if you are unsure how to proceed, provided that your objective fits with the predefined settings. Options are **Color Management Off, Colorsync Workflow (Mac only), Emulate Photoshop 4, Web Graphics Defaults, Photoshop 5 Default Spaces,** as well as **Europe, Japan,** and **US Prepress Defaults.** Changing any of the menu listings that follow converts this setting to **Custom.**

2 **Advanced Mode check box:** Expands the window to show advanced controls.

Working Spaces Section

3 **RGB pop-up menu:** Click the arrow to display a list of RGB working space options:

Adobe RGB (1998): Presents a wide range of colors and works well for RGB-to-CMYK color conversions. As do all RGB models, the Adobe RGB option includes colors that fall outside the CMYK color range.

Apple RGB: Based on the original Apple RGB monitor (gamma 1.8, Trinitron primaries, 6500K white point). Works well for legacy graphics files because this was the standard for older versions of Adobe Photoshop and Illustrator.

ColorMatch RGB: Matches the color space of Radius Pressview monitors. This option should be used when working within that workflow environment.

SRGB IEC61966-2.1: Matches the native color range for most PC monitors and is becoming standard for many scanners, printers, and software applications. This option is ideal for Web work, but its small color range will cause problems for print production.

Monitor Profiles: If you have loaded a monitor profile for your current monitor, you may see a profile option for it in the **RGB** list. In this case, Photoshop acts as though all color management were turned off. This option should be used only if other applications in your workflow do not support color management.

Color Management Profiles: If other color management options are loaded on your system (such as **ColorSync RGB**), you may see profiles for them listed in the **RGB** list. The profiles you see listed usually reflect the current settings for each option.

4 **CMYK pop-up menu:** Click the arrow to display a list of CMYK color spaces—from generic to industry-standard and custom settings. Choose from the **Custom, Load,** or **Save CMYK, Euroscale, Japan,** and **US Prepress** options. Check with your printer if you're unsure which setting to use.

5 **Gray pop-up menu:** This option specifies how grayscale images are displayed. Options reflect dot gain percentages (10%–30%), 1.8 Gamma (Mac), and 2.2 Gamma (PC). Use dot gain percentages if you're going send the image to offset printing, as dictated by your printer.

6 **Spot pop-up menu:** This option specifies how spot color channels and duotones are displayed. Options reflect dot gain percentages (10%–30%).

Continues →

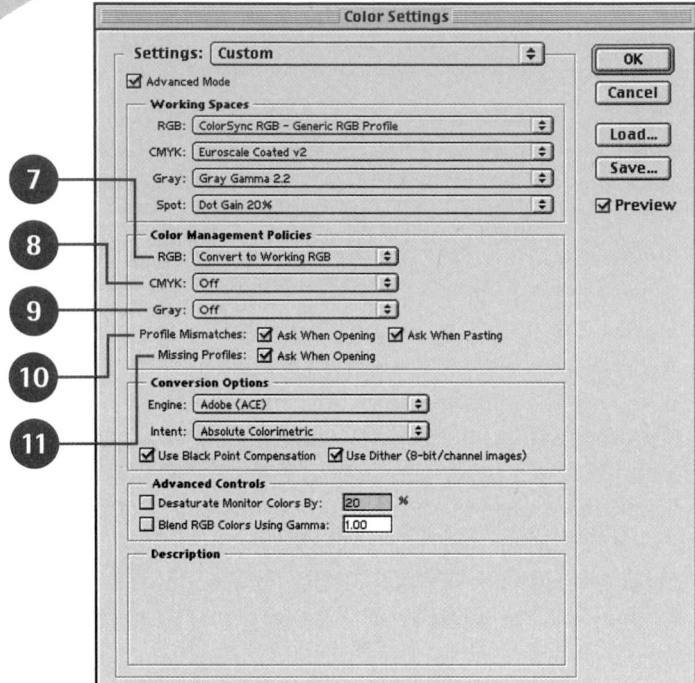

Color Management Policies Section

7 **RGB pop-up menu:** Specifies mapping between different RGB color spaces, as may occur with embedded profile conflicts and the moving of profiles between multiple documents. Options include the following:

> **Off:** Turns off color management when you are opening files or creating new files. In the case of mismatches between the working space and the embedded profile, the working space color model is used.

> **Preserve Embedded Profiles:** Gives precedence to embedded profiles when you are opening files or creating new files. In the case of mismatches between the working space and the embedded profile, the embedded profile is used.

> **Convert to Working RGB:** Gives precedence to the current RGB working space when you are opening files or creating new files. In the case of mismatches between the working space and the embedded profile, the working space color model is used.

8 **CMYK pop-up menu:** Specifies mapping between different CMYK color spaces, as may occur with embedded profile conflicts and the moving of profiles between multiple documents. Options include the following:

Off: Turns off color management when you are opening files or creating new files. In the case of mismatches between the working space and the embedded profile, the working space color model is used.

Preserve Embedded Profiles: Gives precedence to embedded profiles when you are opening files or creating new files. In the case of mismatches between the working space and the embedded profile, the embedded profile is used.

Convert to Working CMYK: Gives precedence to the current working space when you are opening files or creating new files. In the case of mismatches between the working space and the embedded profile, the working space color model is used.

9 **Gray pop-up menu:** Specifies mapping between different grayscale images, as may occur with embedded profile conflicts and the moving of profiles between multiple documents. Options include the following:

Off: Turns off color management when you are opening files or creating new files. In the case of mismatches between the working space and the embedded profile, the working space color model is used.

Preserve Embedded Profiles: Gives precedence to embedded profiles when you are opening files or creating new files. In the case of mismatches between the working space and the embedded profile, the embedded profile is used.

Convert to Working Gray: Gives precedence to the current working space when opening files or creating new files. In the case of mismatches between the working space and the embedded profile, the working space color model is used.

10 **Profile Mismatches check boxes:** Specify when you should be notified about profile conflicts. The **Ask When Opening** check box notifies you of mismatches as a file is opened and offers the option of overriding the embedded profile in favor of the current working space. The **Ask When Pasting** check box notifies you of mismatches when image data is brought into an existing file, as would occur through pasting, drag-and-drop, or importing.

11 **Missing Profiles Ask When Opening check box:** When you are opening a file, this option notifies you that there are no associated profiles and allows you to select one. Requires the related profile option to be turned on.

Continues

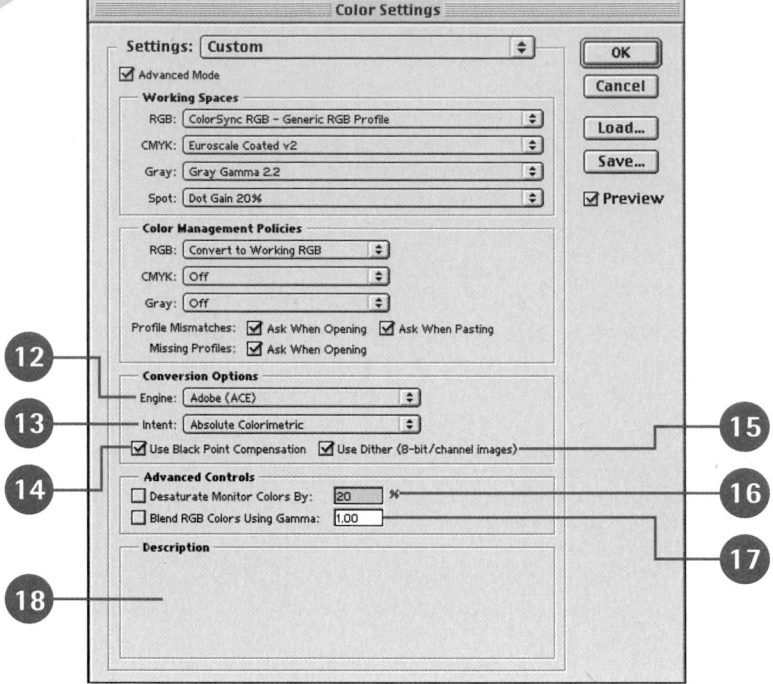

Conversion Options Section

If the **Advanced Mode** check box at the top of the dialog box is enabled, the following options are available:

12 **Engine pop-up menu:** Specifies the color management system or method to be used when converting between color spaces. Options include the following:

>**Adobe (ACE):** The Adobe Color Management System and Color Engine. Adobe recommends this option for most users.

>**Apple ColorSync (Mac only):** Uses the Apple ColorSync color management and matching system, including associated hardware or software profiles.

>**Apple CMM (Mac only):** Uses the Apple ColorSync color management system and the CMM color matching system.

>**Heidelberg CMM (Mac only):** Uses the Apple ColorSync color management system and the Heidelberg CMM color matching system.

>**Kodak ColorSyncTM 2.0 compatible (Mac only):** Uses the Apple ColorSync color management system and the Kodak ColorSync color matching system.

>**Color Management Profiles (Mac only):** If other color management options are loaded on your system, such as ColorSync RGB, the **Engine** menu may list these profile options. The profiles you see listed usually reflect the current settings for each option.

>**Microsoft ICM (Windows only)** Uses the Microsoft Windows color matching system.

13 **Intent pop-up menu:** Controls the method for mapping one color space into another. Options include the following:

Perceptual: Attempts to preserve the relative visual relationships between colors. This option works well with wide gamut images where exact color matching is not critical but a natural color space is desired.

Saturation: Requests high color saturation and bright colors. This option is good for business graphics or dynamic color effects.

Relative Colorimetric: Attempts to replicate the white point of the source file to the white point of the destination image. This option works well when the color range of both images is within the working color space.

Absolute Colorimetric: Does a direct match of source and destination images, without adjusting the white point. This option should be used when the exact match of a specific color is required (as with a logo). Colors outside the working color space will be flattened, and all contrast within these areas will be lost.

(14) Use Black Point Compensation check box: Maps the black point as well as the white point when either of the colorimetric **Intent** options are selected. Selecting this check box ensures that the full color range of the working space is optimized.

(15) Use Dither (8 bit/channel images) check box: Uses a color dithering method to specify colors when converting between color spaces. This option reduces banding but increases file size.

Advanced Controls Section

(16) Desaturate Monitor Colors By check box and field: Allows you to desaturate colors by a prescribed percentage. This is a good option to use if you're trying to view an image with a color range that's larger than that of the current monitor.

(17) Blend RGB Colors Using Gamma check box and field: Allows image colors to be created and combined using a specified gamma value. Gamma 1.0 is considered to be the most accurate with the sharpest detail. This option overrides any existing color spaces and is similar to the basic color controls used by other applications. The only reason I can think of for using this option is to match Photoshop to another application's color conversion process.

(18) Description field: When you drag the mouse pointer over any of the sections and menus in the **Color Settings** dialog box, a short description of each appears in this field.

End

How-To Hints

Opening Files and Dialog Boxes

If you have checked the **Ask When Opening** check boxes in the **Profile Mismatches** section, you will get a dialog box each time a file is opened with a profile that does not match the current working space profile (as specified in the **Working Spaces** section). If **Ask When Opening** is selected in the **Missing Profiles** section, the dialog box appears each time a file is opened that has no profile at all. Although you can avoid these dialog boxes by disabling the **Ask When Opening** check boxes, you run the risk of unwanted color shifts as you open images. You're better off taking some time to understand which space works best for your workflow and image types, and managing the profiles through the controls described here.

How to Set Photoshop Preferences

General Controls

Choose **Edit, Preferences, General** to open the **Preferences** box to the **General** page. You use this page to control interpolation, the **Color Picker** option, and a number of other general application parameters.

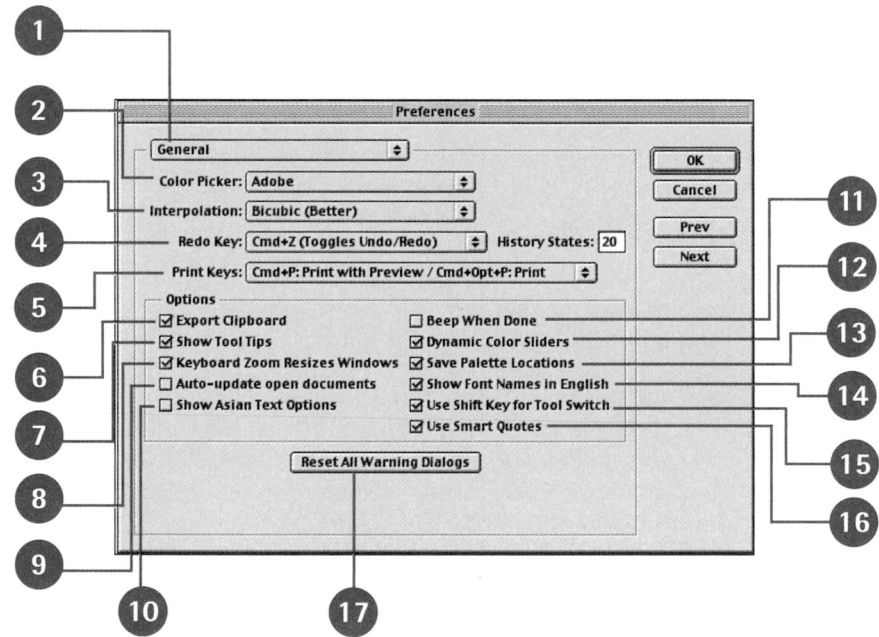

1 **Preferences Title pop-up menu:** Click the arrow to display a list of other pages in the **Preferences** box; select an option to open that page.

2 **Color Picker pop-up menu:** Click the arrow to display a list of color picker options; select the Adobe or Apple/Windows color picker.

3 **Interpolation pop-up menu:** Click the arrow to display a list of interpolation options. Choose **Bicubic, Bilinear,** or **Nearest Neighbor.** In most cases, leave this option set at **Bicubic** for best results.

4 **Redo Key pop-up menu:** Allows you to select a key combination that reapplies the undo/redo commands. Select from the three keyboard combinations to toggle between redo and undo. The **History States** field contains the number of actions to be held in memory and through which the undo/redo commands will cycle.

5 **Print Keys:** Use pull-down menu to select the keyboard combination you want to use for the print and print-with-preview options.

6 **Export Clipboard check box:** This option attempts to export the current Clipboard contents when Photoshop is closed. Leave this option disabled because it slows the shutdown process and because the exported format is almost always incompatible.

7 **Show Tool Tips check box:** Activates the pop-up tool descriptions when you hover the cursor over the interface elements.

8 **Keyboard Zoom Resizes Windows:** Resizes image windows when zooming in and out of the image from the keyboard.

9 **Auto-update open documents check box:** Updates and saves open documents automatically.

10 **Show Asian Text Options check box:** Changes text options to any installed Asian character sets in the character and paragraph text palettes.

11 **Beep When Done check box:** Emits an audible beep when a task is complete.

12 **Dynamic Color Sliders check box:** Updates the current color selections in the **Color** palette in real-time as the sliders are adjusted. Disable this check box for a slight performance increase.

13 **Save Palette Locations check box:** Reopens palettes in the same place and at the same size as they were when they were closed.

14 **Show Font Names in English check box:** Translates all font names into English.

15 **Use Shift Key for Tool Switch:** Allows the use of the **Shift** key to toggle tool selection.

16 **Use Smart Quotes:** Changes typed quotation marks to directional quotation marks.

17 **Reset All Warning Dialogs button:** Resets all warning messages to their defaults.

Continues

File Handling

Choose **Edit, Preferences, File Handling** to launch the **File Handling Preferences** box. You use this page to specify how a file is saved, including previews, thumbnails, and for compatibility with files created in older versions of Photoshop.

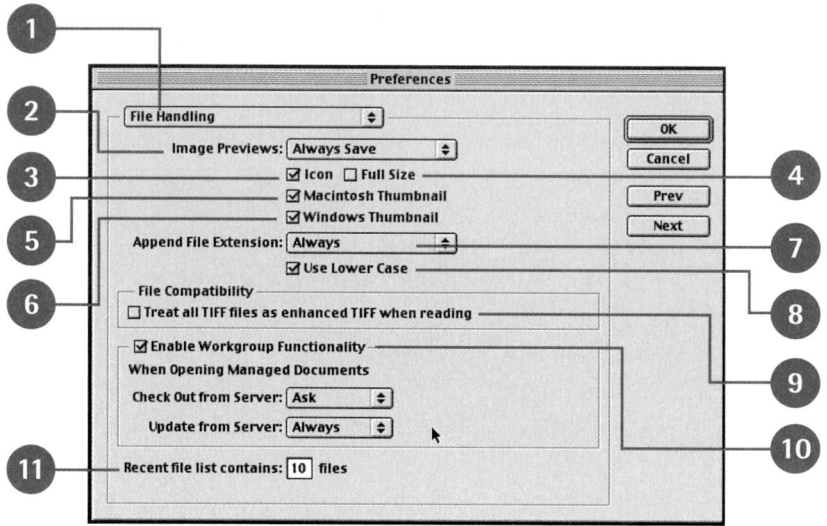

① **Preferences Title pop-up menu:** Click the arrow to display a list of other pages in the **Preferences** box; choose an option to open that page.

② **Image Previews pop-up menu:** Click the arrow to display a list of save options and then choose one of these options: **Always Save, Never Save,** or **Ask When Saving.**

③ **Icon check box (Mac only):** Saves an icon preview for viewing within windows on the desktop.

④ **Full Size check box (Mac only):** Saves a 72dpi file version for applications that can open only low-resolution Photoshop files.

⑤ **Macintosh Thumbnail check box (Mac only):** Creates a thumbnail that will be displayed in Macintosh systems in the **Open** dialog box.

⑥ **Windows Thumbnail check box (Mac only):** Creates a thumbnail that will be displayed in Windows systems.

⑦ **Append File Extension pop-up menu (Mac only):** Adds file extensions as a file is saved, based on the file format. Click the arrow to display a list: **Always, Never,** and **Ask When Saving.**

8 **Use Lower Case check box:** Adds the file extension using lowercase letters. In Windows, the **File Extension** drop-down list offers the choice between automatically adding extensions to filenames in **Upper Case** or **Lower Case** letters.

9 **Treat All TIFF Files as Enhanced TIFF When Reading check box:** Allows additional save options when saving TIFF files.

10 **Enable Workgroup Functionality:** Allows Photoshop to recognize workflow and version-control servers for file check-out capabilities. Pull-down menus control file check-out and check-in.

11 **Recent File List Contains field:** Type a number in the box to set the number of recent files to be displayed in the **Recent Files** pop-up menu that appears when you select **File, Open Recent.**

Continues

Display & Cursors

Choose **Edit, Preferences, Display & Cursors** to open the **Preferences** box to the **Display & Cursors** page. You use this page to specify brush and cursor shapes and sizes.

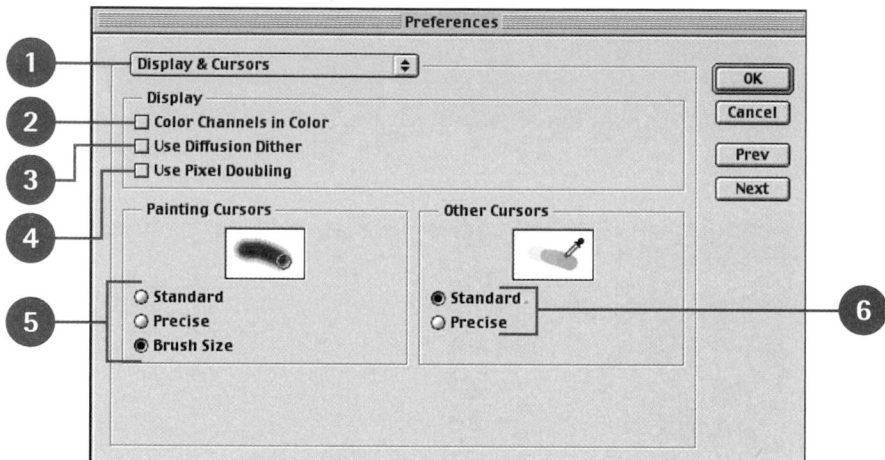

① **Preferences Title pop-up menu:** Click the arrow to display a list of other pages in the **Preferences** box; choose an option to open that page.

② **Color Channels in Color check box:** Displays the color channels in color rather than in grayscale.

③ **Use Diffusion Dither check box:** Employs a random dot pattern for dithering (which generally has a smoother result) instead of the default pattern dither.

④ **Use Pixel Doubling check box:** Allows faster previews when using the **Move** tool.

⑤ **Painting Cursors radio buttons:** Enables you to select **Standard** (icon), **Precise** (cross hairs), or **Brush Size** (circular) for the painting cursor.

⑥ **Other Cursors radio buttons:** Enables you to select between a **Standard** (icon) and **Precise** (cross hairs) cursor.

Transparency & Gamut

Choose **Edit, Preferences, Transparency & Gamut** to open the **Preferences** box to the **Transparency & Gamut** page. You use this page to specify how transparency is shown in a file, as well as to select the gamut warning color format.

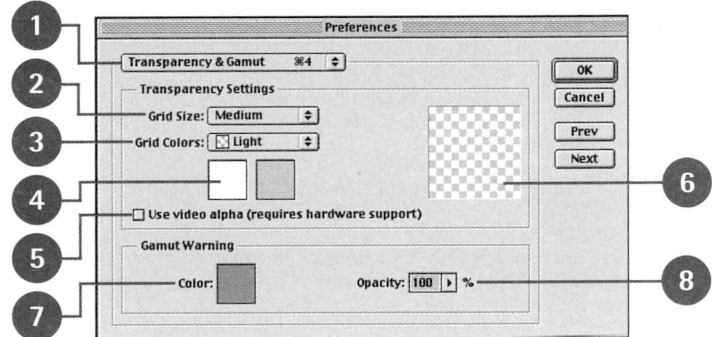

1 **Preferences Title pop-up menu:** Click the arrow to display a list of other pages in the **Preferences** box; choose an option to open that page.

2 **Grid Size pop-up menu:** Controls the size of the checkerboard used to indicate transparency. Options are **None, Small, Medium**, and **Large.**

3 **Grid Colors pop-up menu:** Controls the color of the checkerboard used to indicate transparency. Options are **Light, Medium, Dark, Red, Orange, Green, Blue, Purple,** and **Custom.**

4 **Custom color swatches:** Click one or both of the swatches to select specific colors for the transparency checkerboard.

5 **Use Video Alpha check box:** Enables video alpha capability (a special effect transparency technique available with certain video boards).

6 **Transparency preview window:** Shows the current checkerboard pattern.

7 **Gamut Warning Color swatch:** Click to display the **Color Picker** so that you can select the color that will show in place of the out-of-gamut color.

8 **Gamut Opacity slider:** Click and drag the slider to control the transparency of the color you've chosen to replace the out-of-gamut color.

Continues

Units & Rulers

Choose **Edit, Preferences, Units & Rulers** to open the **Preferences** box to the **Units & Rulers** page. You use this page to specify the format and measurements for rulers and columns.

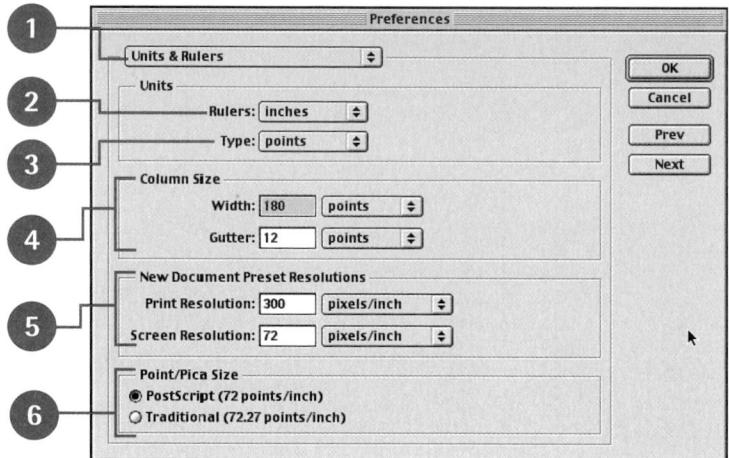

① **Preferences Title pop-up menu:** Click the arrow to display a list of other pages in the **Preferences** box; choose an option to open that page.

② **Rulers Units pop-up menu:** Click the arrow to display a list of the units of measurement for Photoshop rulers. Options include **pixels**, **inches**, **centimeters**, **points**, **picas**, and **percent.**

③ **Type Units pop-up menu:** Click the arrow to display a list of the units of measurement for type specifications. Options include **pixels, points,** and **millimeters.**

④ **Column Size Width and Gutter pop-up menus:** Enter the width of a target column and the width of the *gutter* (the space between columns) for layout purposes. When resizing an image or canvas, the units you specify here are the ones you'll see in the **Resize** dialog box.

⑤ **New Document Preset Resolutions fields:** Pull-down menus control pixels per inch or centimeter. Enter default new document resolutions for print or screen in the fields.

⑥ **Point/Pica Size radio buttons:** Select either the **PostScript** or the **Traditional** measurement system.

Guides, Grid & Slices

Choose **Edit, Preferences, Guides, Grid & Slices** to open the **Preferences** box to the **Guides, Grid & Slices** page. You use this page to control interpolation, the **Color Picker** option, and a number of other general application parameters.

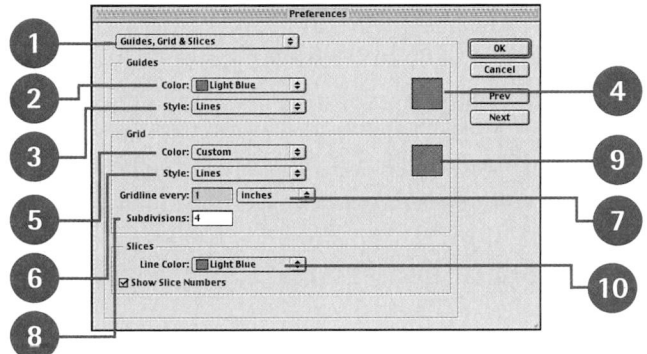

Preferences Title pop-up menu: Click the arrow to display a list of other pages in the **Preferences** box; choose an option to open that page.

Guides Color pop-up menu: Select the color of the guide lines. Choices are **Light Blue, Light Red, Green, Medium Blue, Yellow, Magenta, Cyan, Light Gray, Black,** and **Custom.**

Guides Style pop-up menu: Determines the format of the guides. Options are solid **Lines** and **Dashed Lines.**

Guides color swatch: Click to open the **Color Picker** so that you can select a custom guide color.

Grid Color pop-up menu: Select the color of the grid. Choices are **Light Blue, Light Red, Green, Medium Blue, Yellow, Magenta, Cyan, Light Gray, Black,** and **Custom.**

Grid Style pop-up menu: Determines the format of the grid. Options are solid **Lines, Dots,** or **Dashed Lines.**

Gridline controls: Select the unit of measurement from the pop-up menu for the main grid divisions. Choices are **pixels, inches, centimeters, points, picas,** and **percent.** After you select a unit, type the number of units between gridlines.

Subdivisions: Determines how many subdivisions fall between each main gridline. Enter the desired value in the field.

Grid color swatch: Click to open the **Color Picker** so that you can select a custom grid color.

Slices options: Select slices line color from the **Line Color** pop-up menu. To show slice numbers, enable the **Show Slice Numbers** check box.

Continues

Plug-Ins & Scratch Disks

Choose **Edit, Preferences, Plug-Ins & Scratch Disks** to open the **Preferences** box to the **Plug-Ins & Scratch Disks** page. You use this page to tell Photoshop where to look for plug-ins and scratch disks.

Plug-ins are commands and filters that extend Photoshop's core functionality. They all should be stored in a single folder so that Photoshop can access them as needed. This page of the **Preferences** box allows you to specify the proper folder for Photoshop to access.

As Photoshop manipulates files, it temporarily appropriates hard disk space to cache image data as things are copied and layered. When you work with larger files, it's even more important to have free disk space for the scratch disk. This page of the **Preferences** box is also the place for you to tell Photoshop which drives to use for the scratch disk.

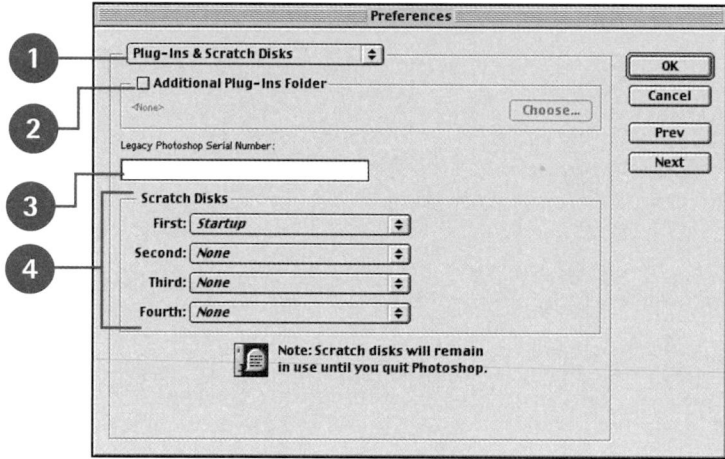

1. **Preferences Title pop-up menu:** Click the arrow to display a list of other pages in the **Preferences** box; choose an option to open that page.

2. **Additional Plug-Ins Folder check box and Choose button:** Enable the check box and click **Choose** to navigate to an additional plug-ins folder. This folder usually is located in the Photoshop 7 application folder and is the folder in which you normally install your plug-ins.

3. **Legacy Photoshop Serial Number field:** Enter the old-style serial number in the field as required by certain plug-ins.

4. **Scratch Disks pop-up menus:** Click to select up to four disks that will serve as scratch disks. All mounted disks are listed as scratch disk options. You may need more than one scratch disk if you work with particularly large image files.

Image Cache

Choose **Edit, Preferences, Image Cache** to open the **Preferences** box to the **Image Cache** page. You use this page to set the number of *caching levels*—a Photoshop method for speeding screen redraw. Note that in Windows, this page is called **Memory & Image Cache**.

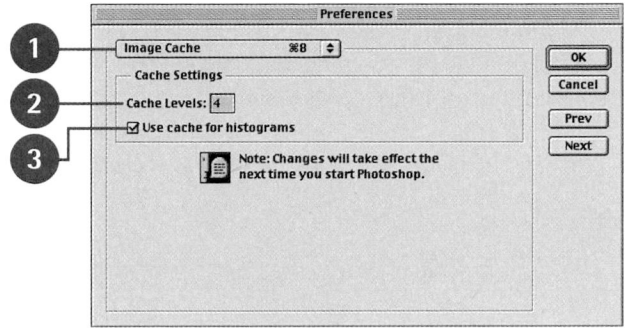

① **Preferences Title pop-up menu:** Click the arrow to display a list of other pages in the **Preferences** box; choose an option to open that page.

② **Cache Levels field:** Enter the number of cache levels you want to use. A higher number speeds redraws but requires more RAM and can increase the time it takes to open an image.

③ **Use Cache for Histograms check box:** Enable this box to use image caching (using memory to temporarily hold information) for calculating histograms (graphs of the colors and brightness/darkness of an image).

Physical Memory Usage (Windows only): Set the amount of memory (in percentage of total memory) that you want to dedicate to Photoshop while it's running. The more memory you can give Photoshop, the better it will run. Keep in mind, however, that this setting may take memory away from other applications you may be running.

End

How to Set ImageReady Preferences

General Controls

Choose **Edit, Preferences, General** to open the **Preferences** box to the **General** page. You use this page to control interpolation, the **Color Picker** option, and a number of other general application parameters.

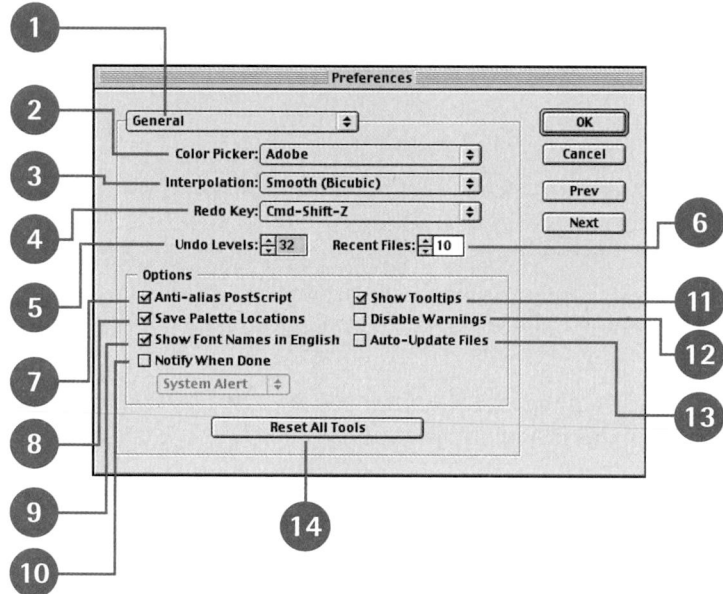

1 **Preferences Title pop-up menu:** Click the arrow to display a list of other pages in the **Preferences** box; choose an option to open that page.

2 **Color Picker pop-up menu:** Click the arrow to display the list of options; then select the **Adobe** or **System** option.

3 **Interpolation pop-up menu:** Click the arrow to display the options: **Smooth (Bicubic)** and **Jagged (Nearest Neighbor).** In most cases, leave this option set at **Smooth (Bicubic)** for best results.

4 **Redo Key pop-up menu:** Click the arrow to select the key combination that reapplies a command.

5 **Undo Levels spinbox:** Determines the number of undo states supported by the **History** palette. Type a value in the field to change the setting. The higher you set this number, the more memory ImageReady uses to store the changes.

6 **Recent Files spinbox:** Enter the number of recent files you want to appear in the **Recent Files** submenu. Use the up/down arrows if desired.

7 **Anti-alias PostScript check box:** Select this option to achieve smooth results when placing or importing PostScript images.

8 **Save Palette Locations check box:** Reopens palettes in the same place and at the same size as when they were closed.

9 **Show Font Names in English check box:** Translates all font names into English.

10 **Notify When Done check box and pop-up menu:** Enable the check box to produce a notification when tasks are completed. Choose **System Alert** or **Text to Speech** from the pop-up menu as the notification method.

11 **Show Tooltips check box:** Activates the pop-up tool descriptions when you hover the mouse pointer over the interface elements.

12 **Disable Warnings check box:** Disables layer effect and selection warnings.

13 **Auto-Update Files check box:** Updates and saves files automatically.

14 **Reset All Tools button:** Resets all tools to their default configurations specified at the initial installation.

Continues

Slices

Choose **Edit, Preferences, Slices** to open the **Preferences** box to the **Slices** page. You use this page to specify how ImageReady generates slices, including naming conventions, colors, and slice lines. A *slice* is the portion of the image when ImageReady divides an image into smaller pieces for optimization and display in an HTML table.

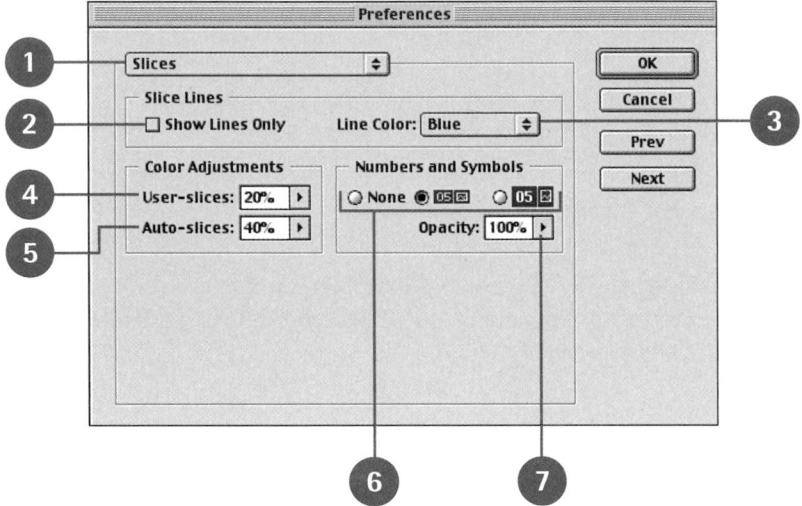

①   **Preferences Title pop-up menu:** Click the arrow to display a list of other pages in the **Preferences** box; choose an option to open that page.

②   **Show Lines Only check box:** Shows only the slice lines when you view slices, omitting the transparent coloring.

③   **Line Color pop-up menu:** Specifies the color of the slice lines. Choices include 24 color options.

④   **Color Adjustments User-slices box and slider:** Determines the opacity for the color shading of the user slices. Click the arrow and drag the slider or type a number value to change the setting.

⑤   **Color Adjustments Auto-slices box and slider:** Determines the opacity for the color shading of the auto slices. Click the arrow and drag the slider or type a number value to change the setting.

⑥   **Numbers and Symbols radio buttons:** Control the size of slice numbers and icons. Select **None** or the small or large icon button.

⑦   **Numbers and Symbols Opacity box and slider:** Click the arrow and drag the slider or type a number value to control the opacity of the slice numbers and symbols.

Image Maps

Choose **Edit, Preferences, Image Maps** to open the **Preferences** box to the **Image Maps** page. You use this page to specify how ImageReady displays imagemap information. An *imagemap* refers to the process of creating hot spots in Web images that serve as links or triggers for other actions.

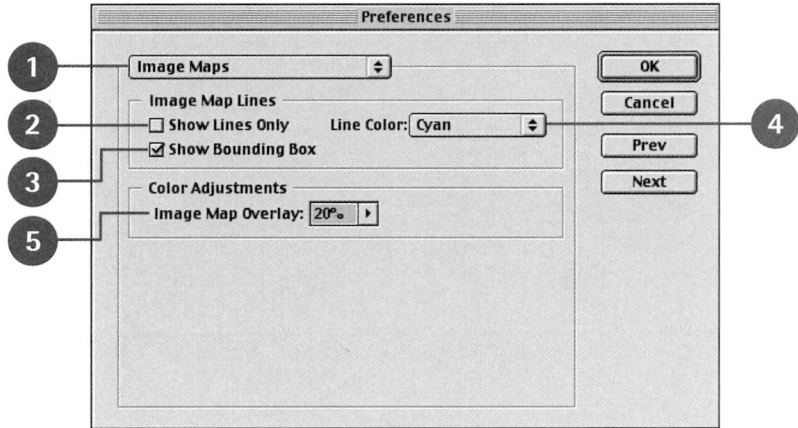

1 **Preferences Title pop-up menu:** Click the arrow to display a list of other pages in the **Preferences** box; choose an option to open that page.

2 **Show Lines Only check box:** Uses an outline to designate an imagemap.

3 **Show Bounding Box check box:** Creates a rectangular bounding box around an imagemap.

4 **Line Color pop-up menu:** Allows you to choose the line color for outlining imagemaps from a list of 24 different line colors.

5 **Image Map Overlay box and slider:** Designates an imagemap with a tinted white fill to separate it from the rest of the image. The slider value determines the fill opacity.

Continues

Optimization

Choose **Edit, Preferences, Optimization** to open the **Preferences** box to the **Optimization** page. You use this page to specify how optimization settings are calculated and displayed.

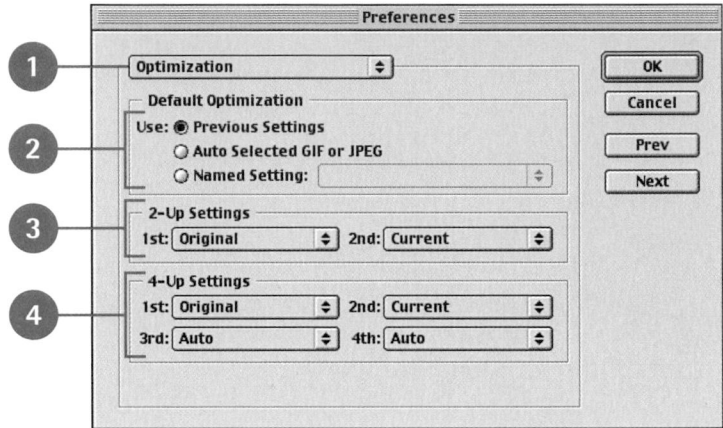

1 **Preferences Title pop-up menu:** Click the arrow to display a list of other pages in the **Preferences** box; choose an option to open that page.

2 **Default Optimization radio buttons:** Select how you want to generate optimization defaults for an image. Choices are **Previous Settings, Auto Selected GIF or JPEG,** and **Named Setting.** Named setting allows you to select from a list of standard optimization defaults.

3 **2-Up Settings pop-up menus:** Determine which iterations of the image are displayed in the **2-Up** window. Defaults for the first menu are **Original** and **Current,** but the second menu allows you to choose from a long list of optimized presets.

4 **4-Up Settings pop-up menus:** Determine which iterations of the image are displayed in the **4-Up** window. Defaults are **Original** and **Current,** but you also can choose from a long list of optimized presets, including **Auto,** which uses the next logical level of compression.

Cursors

Choose **Edit, Preferences, Cursors** to open the **Preferences** box to the **Cursors** page. You use this page to specify brush and cursor shapes and sizes.

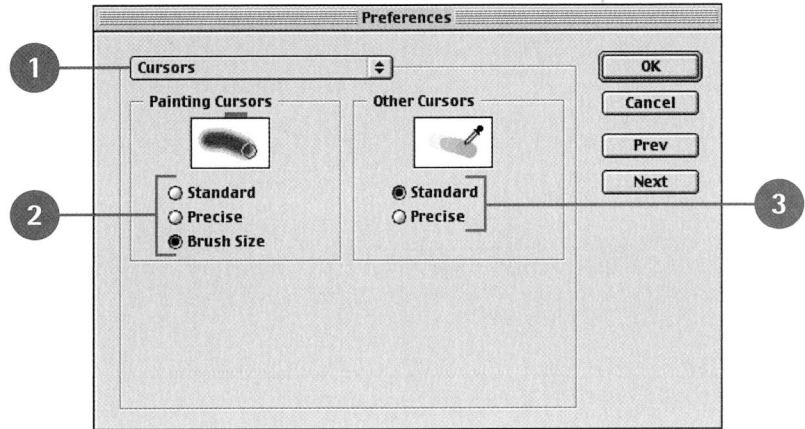

1   **Preferences Title pop-up menu:** Click the arrow to display a list of other pages in the **Preferences** box; choose an option to open that page.

2   **Painting Cursors radio buttons:** Select **Standard** (icon), **Precise** (cross hairs), or **Brush Size** (circular) as the shape of the painting cursor.

3   **Other Cursors radio buttons:** Select **Standard** (icon) or **Precise** (cross hairs) for the cursor shape.

Continues

Transparency

Choose **Edit, Preferences, Transparency** to open the **Preferences** box to the **Transparency** page. You use this page to specify how transparency is depicted in a file.

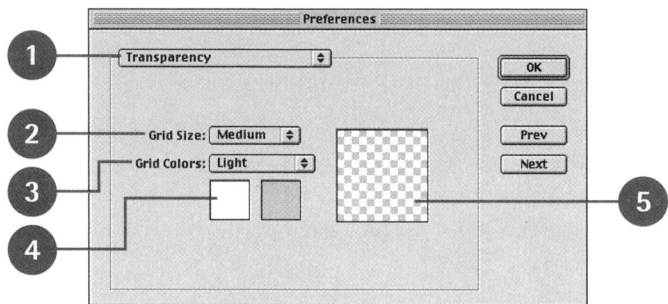

1 **Preferences Title pop-up menu:** Click the arrow to display a list of other pages in the **Preferences** box; choose an option to open that page.

2 **Grid Size pop-up menu:** Controls the size of the checkerboard used to indicate transparency. Options are **None, Small, Medium,** and **Large.**

3 **Grid Colors pop-up menu:** Controls the color of the checkerboard used to indicate transparency. Options are **Light, Medium, Dark, Red, Orange, Green, Blue, Purple,** and **Custom.**

4 **Custom color swatches:** Click one or both of the swatches to select specific colors for the transparency checkerboard.

5 **Transparency preview window:** Shows the current transparency checkerboard pattern.

Plug-Ins & Scratch Disks

Choose **Edit, Preferences, Plug-Ins & Scratch Disks** to open the **Preferences** box to the **Plug-Ins & Scratch Disks** page. You use this page to tell ImageReady where to look for plug-ins and scratch disks. Note that in Windows, this page is called simply **Plug-Ins**; the Windows version does not allow you to specify a scratch disk location.

Plug-ins are commands and filters that extend ImageReady's core functionality. They all should be stored in a single folder so that ImageReady can access them as needed. This page of the **Preferences** box allows you to specify the proper folder for ImageReady to access.

As ImageReady manipulates files, it temporarily appropriates hard disk space to cache image data as things are copied and layered. When you work with larger files, it's even more important to have free disk space for the scratch disk. This page of the **Preferences** box is also the place for you to tell ImageReady which drives to use for the scratch disk.

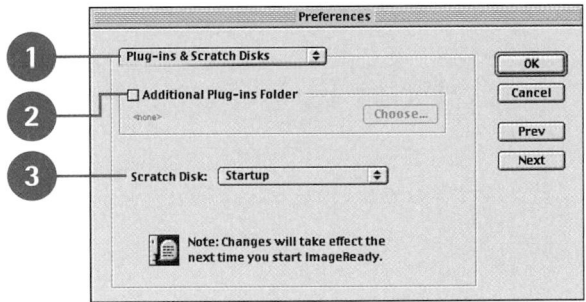

① **Preferences Title pop-up menu:** Click the arrow to display a list of other pages in the **Preferences** box; choose an option to open that page.

② **Additional Plug-ins Folder check box and Choose button:** Enable the check box and click **Choose** to navigate to an additional plug-ins folder.

③ **Scratch Disk pop-up menu (Mac only):** Click the arrow to display a list of potential scratch disks. All mounted disks are listed as scratch disk options.

End

Task

Optimizing Photoshop Projects

Although Photoshop often is thought of as a high-powered creative tool, it's also a nuts-and-bolts production tool. Even though most designers would rather spend their time building montages and creative designs, too often they're saddled with less glamorous tasks such as cropping images and cataloging files.

The tasks in this part look at how to optimize your workflow, with tips and ideas on how to work faster and more efficiently. These tasks are valuable to master because you can apply them to other tasks, making everything you do a bit easier. In some situations, such as the tasks involving actions, these tips let you automate the entire process. Other tasks allow you to categorize groups of images into contact sheets, to share files, and to optimize the features in the **History** palette. ●

How to Build a Contact Sheet

A *contact sheet* is a Photoshop file with thumbnail references for all the images in a given folder. You can use contact sheets for a number of tasks, such as sending clients a list of images for approval, archiving, or just organizing your graphics visually rather than with archaic filenames. When you set up contact sheets, you have full control over the page size, the thumbnail size, and the spacing on the page. You can optimize the format of contact sheets for any printer or format.

Begin

1 Load Images into a Single Folder

All the images for a contact sheet must reside in the same folder or subfolder. Drag the images into the target folder before you do anything else. This contact sheet will include all the images in the folder, so you should remove any image you don't want to appear on the contact sheet.

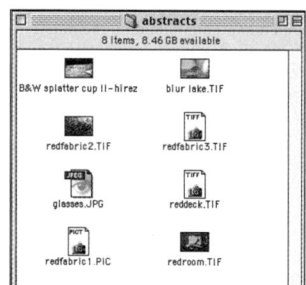

2 Choose Source Folder

To start building a contact sheet, choose **File, Automate, Contact Sheet II.** The **Contact Sheet II** dialog box opens. In the **Source Folder** section, click the **Choose** button. Browse to the target folder (the folder containing the images), select it, and click **Choose** to return to the main **Contact Sheet** dialog box.

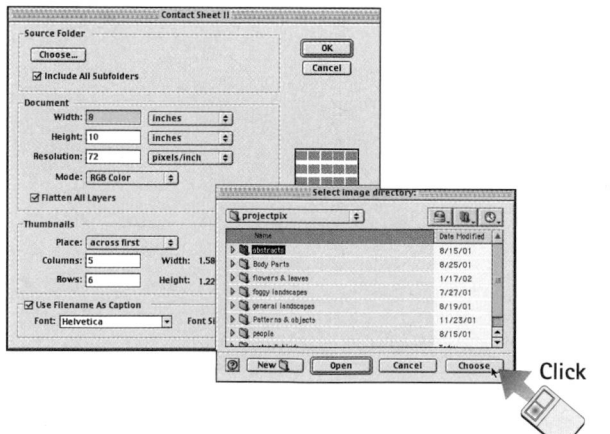

Click

3 Specify Size of Contact Sheet

In the **Document** area of the dialog box, specify the size of the contact sheet you're building. Enter the dimensions and resolution in the spaces provided. Keep the resolution at 72dpi if you're just viewing onscreen, or use a setting of 150dpi for basic-quality laser or inkjet printing. Watch the preview area on the right side of the dialog box change as you modify these values.

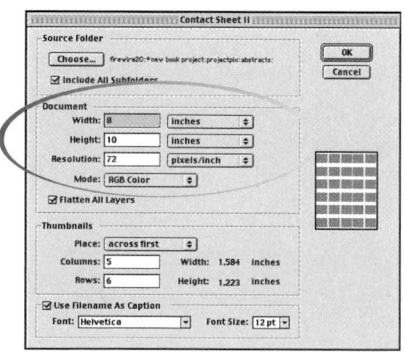

4 Set Color Mode

From the **Mode** drop-down list, select the color mode for your contact sheet: **RGB Color, CMYK Color, Lab Color,** or **Grayscale.** Make your choice based on the color modes of the images you're working with.

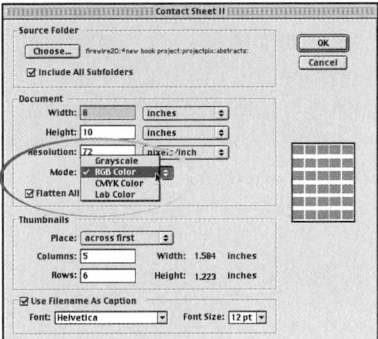

5 Determine Page Grid

Make a selection from the **Place** drop-down list and specify the numbers of **Columns** and **Rows** you want on your contact sheet. Watch the preview area to see how the values you provide affect the size of the thumbnails (based on the overall page dimensions).

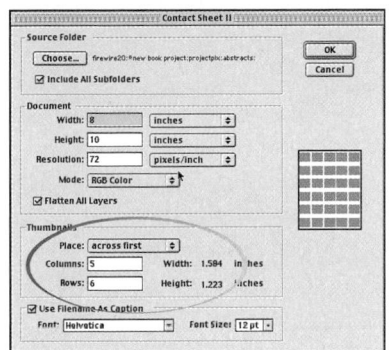

6 Set Captions and Fonts

Enable the **Use Filename as Caption** check box if you want the filenames of the images to appear below the thumbnails on the contact sheet. From the **Font** drop-down menu, select the font you want to use for the captions and enter the caption font size in the **Font Size** box.

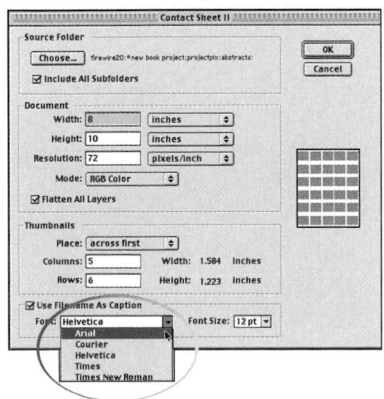

7 Build the Sheet

Click **OK** to start the script and build the contact sheet image. Note that the contact sheet is a Photoshop file; you can modify it any way you want. Consider saving the file as a PDF file. This compact Adobe file format is especially suited for e-mailing to clients or if disk space is limited. To save an image as a PDF file, choose **File, Save As** and select **Photoshop PDF** from the **Format** drop-down menu.

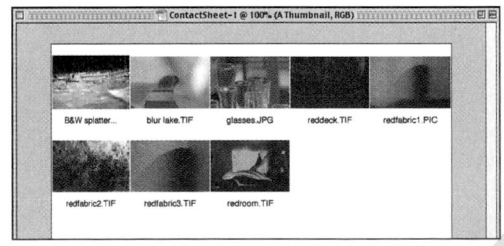

End

How to Use the File Browser

The **File Browser** is a floating window and palette that allows you to quickly view, reference, and launch any image file on your local computer or server. It allows you to visually browse multiple images and folders, and it is a real timesaver if you have a multitude of images or nondescript filenames

Begin

1 Open the File Browser

By default, the **File Browser** is located in the palette well on the right edge of the **Options** bar. To open it, click the tab labeled **File Browser**. The browser is also listed in the **Window** menu; you can launch it from there by selecting **Window, File Browser**.

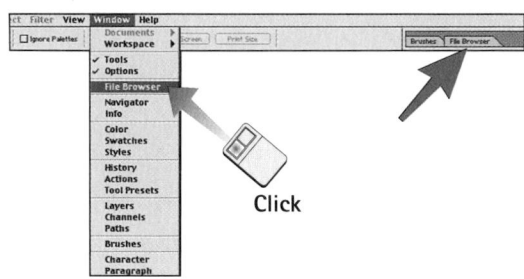

Click

2 View the Content Areas

The **File Browser** window is divided into four main areas. In the left column is the file list, the image preview section, and the file info section. The right column displays the image thumbnails for the selected folder.

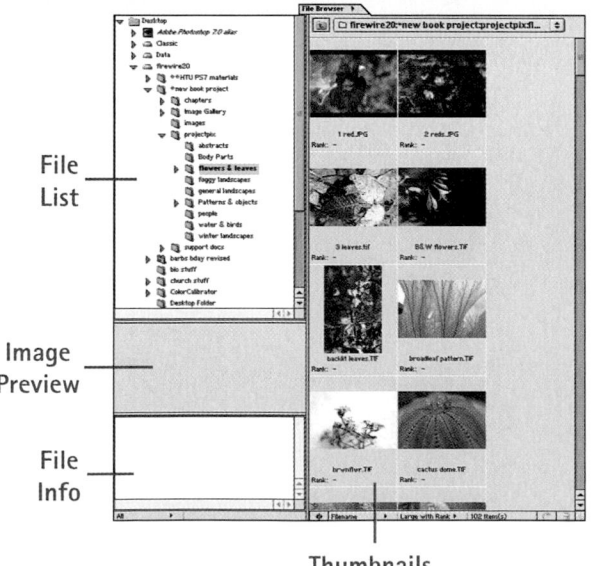

File List

Image Preview

File Info

Thumbnails

3 Access a Folder of Images

Navigate the hierarchical menus in the file list to locate the desired folder of images. Click the folder to highlight it; this action also loads the thumbnails for the images in the folder in the thumbnail section of the window.

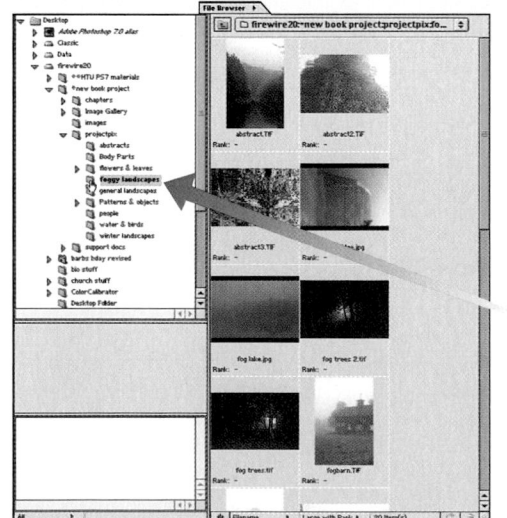

Click

4 Format Thumbnail Display Area

Thumbnail previews can be displayed in a variety of ways. Use the **Sort By** menu at the bottom of the **File Browser** window to sort by 11 different variables, including name, size, file type, and copyright. The **View By** menu controls thumbnail size and data display.

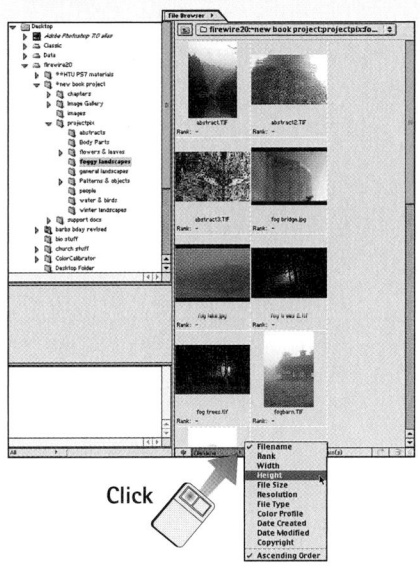

Click

5 Select an Image

Click a thumbnail to display a larger preview in the image preview section of the **File Browser** window. Information about file size, format, modification dates, and more is listed in the file info section of the window.

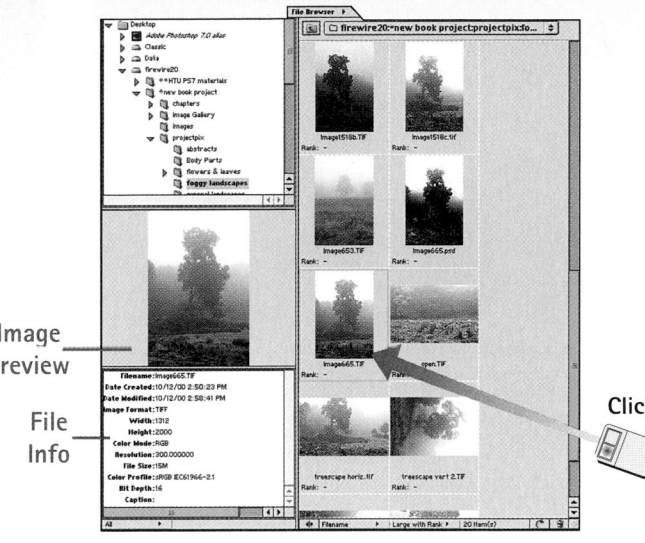

Image Preview

File Info

Click

6 Open an Image

Double-click a thumbnail to open the image. While the browser is open, you can continue to open multiple files in sequence.

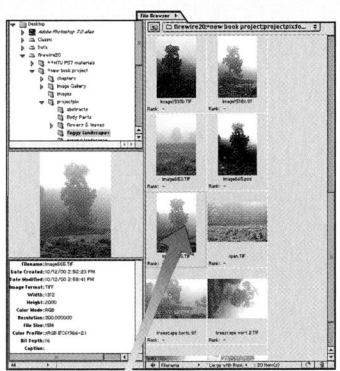

Double-click

End

How-To Hints

Repositioning the Browser

If you drag the **File Browser** tab out of the palette well, it becomes a floating window, and you can close, expand, or minimize it. To redock it, choose **Dock to Palette Well** from the **File Browser Options** menu.

Rotating Files and Thumbnails

Occasionally, a scanned or digital photo image requires rotation. The **File Browser** features a **Rotate** button next to the **View By** menu at the bottom of the window. Select a thumbnail and click the **Rotate** button to rotate the thumbnail 90 degrees clockwise. Hold the **Option** key (Mac users) or the **Ctrl** key (Windows users) and click the **Rotate** button to rotate 90 degrees counterclockwise. When you open the file, Photoshop automatically applies the rotation shown in the thumbnail.

How to Use Multiple Views

People are working with larger images than ever before. One challenge is being able to zoom in on work at a pixel level while still monitoring the overall look of the piece. The best way to address this issue is by using *multiple views*. Just open two separate windows of the same file, specify a high rate of magnification for editing in one window, and leave the other at full screen size to check your progress as you work.

Begin

1 Open the Main File

Choose **File, Open** to display the **Open** dialog box. Select the file you want to work on and click **OK.**

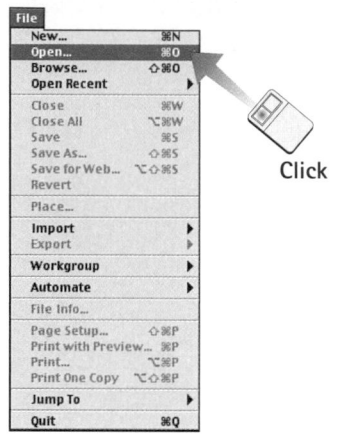

Click

2 Set Desired Magnification

Click the **Zoom** tool in the toolbox and click the image. Watch the zoom percentage numbers in the lower-left corner of the screen. Continue clicking to zoom in to the magnification level that lets you see the area clearly. To zoom in on a particular area of the image, click the **Zoom** tool and drag to draw a marquee around the area you want to magnify.

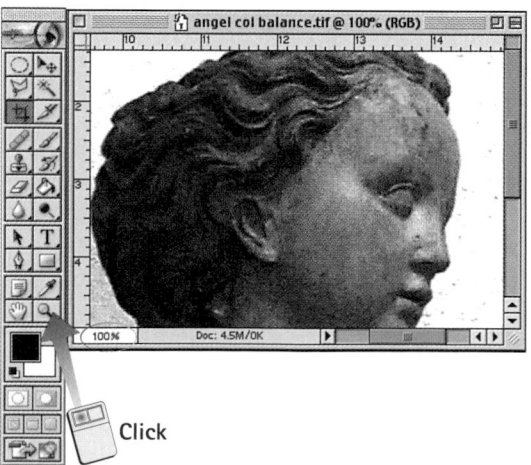

Click

3 Open a New View

To create a second window on this same image, choose **Window, Documents, New Window.** You now have two windows with the same image on your desktop: One shows the full image, and the other shows a detailed zoom of a single area. At this point, you can create additional views for as many areas as necessary. (Don't worry about "using up" system resources when using multiple views. Your computer can handle it!)

4 Drag Windows into Position

Because the active window automatically appears on top of any other open windows, you should arrange the image windows so that they're side by side. This arrangement allows you to see both the zoomed screen and the full screen at the same time.

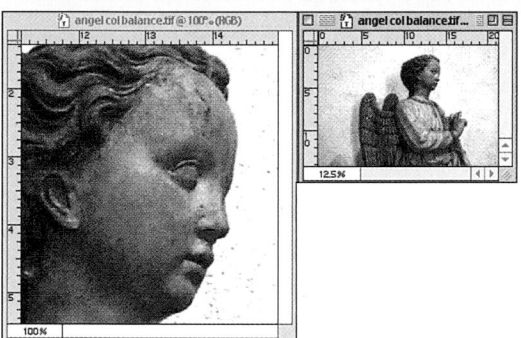

5 Edit the Image

Make any local edits to the image in either window. For example, you can paint, erase, or silhouette. (These and other tasks are explained later in this book.) As you work in one window, notice that the image is updated in real time in the other window.

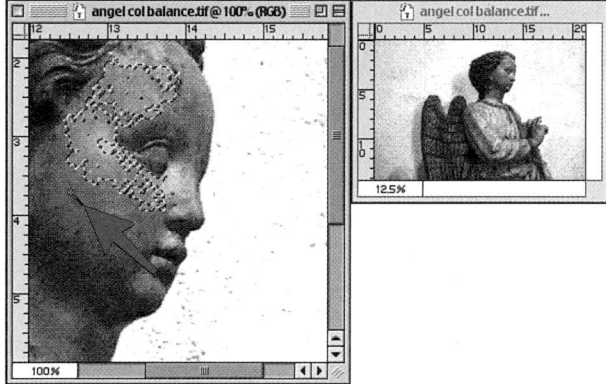

6 Close Window to Reduce Number of Views

When you finish editing the image, close either of the view windows (click the **Close box** in the title bar) to revert to a single view and reduce onscreen clutter.

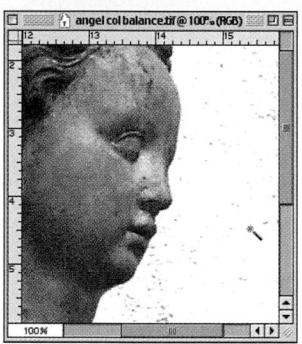

End

How-To Hints

Using Macro and Micro Views

When necessary, you can open a third window to show a high magnification, normal size, and reduced views.

Views and Proofing

Views can be very useful when you're proofing an image in different color spaces. Open multiple views of the same image and select **View, Proof Setup;** then select the color model of your choice (such as **Macintosh RGB** or **Monitor RGB**). You can even select **Custom** and choose the Colorsync profile of your choice. This is a great way to compare multiple color spaces side by side, using the same image.

How to Annotate Files with Text and Audio

Photoshop 7 allows you to add comments to your images in the form of text and voice annotations. These notes are helpful for communicating comments or questions in the approval process, so that several people can evaluate an image and suggest modifications or improvements. Photoshop files can get complex, making the accumulation of layers, filters, and effects difficult to keep straight. Annotations are a great way to ensure that you remember how an effect was created, where the image was taken, or any other details.

Begin

1 Select the Notes Tool

Select **File, Open** to open the file you want to annotate. Then select the **Notes** tool from the toolbox.

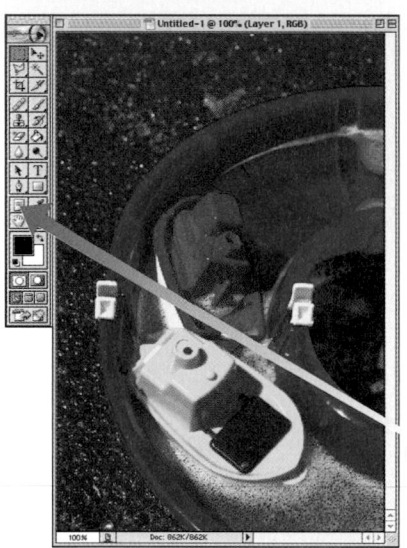

Click

2 Set the Tool Options

Change any of the tool options in the **Options** bar. The **Author** field allows you to specify the name that appears in the note's title bar. You can also change the font, size, and color of the note.

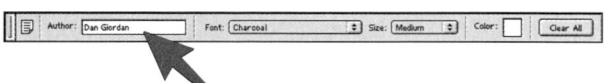

3 Place the Note

Click within the image to insert the notes window. If you want to create a note of a specific size or shape, you can drag a window of the appropriate size. Notice that a little note icon appears on the image; later, you can click this icon to view the note.

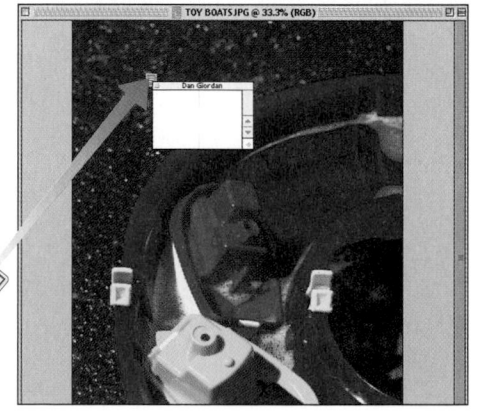

Click

4 Enter the Text

Click inside the notes window to position the cursor and then type text as desired. You can use the standard editing commands (such as basic formatting or cut and paste) for your operating system. When you're finished typing comments, click the **Close** box in the upper-left corner of the notes window to close it.

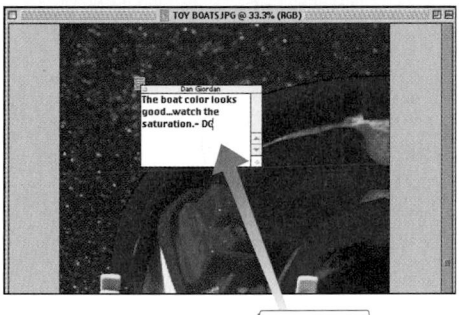

5 Select the Audio Annotation Tool

To create audio notes, select the **Audio Annotation** tool from the toolbox. This tool shares the same pop-up menu as the **Notes** tool. Click and hold the **Notes** tool and select the **Audio Annotation** tool from the pop-out menu that appears.

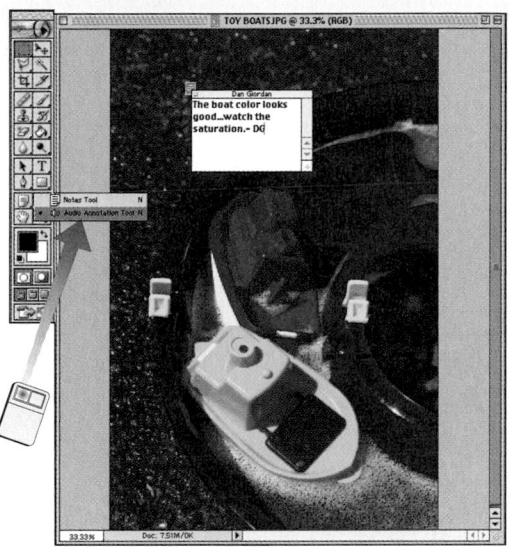

Click

6 Record the Audio

Click within the image to insert the audio notes icon. To record the message on a Windows system, click **Start** in the **Audio Annotation** dialog box and speak into your computer's microphone. Click **Stop** when you're finished. To record on the Mac OS, click **Record** and speak into your computer's microphone. Click **Stop** when you're finished. For both systems, click **Save** to save your audio note. Double-click the audio icon to play it back.

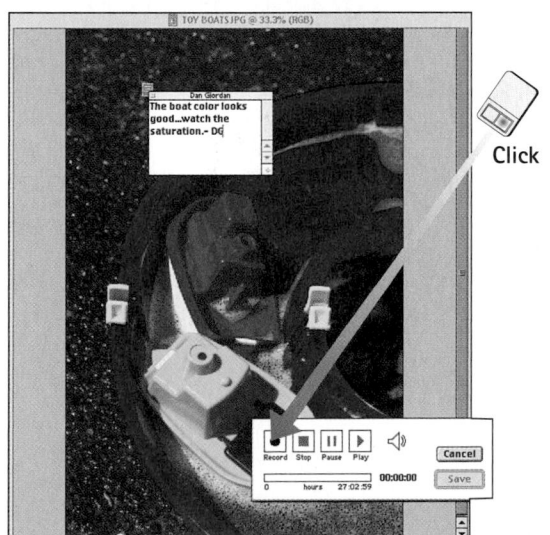

Click

How-To Hints

Building Annotated PDF Files

When you save an annotated file in PDF format, the voice or note annotations are saved with it. Select **File, Save As** and select **Photoshop PDF** from the pop-up menu in the **Save As** dialog box. Be sure to select the **Annotations** check box in this dialog box, or the notes will not be included.

Hiding the Icons

The notes and audio icons indicating that an image contains annotations can be distracting when you're working on an image. To hide these icons, select **View, Extras** to remove the check mark next to the command. Select the command again to get the icons back.

End

How to Undo with the History Palette

The **History** palette is the control center for Photoshop's multiple undo capability. It allows you to revert an image back beyond what the simple **Edit, Undo** command can do. The **History** palette records each edit or command as a *layer tile*. Click a tile to revert the image back to that earlier state. You can set features and options to optimize how the **History** palette works for you.

Begin

1 Open the History Palette

Choose **Window, History** to open the **History** palette. The palette shows a snapshot at the top, representing the original state of the file as it was opened. As you make changes to the file, those changes are displayed as tiles running in descending order in the palette.

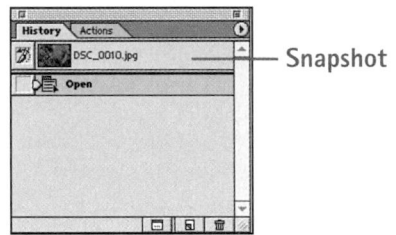

— Snapshot

2 Set the Number of History States

Select **Edit, Preferences, General** to open the **General Preferences** dialog box. Set the number of states you want to record, with the understanding that any states that exceed this limit will be lost. If you set **History States** to **20,** for example, you cannot go back to what you did 21 steps ago. On the other hand, having more states is memory-intensive, so you must strike a happy medium between a **History** palette safety net and efficient allocation of memory and disk space. Click **OK** to save the history states and close the dialog box.

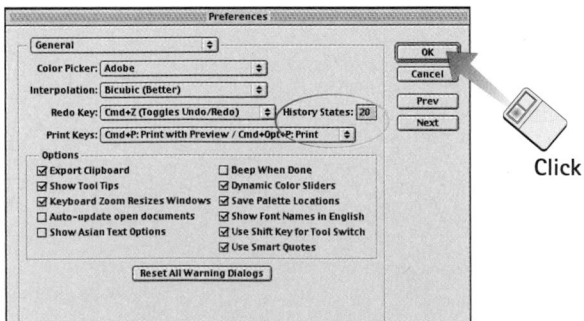

Click

3 Take Snapshots

Another way to preserve a specific image state is to take a *snapshot*. Snapshots are independent of the standard image states mentioned in Step 2 and remain available until you close or save the file. To take a snapshot, display the **History** palette menu and select **New Snapshot.** Give the snapshot a name in the dialog box that appears and click **OK.** A thumbnail of the snapshot appears in the upper part of the palette.

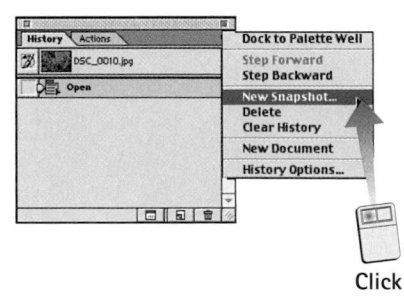

Click

4 Revert to a Previous State

To revert to a previous state or snapshot, select the corresponding tile in the **History** palette. The image in the active window reverts to the point in the editing process you selected. All tiles below the active tile are dimmed, but you can still revert to them by clicking them.

Click

5 Create Duplicate Files

The **History** palette also lets you create a duplicate image file. After you create a duplicate, you can continue editing that duplicate, leaving the original in its previous state. To make a duplicate, choose **New Document** from the **History** palette menu. Photoshop copies the image in a new window (without keeping track of any of the previous history states), which you can modify further or rename and save.

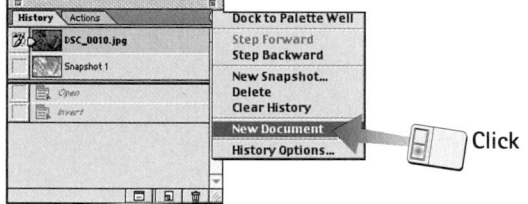

Click

End

How-To Hints

Watching Those Brushstrokes

Remember that each time you click the mouse to apply a brushstroke, you "consume" a history state. Clicking away with multiple brushstrokes can consume all your history states in a hurry. Be sure to grab a snapshot before you start brushing, leaving you an escape route to a previous version.

Using the History Brush

You also can do great things with the Photoshop **History** brush, which allows you to brush in corrections using history states as a source. See Part 8, Task 4, "How to Use the History Brush," for details.

Snapshot Options

In the **Snapshot** dialog box that appears in Step 3, you can control what portions of the image are archived. Select **Full Document, Merged Layers,** or **Current Layer** from the **From** menu as desired.

How to Create Custom Tool Presets

The custom tool preset options in Photoshop 7 allow you to save all the variable settings associated with that tool. Specific brush sizes, feathering, blending modes, transparency, and other settings can be customized and loaded with a single click of the mouse. With the custom tool presets, you can create customized brushes for specific tasks and store them in a floating palette or in tool sets for easy access.

Begin

_1_ Select the Tool

Tool presets can be created for any Photoshop tool. Select the desired tool from the toolbox. In this example, the **Paintbrush** tool is selected.

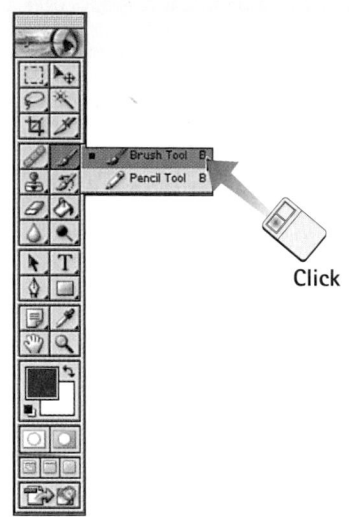

Click

_2_ Set the Tool Parameters

Modify the tool settings in the **Options** bar. You can save in the preset any settings you specify in the **Options** bar, along with the foreground and background colors, if desired.

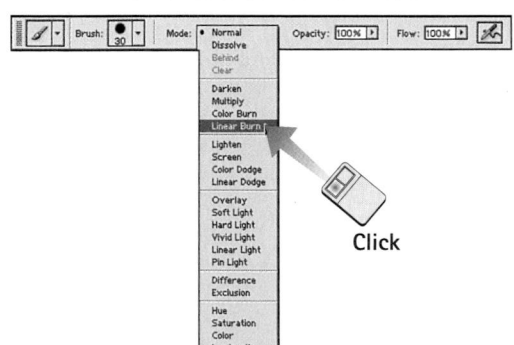

Click

_3_ Open the Tool Preset Palette

Select **Window, Tool Presets** to open the **Tool Presets** palette. The palette allows the option of showing all presets in the system, or only the presets for the currently selected tool. Select the **Current Tool Only** check box at the bottom of the palette to restrict the selection to only the presets for the current tool.

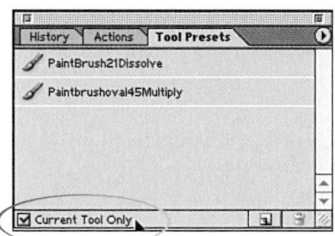

4 Save the Preset

Select **New Tool Preset** from the palette menu, or click the **New Tool Preset** icon at the bottom of the palette. Name the preset in the **New Tool Preset** window that appears. If desired, enable the **Include Color** check box to preserve the current foreground color selection as part of the preset.

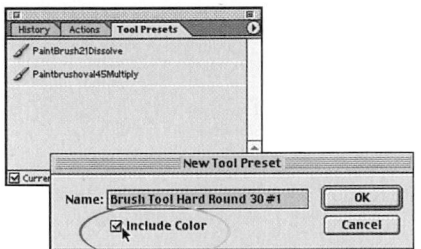

5 Load the Preset

Click the preset bar in the **Tool Presets** palette to load the preset options for the selected tool.

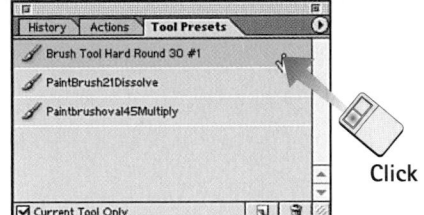

Click

End

How-To Hints

An Alternative Toolbox

If you leave the **Current Tool Only** check box disabled, all the presets for all the tools are visible in the **Tool Presets** palette. Now you can access specific presets as you need them, intuitively changing tools and parameters. It's like using the toolbox to select different tools, only now you can have a dozen variations on a tool instead of just one.

Saving and Loading Sets

Sometimes, specific projects require unique tool presets. You can create groups of presets and load them into the **Tool Presets** palette as needed. Use the **Save**, **Load**, or **Replace** tool preset commands in the palette menu. You can also select **Preset Manager** from the palette menu to launch the **Preset Manager** dialog box, where you can sort, load, save, rename, or delete your tool presets.

How to Use the Preset Actions

Photoshop uses preset scripts called *actions* to automate repetitive tasks. For example, creating a drop shadow can involve inverting a selection, deleting a background, inverting the selection again, offsetting it, feathering it, and filling it with a transparent fill. Actions allow you to apply multiple steps such as these with a single mouse click. This can save you time—especially when you're processing multiple images in the same way. You can view actions in a simplified button mode (which allows for one-click application) and in a more detailed mode (in which you can examine each step in the action). In this task, you'll work in **Simplified Button** mode. You'll get more detailed information in the following tasks.

Begin

1 Open the Actions Palette

Choose **Window, Actions** to open the **Actions** palette.

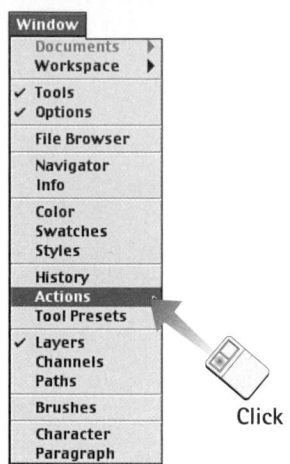

Click

2 Set Palette to Button Mode

Click and hold the arrow in the upper-right corner of the palette and drag to select **Button Mode.** The **Actions** palette changes to display all the actions as clickable buttons. Select this option again to disable **Button** mode and return the palette to the simple **List** mode.

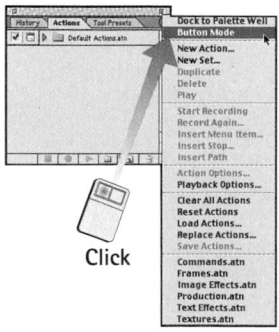

Click

3 Select an Area of the Image

Actions can be applied to a selected area of the image; in many cases, actions can be applied to the entire image. Click the **Marquee** tool and drag to select the area of the image you want to modify with an action.

Drag

4 Click the Action Button

Click the desired action button in the **Actions** palette to execute the effect. You can apply multiple actions to the same selection—just click another Action button.

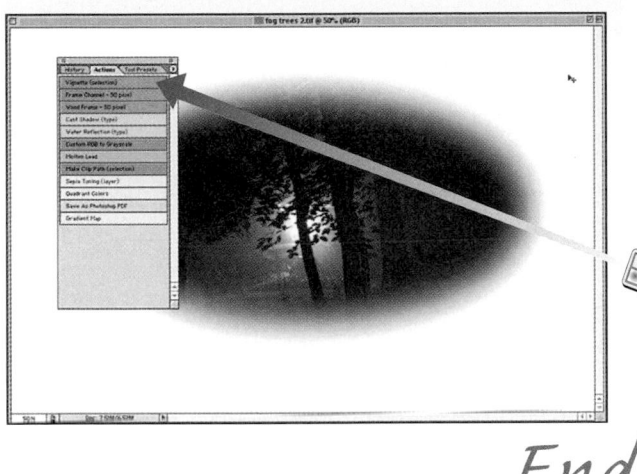

Click

End

How-To Hints

Keystroke Applications

If you deselect **Button Mode** from the **Actions** palette menu, you can set custom keystrokes for each action. For example, instead of going to the **Actions** palette to click the **Vignette** button, you could assign a keystroke such as **Shift+Ctrl+F2** that executes the Vignette action. In the **Actions** palette, select the action you want; open the palette menu and drag down to select **Action Options.** In the dialog box that opens, specify a keystroke to launch the action.

More Actions with Photoshop 7

In previous versions of Photoshop, it was generally acknowledged that the default set of actions was not very useful. Sure, you could create fake wood-frame effects with a push of a button, but that's not an effect you would use on a daily basis. The presets were there as examples of what you could build yourself, but nothing that anyone would call a useful library.

To address this, Photoshop 7 includes a host of new action sets, accessible from the **Actions** palette menu. Select any of the files with the **.atn** suffix to load the action set in the palette. Each action set includes numerous actions that are useful in daily applications. The topics for the new action sets are **Buttons, Commands, Frames, Image Effects, Production, Text Effects,** and **Textures.**

How to Create Custom Actions

Although the preset actions that ship with Photoshop are useful, it won't be long before you'll feel the need to build your own. An action should be generic enough to work in a number of situations and on multiple images. There may be some editing tasks that just don't translate into actions. Keep trying, though, because building a clean action can give you a great deal of satisfaction—as well as save you a lot of time.

Begin

1 Open the Actions Palette

If the **Actions** palette is not currently displayed on your desktop, choose **Window, Actions** to display the palette. If necessary, exit **Button** mode and return the palette to **List** mode (see Step 2 in Task 7).

Click

2 Create a New Action

From the palette menu, select **New Action** to open the **New Action** dialog box. Type a name for the action you're going to record and select the **Set** orientation. You can create multiple sets of actions, which you can then select from the **Set** menu. If no other sets of actions are created, select from the **Default Actions** set that appears.

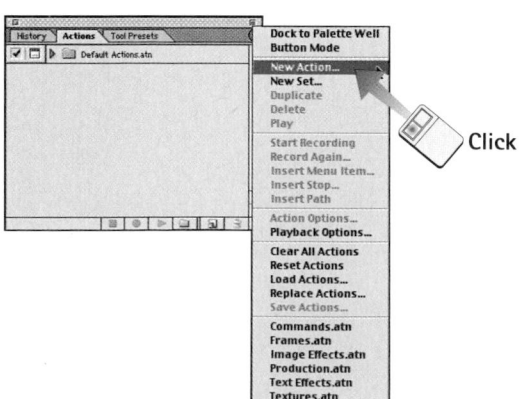

Click

3 Execute the Action

Click the **Record** button in the dialog box to begin recording the action. The **New Action** dialog box disappears to give you free access to your desktop. In this example, I converted a file to grayscale, changed it to index color, and inverted it to create a negative image.

4 Select Stop Recording

After you perform all the steps of the action you want to record, choose **Stop Recording** from the **Actions** palette menu to end the recording process.

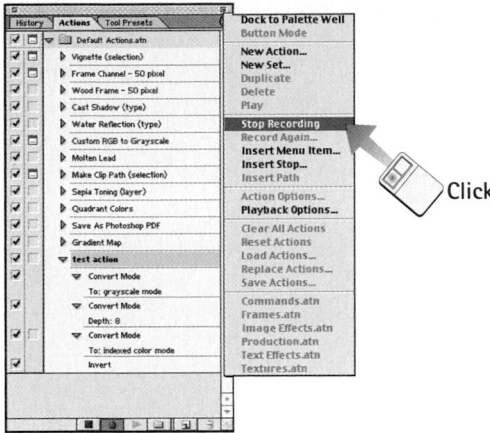

Click

5 Check the Action Sequence

Go to the **Actions** palette and find your newly created action in the list. Click the right-facing arrow to display the list of steps you recorded for that action.

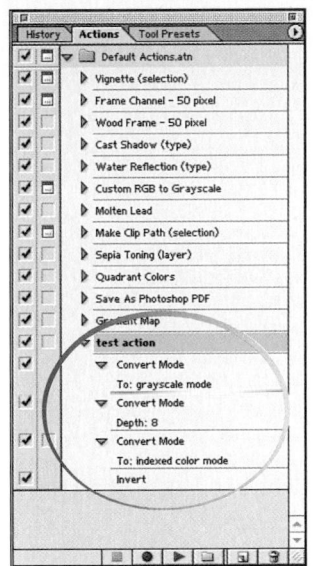

6 Add Any Missing Steps

If necessary, you can add steps to the action sequence by selecting a step as an insertion point (here I selected **Convert Mode**) and then selecting **Insert Menu Item** from the palette menu. Then type the name of the command as desired; Photoshop automatically records it and adds it to the action sequence *after* the selection. You also can select **Start Recording** and execute the commands to add steps after the selected command.

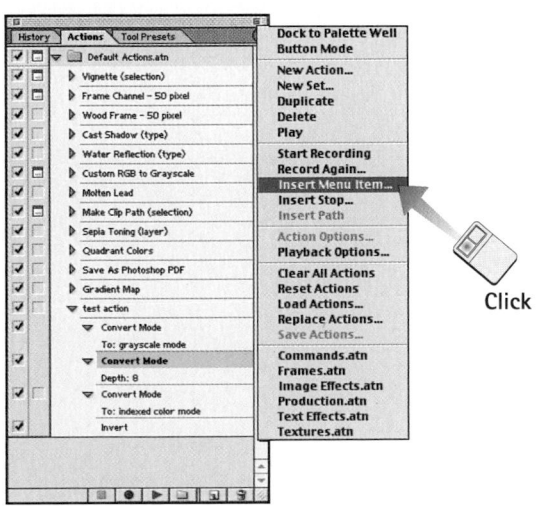

Click

How-To Hints

Cutting and Duplicating Actions

In the course of recording actions, certain tasks may become obsolete. To delete an action, select it in the **Actions** palette and choose **Delete** from the **Actions** palette menu. In the dialog box that appears, click **OK** to delete the action.

It can also be helpful to duplicate an action and modify it to create a new result. Highlight the action to be copied and select **Duplicate** from the **Actions** palette menu. Click the triangle next to the action to expand it, showing the associated parameters. To change the settings, double-click the action, which launches an appropriate dialog box. Enter the new information and click **OK** to create the new action.

End

How to Set Up Batch Processing Options

As described in the preceding tasks, actions allow you to apply multiple commands to one image with a single mouse click. But what do you do if you have a folder of 200 image files that all need the same action? Although you could open each image file and apply the action, it would be much better to process all 200 images with just a single command. This is what the Photoshop **Batch** command does. The process involves specifying a target folder that contains all the images to be processed and then detailing how and where Photoshop saves the images created by the action.

Begin

1 Open the Actions Palette

If the **Actions** palette is not currently displayed on your desktop, choose **Window, Actions** to display the palette. If necessary, exit **Button** mode and return the palette to **List** mode (see Step 2 in Task 7).

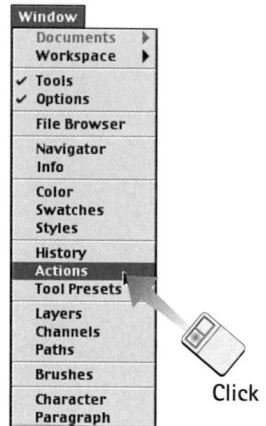

Click

2 Highlight the Action to Be Applied

In the **Actions** palette, click the action to be applied. The action is highlighted in the list. Ideally, you'll create the action first (refer to Task 8) and then select that action for the **Batch** command to use when it processes the files.

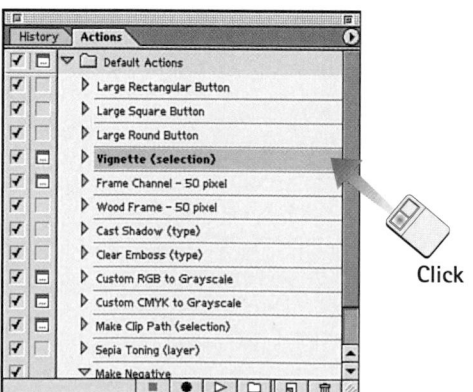

Click

3 Open the Batch Dialog Box

From the menu bar, choose **File, Automate, Batch.** The **Batch** dialog box opens. The action you highlighted in Step 2 appears in the **Play** section.

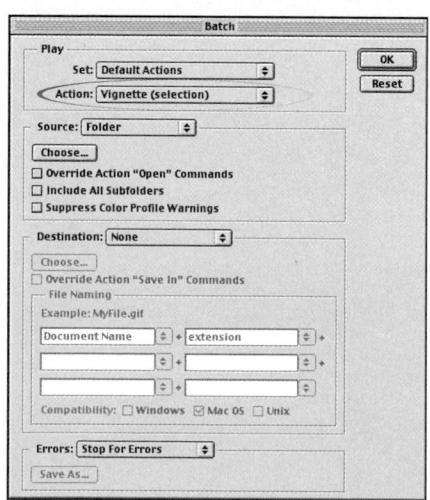

4 Select the Source Folder

From the **Source** drop-down list, select the **Folder** option and then click the **Choose** button. In the **Choose a Batch Folder** dialog box that appears, navigate to highlight the folder containing the images you want to process and click the **Choose** button. Back in the **Source** section, choose options if you want to process images in subfolders. (In Windows, note that the file-selection dialog box is different than the Mac version shown here; use standard navigation techniques to select a source folder.)

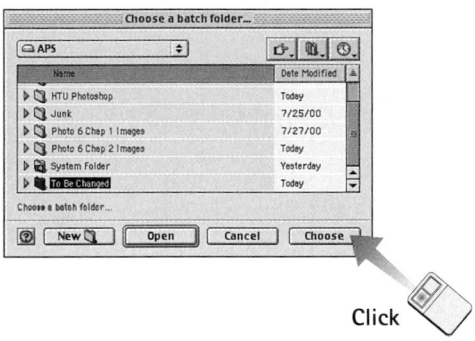

Click

5 Select the Destination Folder

Now specify where you want the changed images to be stored. From the **Destination** drop-down list, choose **None** (the changed images remain open onscreen), **Save and Close** (the changed images are saved and stored in their original location), or **Folder** (you then click the **Choose** button and navigate to the folder in which you want copies of the changed images to be stored). You can also specify a desired naming convention, using the pop-up menus in the **File Naming** section of the **Batch** dialog box.

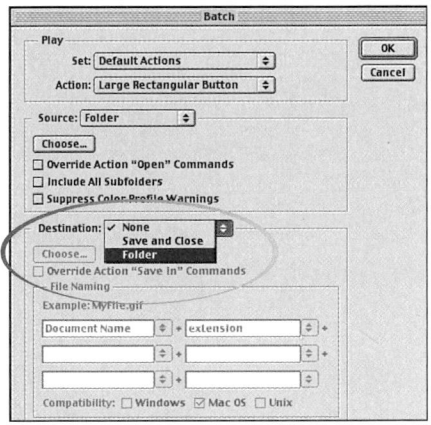

6 Specify Error Handling

From the **Errors** drop-down list, select **Stop for Errors** (the process stops until errors are resolved) or **Log Errors to File** (the process continues and a list of errors is generated for later review). Click **OK** to begin running the selected action on the selected folders and subfolders.

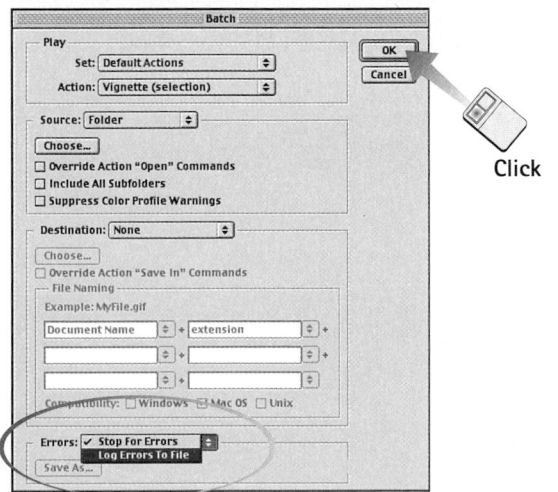

Click

How-To Hints

The Open and Save Commands

The **Batch** dialog box lets you designate special handling for opening and saving files. In many cases, individual actions include an **Open** command for a specific file, or a **Save** or **Save As** command that stores files in a unique place.

Because these specific commands could conflict with processing a whole folder of different images, Photoshop lets you override a specific "Open" command in an action with a generic one that opens each image in the folder, regardless of how it is named. In a similar manner, the override "Save in" command stores each file in the folder specified, rather than in a unique place as specified in the action.

End

Task

Selection Techniques

There are times when you need to change just a portion of an image rather than make global changes. To do this effectively, you'll usually select just the portion of the image you want to change, isolating it from the rest of the image. Then you can use all of Photoshop's editing tools to change just the selected area, leaving the remaining image unchanged.

As you select objects or areas in an image, take the time to select those areas as accurately as possible. Selections that include fringe elements from the background or that have poorly defined edges can destroy the realism and professional look of an image.

Photoshop goes to great lengths to provide a wide array of selection tools. The tasks in this part provide a solid overview of the different kinds of selections you can make in Photoshop, as well as how to modify, combine, and save selections after you've made them. The Photoshop selection tools let you isolate just about any kind of image area. It's well worth your time to learn as much as you can about image selections. ●

How to Select Geometric Areas

Selecting geometric areas such as circles, ovals, and rectangles is a common Photoshop task. Reasons for selecting geometric areas include lightening an area to place text on it, deleting a section of the image, or preparing to crop the image.

1 Open the File

Choose **File, Open** to open the desired file.

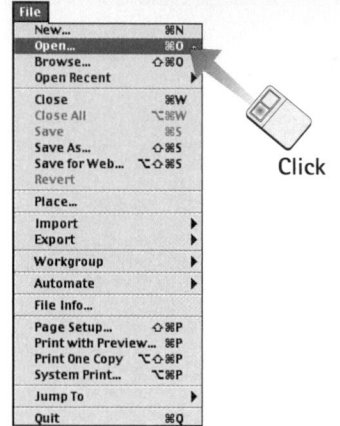

Click

2 Select the Marquee Tool

Select the **Rectangular Marquee** tool to draw a rectangular selection; select the **Elliptical Marquee** tool to draw an oval selection. (Other tools offer you the option of selecting a vertical or horizontal row of a single pixel.) To select any tool not currently visible in the toolbox, click and hold the current marquee tool and drag to the desired tool in the pop-out menu that appears. Note that the selected tool now appears on the toolbox button and in the **Options** bar at the top of the screen.

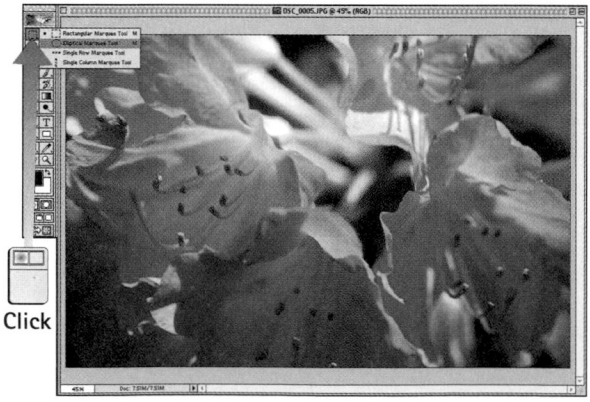

Click

3 Drag the Selection

Move the cursor onto the image and click and drag to draw the selection. If the selection is not where you want it, click once outside the selection to deselect the area, and drag to redraw the selection.

Drag

4 Move the Selection as Needed

After you create the selection, you can move the selection area (the ellipse or the rectangle, for example) to another area in the image. With the **Marquee** tool still selected, click inside the active selection and drag to move its location.

Drag

5 Deselect as Necessary

If you need to deselect the area and start over, choose **Select, Deselect** to deactivate the current selection. You also can deactivate a selection by clicking outside the selected area or by pressing ⌘+**D** (Mac users) or **Ctrl+D** (Windows users) when using any of the marquee tools.

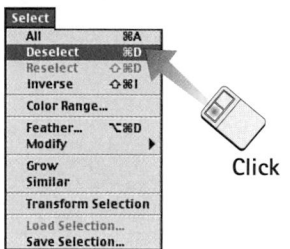
Click

End

How-To Hints

Selecting a Specific Size

To make a selection of a specific size, choose **Fixed Size** from the **Style** menu in the **Options** bar and type the dimensions, in pixels, in the **Height** and **Width** fields. Click in the image to create a selection matching the dimensions you entered.

Selecting a Size Ratio

To select a perfect circle or square, press and hold the **Shift** key as you drag the selection. To constrain any other size ratio (that is, to drag a selection area that preserves a height/width ratio), select **Constrained Aspect Ratio** from the **Style** menu in the **Options** bar and type values for the desired width-to-height ratio.

Drawing from the Center Out

To draw a selection from the center out instead of drawing it from a corner down, hold the **Option** key (Mac users) or the **Alt** key (Windows users) as you drag.

How to Use the Polygonal Lasso Tool

The **Polygonal Lasso** tool lets you create selections with straight-line segments so that you can create complex geometric areas such as starbursts and objects in perspective. It does not let you create curved segments, however, so make sure that the area you want to select is suited for this tool.

Begin

1 Open the File

Choose **File, Open** and select the desired file.

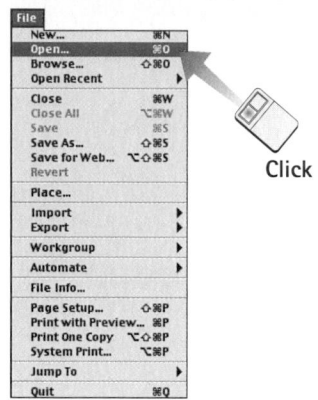

Click

2 Select the Polygonal Lasso Tool

Click and hold on the **Lasso** tool in the toolbox and drag to select the **Polygonal Lasso** tool from the pop-out menu that appears. Note that the selected tool now appears on the toolbox button and in the **Options** bar at the top of the screen.

Click

3 Click the First Point

Move the pointer onto the image and click to place the first anchor point. After placing the first point, notice that a straight line extends between the anchor point and the mouse pointer. This line indicates the selection line that will be created when you click to place another anchor point.

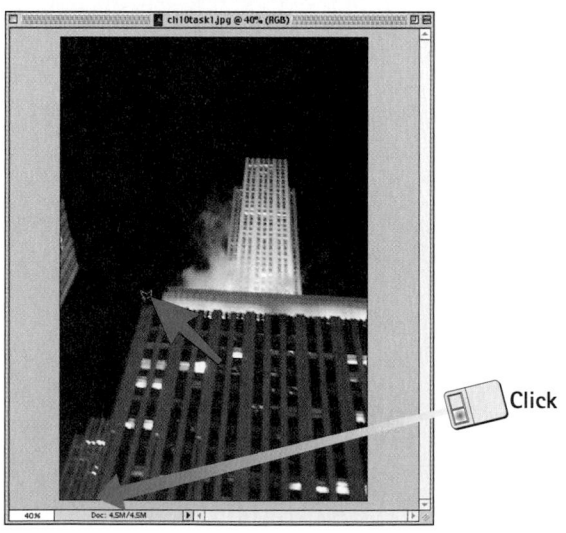

Click

4 Add Other Points as Needed

Click once at each location on the image, and place as many anchor points as necessary to surround the area you're selecting.

5 Close the Selection

To define an enclosed area, you can close the selection shape by clicking back on the starting anchor point. Alternatively, you can double-click or ⌘+click (Mac users) or **Ctrl**+click (Windows users) to connect the current point to the starting point. When you do this, the selection process is complete.

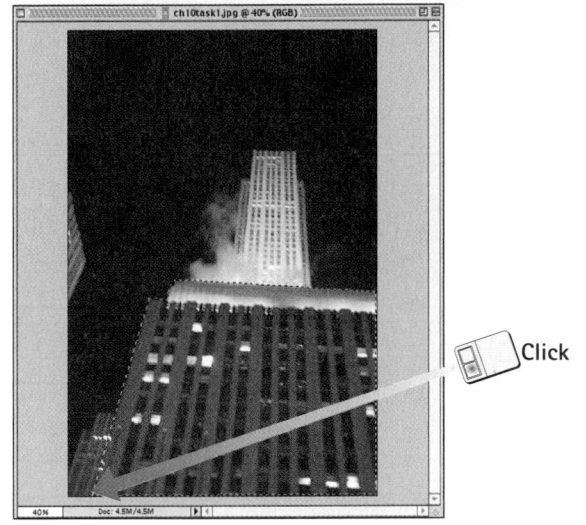

Click

End

How-To Hints

Using the Shift Key for Right Angles

Press and hold the **Shift** key to constrain the line segments you draw with the **Polygonal Lasso** tool to increments of 45-degree angles.

For Organic Selections

Select the **Lasso** tool instead of the **Polygonal Lasso** tool to draw freeform shape selections. You can switch to the **Lasso** tool from the **Polygonal Lasso** tool on-the-fly by pressing and holding the **Option** key (Mac users) or **Alt** key (Windows users) as you drag freeform shapes. Release the **Option/Alt** key to go back to dragging straight lines.

A Geometric Alternative

If you want a little help with geometric selections, try the **Magnetic Lasso** tool, found in the pop-out menu of the **Lasso** tool in the toolbox. Click and drag the tool around the selection area, and the selection snaps to the nearest contrast edge. The settings in the **Options** bar allow you to control the "snap-to" qualities of the tool, which you can adjust as needed.

How to Select by Color Range

When the area you want to select is predominantly one color, try using the color range as a selection criterion. This approach selects all the pixels in an image based on a specified color value. The color-range controls let you designate the exact range so that you can fine-tune the selection to a specific set of colors.

Begin

1 Open the File

Choose **File, Open** to launch the desired file.

2 Select the Color Range Command

Choose **Select, Color Range** to launch the **Color Range** dialog box.

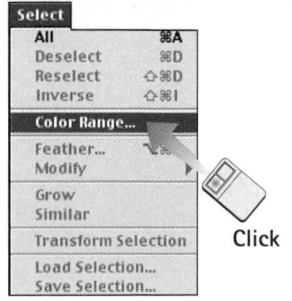

Click

3 Configure the Dialog Box

Click the arrow to the right of the **Select** field to access the menu and drag to select **Sampled Colors.** Start with the **Fuzziness** slider set to **40,** choose the **Selection** radio button, and set the **Selection Preview** option to **None.**

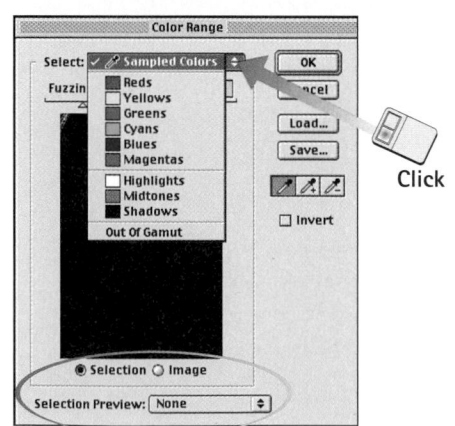

Click

4 Sample a Color

Move the cursor onto the image; notice that the cursor changes to an eyedropper as it moves over the image. Then click on a color you want to select. In this example, I clicked to select the purple in the flower; the preview in the dialog box shows how much of the image has that color. You can control how much variation of that color is selected by adjusting the **Fuzziness** slider.

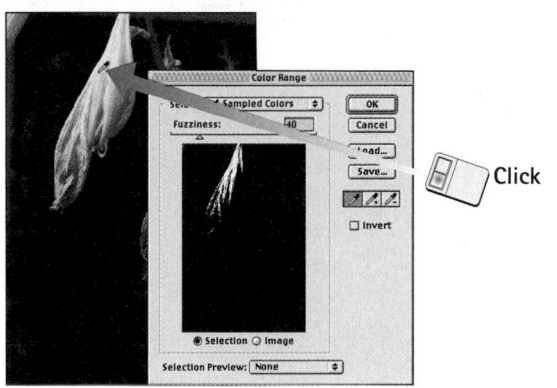

Click

5 Adjust the Fuzziness Slider

Increase or decrease the **Fuzziness** slider to include more or less of the color in the selection. Choose the **Black Matte** and **White Matte** options in the **Selection Preview** list in the **Color Range** dialog box to evaluate the selection area.

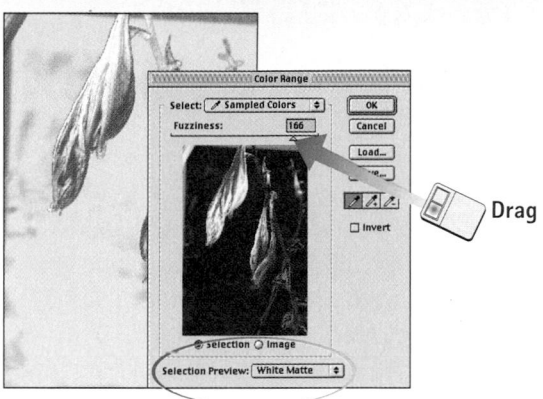

Drag

6 Add Additional Colors

Select the **Plus Eyedropper** from the dialog box and click on the image to add additional colors to the selected range. Click **OK** to close the dialog box and make the selection. If the selection is not to your satisfaction, adjust the **Fuzziness** slider and try again.

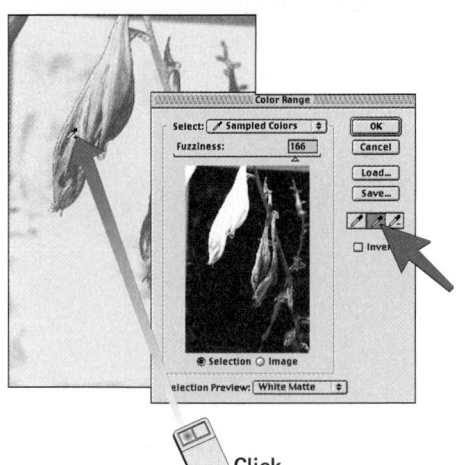

Click

End

How-To Hints

Image Previews

To check the selection in more detail, select **Grayscale, Black Matte, White Matte,** or **Quick Mask** from the **Selection Preview** drop-down list to show the selection results in the main image window. **Grayscale** shows selected areas in white and unselected areas in black. **Black Matte** shows selected areas as normal and unselected areas as flat black. **White Matte** shows selected areas as normal and unselected areas as white. **Quick Mask** places a mask over the selected or unselected areas, depending on how the **Quick Mask Options** are set (see the following task for details). To select all of a particular color or tonal range in an image, choose the desired color from the **Select** drop-down list. You also can select **Out of Gamut** to show which colors would be lost in an RGB-to-CMYK file conversion.

How to Use Quick Mask

Quick Mask is an intuitive way of selecting complex image areas using Photoshop's paint tools to define the selection area. The area is painted in as a mask, and you can erase or add to the mask to define the exact area you want to select. After you define the area, you exit Quick Mask to select the area. When you use Quick Mask with Photoshop's other painting tools (such as the **Paintbrush** tool), you can literally paint a mask or selection using the actual image as a guide-line. In fact, you won't need to worry about staying within the lines because you can easily reverse the painting by switching the color you're painting with.

Begin

1 Open the File

Choose **File, Open** to launch the desired file.

2 Make a Basic Selection

Although you can start the selection process with Quick Mask, I find it's easier to make an initial selection first, just to set up a relationship between the mask and the rest of the image. Use any of Photoshop's selection tools and select the general area you want to define. Here, I used the **Magic Wand** tool to select a portion of the statue's back.

3 Set Quick Mask Options

Double-click the **Quick Mask** button in the toolbox to launch the **Quick Mask Options** dialog box. Select **Masked Areas** or **Selected Areas** to specify whether the mask represents the selection or the background (that is, whether you're covering or uncovering as you paint the mask). The default mask color is red, but you can click the color swatch and select another color. The selection you made in Step 2 reflects these settings as you make them. When everything looks good, click **OK.**

Double-click

4 Draw or Paint the Selection

Use the Photoshop paint tools to fine-tune the mask. See Part 8, "Drawing, Painting, and Filling with Color," for details. You can choose smaller or larger brushes or zoom in to follow the lines of your image more closely. As you'll see in the next step, you also can easily erase any areas where you painted outside the lines.

5 Erase Unwanted Areas

Select the **Erase** tool and erase the mask to reduce the selection area as necessary. If the eraser *adds* mask instead of *deleting* it, select **Edit, Undo** and change the foreground color to white.

6 Exit Quick Mask

Click the **Standard Mode** button in the toolbox to exit Quick Mask and convert the mask to a selection. Alternatively, press the **Q** key to toggle between standard mode and Quick Mask mode to make sure that the selection is correct for the work you're doing to the image.

End

How-To Hints

Filtering for Graphic Effects

While still in Quick Mask mode, you can use any of Photoshop's filters to apply unique textures to the mask. When you switch to standard mode, the texture of the selection is reflected as you edit the image.

Using the Type Tool for Text Selections

While in Quick Mask mode, you also can use the **Type Mask** tool to create text selections. Fill the selections with the mask to make the selection active, and then modify the selection further with filters or other tools.

How to Select Areas Using Paths

Because *paths* define the edges of an area, it's only natural that you use them to create a selection. Paths are a good selection choice if you need to select areas with smooth, flowing curves and precise angles. Because Part 10, "Using Paths," goes to great lengths to describe how to work with paths, this task focuses only on how to convert a path to a selection.

Begin

1 Open the File

Choose **File, Open** to launch the desired file.

2 Select the Pen Tool

Select the **Pen** tool from the toolbox. Note that the tool you select appears on the toolbox button and in the **Options** bar at the top of the screen.

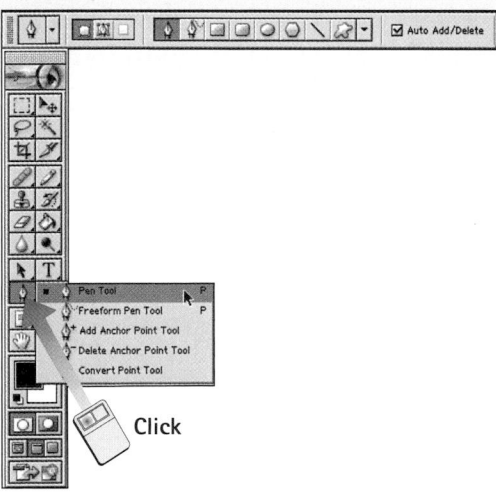

Click

3 Draw a Path or Segment

Starting at one side of the area you want to select, click the **Pen** tool on the image to create the necessary points for a path or segment. (A *segment* is a path that hasn't been joined at both ends.) You're trying to create a contained area. In this example, I've selected the church steeples, but note that the selection path runs off both edges of the image area.

4 Make the Path a Selection

Choose **Window, Paths** to launch the **Paths** palette. From the palette menu, select **Make Selection** to launch the **Make Selection** dialog box. Select the **Feather Radius** and **Anti Alias** options if you want to soften the selection, and then click **OK**. The segmented path line now includes a blinking selection line. If you didn't define a contained area in Step 3, Photoshop joins your first and last points to "complete" the selection area.

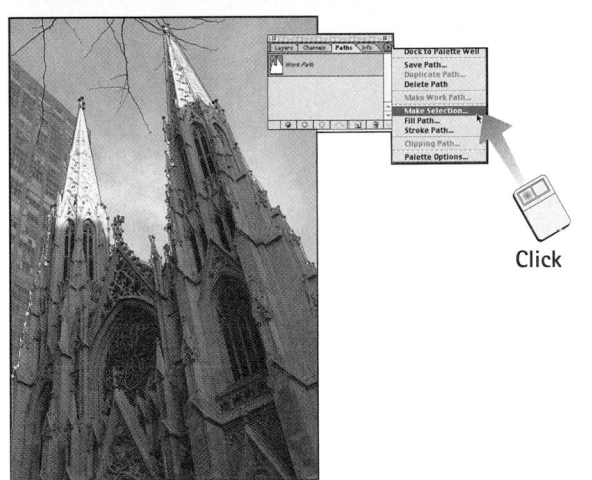

Click

5 Deselect the Path

At this point, both the path and the selection are active. In the **Paths** palette, deselect the path tile so that only the selection is active.

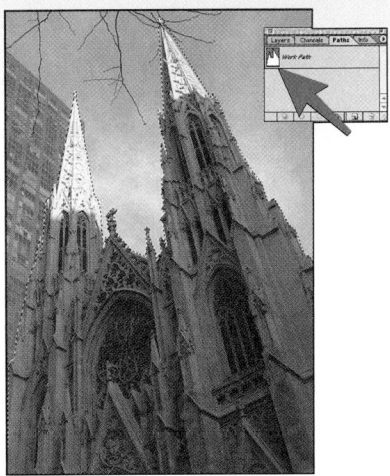

End

How-To Hints

Using Paths Instead of Saving Selections

Paths are a smart alternative to saving selections. This is because paths add very little to the file size and can be modified and resized infinitely. Selections, on the other hand, are saved as channels, which can bloat overall file size very quickly.

Note that there's a difference between *making* a selection and *saving* a selection. Saving a selection actually creates a separate channel that is masked to show the selection area. This channel is used as a base when the selection is reloaded. It's the channel itself that adds to the file size, not the ability to select the channel.

How to Modify Selections

To select complex shapes and areas, you must sometimes combine multiple selection methods. Adding or subtracting from a selection is only the beginning. You also can shrink or grow a selection, smooth out sharp corners, and tweak or skew the selection area in any direction. This task shows the top 12 shortcuts for working with selections. Combine them as you see fit to select exactly the right area of your image.

Begin

1 Adding to Selections

To add to a selection, hold the **Shift** key as you're using any of the Photoshop selection tools. Alternatively, you can also click the **Add To Selection** button in the **Options** bar. A plus sign appears next to the cursor to show that you're adding to the current selection.

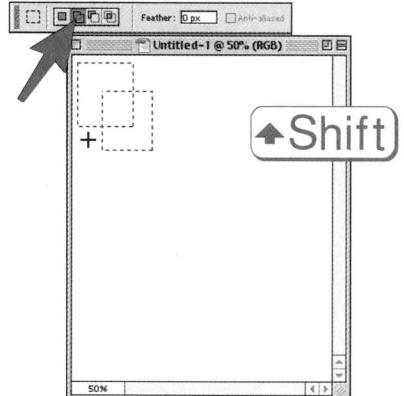

2 Subtracting from Selections

To subtract from a selection, hold the **Option** key (Mac users) or **Alt** key (Windows users) as you're using any of the Photoshop selection tools. Alternatively, you can click the **Subtract from Selection** button in the **Options** bar. A minus sign appears next to the cursor to show that you're subtracting from the current selection.

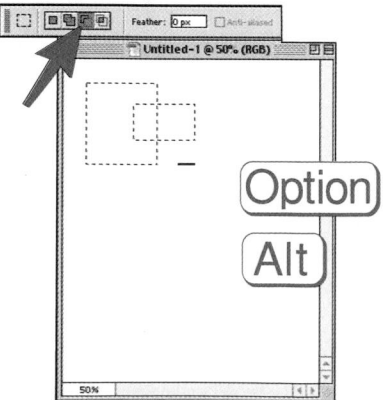

3 Intersecting Selections

With an area selected, it's possible to create a second, overlapping area that leaves only the common, intersecting area selected. First, select an area. Then press **Shift+Option** (Mac users) or **Shift+Alt** (Windows users) as you draw a second selection that overlaps the first. An × appears next to the cursor as you do this. After you release the mouse and the keyboard keys, only the intersecting area remains selected.

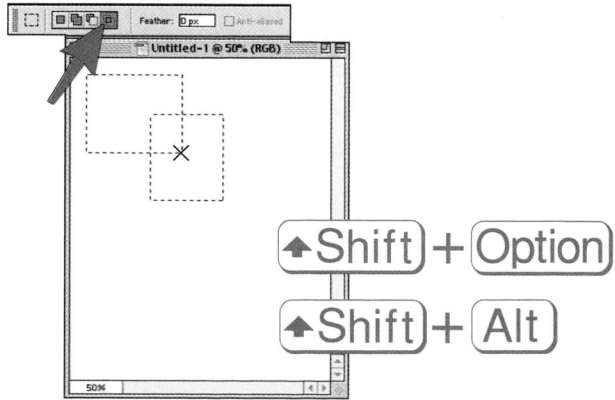

4 Nudging a Selection

After you select an area, you can nudge the selection area up, down, left, or right one pixel at a time. Select one of the **Marquee** tools in the toolbox and press the arrow keys on your keyboard.

5 Inverting Selections

To invert an active selection, choose **Select, Inverse.** This action selects the exact opposite of the current selection. In this example, after you select the menu command, everything on the image area will be selected *except* the rectangle that's currently selected.

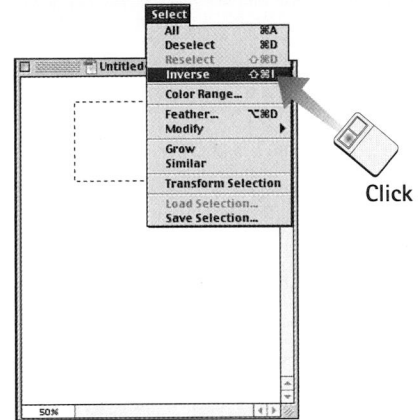

Click

6 Smoothing Selections

Smoothing a selection involves a gradual rounding of corners or sharp edges. To smooth an active selection, choose **Select, Modify, Smooth.** In the **Smooth Selection** dialog box that appears, enter a value from 1 to 16 pixels to determine the degree of smoothing. Click **OK** to modify the selection. Repeat this step as desired to smooth the selection even more.

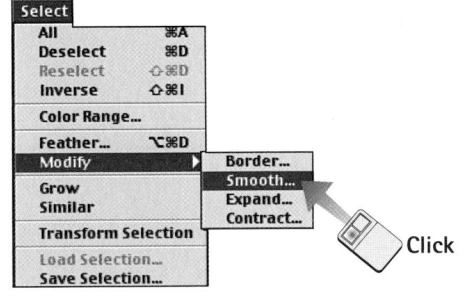

Click

7 Expanding Selections

Expanding a selection means just what it says: expanding the overall area of a selection by a specific number of pixels. To expand an active selection, choose **Select, Modify, Expand.** In the **Expand Selection** dialog box that appears, enter a value from 1 to 16 pixels to determine the degree of expansion. Click **OK** to modify the selection. Repeat this step as desired to expand the selection even more.

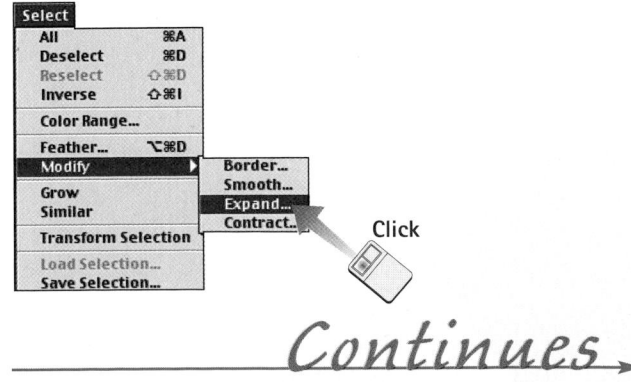

Click

Continues

8 Contracting Selections

Contracting a selection makes the overall selection area smaller. To contract an active selection, choose **Select, Modify, Contract.** In the **Contract Selection** dialog box that appears, enter a value from 1 to 16 pixels. Click **OK** to modify the selection. Repeat this step to contract the selection even more.

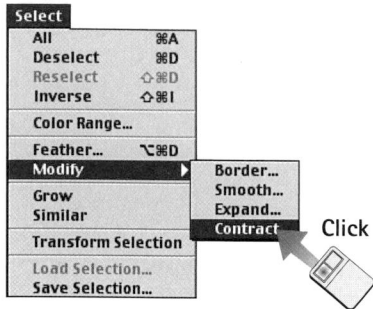

Click

9 Isolating Selection Borders

When you're working with geometric selections, there may be times when you want to apply an effect only to the *border* of a selected area. Choose **Select, Modify, Border.** In the **Border** dialog box that appears, enter a value from 1 to 16 pixels to specify the width of the border. This option thickens the selection line to the width you specify and makes that line the active selection area. Click **OK** to modify the selection.

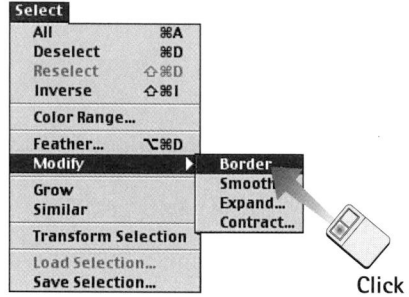

Click

10 Feathering a Selection

Feathering a selection involves vignetting the selection edges, softening any effects that are applied to the selected area. To feather a selection, enter a pixel value in the **Feather** field of the **Options** bar. Alternatively, choose **Select, Feather.** In the **Feather Selection** dialog box that appears, type a feather value from 0.2 to 250 pixels and click **OK.**

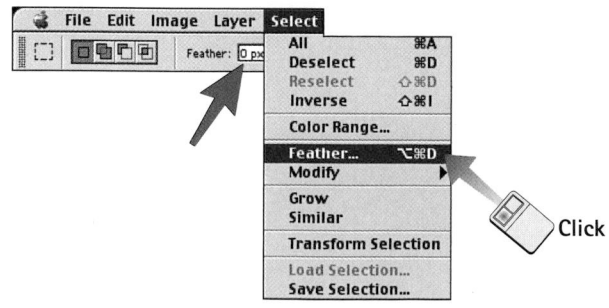

Click

11 Selecting Similar Colors

After you select an area, you can select all other pixels in the image that have the same color value. This capability can be effective if you want to select multiple colored objects or areas. To do this, select a color or range of colors, and then choose **Select, Similar.** All pixels with similar pixel values are selected.

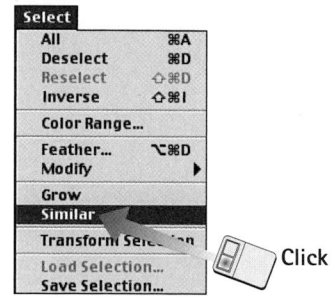

Click

12 Transforming Selections

You can distort or skew a selection using any of the **Transform** options described in Part 11, Task 5, "How to Transform Layers." To transform an active selection, choose **Select, Transform Selection.** A bounding box appears around the selection; drag the handles to modify the selection area. Double-click inside the bounding box or click the **Move** tool and then click **OK** to apply the transformation.

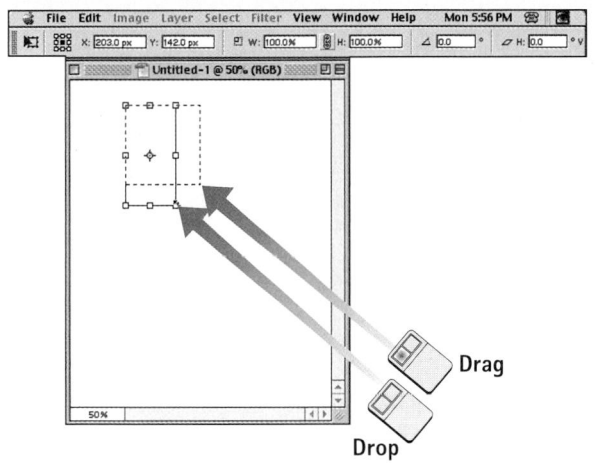

Drag

Drop

End

How-To Hints

Smoothing Selections to Make Rounded Corners

Use the **Smooth Selection** technique from Step 6 to create rounded-corner rectangular selections. The 16-pixel rounding value works very well with 72dpi Web images. The result is ready to be stroked or filled to create a rounded-corner box shape.

Using Tolerance with Select Similar

The **Select Similar** command in Step 11 uses the tolerance setting from the **Magic Wand Options** palette to determine how it selects similar colors. If you set the tolerance high, more "similar" colors are selected; if you set the tolerance low, a more narrow range of colors is selected.

How to Save and Load Selections

After you've gone to the trouble of making the perfect selection, you may want to save that selection for future use. This is especially true if you've selected an object or area you know you're going to be going back to as you work with the image. Photoshop lets you save selections as *alpha channels*, which preserve the exact area and transparency levels and can be reloaded at any time.

Begin

1 Open the File

Choose **File, Open** and launch the desired file.

2 Make the Selection

Select the desired area using any of Photoshop's selection tools. In this example, I used the **Color Range** dialog box to select the green blades of grass. (Sample the color and click **OK** to make the selection.)

3 Choose Save Selection

Choose **Select, Save Selection.** The **Save Selection** dialog box opens.

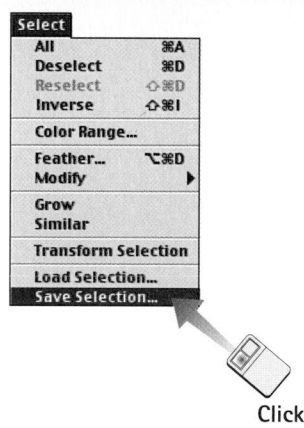

Click

4 Name the Selection Channel

In the **Name** field, type a name for the selection. This is the name that Photoshop gives to the alpha channel, which is where the selection is saved. Click **OK** to save the selection.

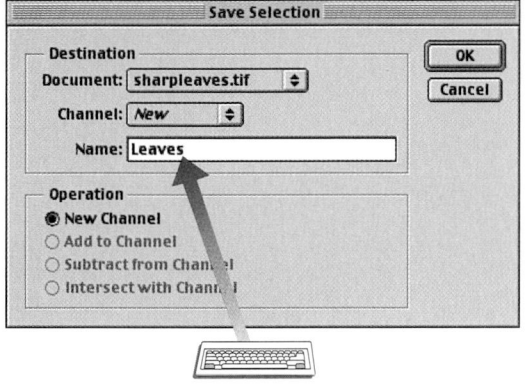

5 Load the Selection

To load a saved selection, choose **Select, Load Selection.** In the **Load Selection** dialog box that appears, choose the selection name from the **Channel** drop-down list and click **OK** to activate the selection. Note that you can load a selection from any open document.

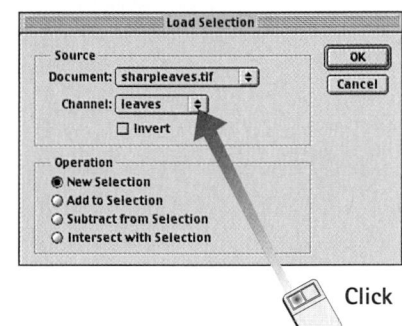

Click

End

How-To Hints

PSD or TIFF?

To preserve the channel along with the saved file in Step 4, you must use either the native Photoshop format (PSD) or the TIFF format. The PSD format is safest, though, and can hold more than one extra channel.

Viewing Saved Selections

All saved selections are visible in the **Channels** palette, listed by the name you entered in Step 4. To review saved selections, choose **Window, Channels** to open the **Channels** palette and examine all saved selections.

File Size Caution

Although saving selections is easy and convenient, these selections can dramatically increase file size if you're not careful. This is especially true if you're saving multiple selections in one file, if your selections are large, or if they include transparent areas. To monitor file size as you work, choose **Document Sizes** from the pop-up menu on the status bar at the bottom of the image window. The value on the left shows the current image's file size if the image were to be flattened; the value on the right shows the image's file size saved with any additional layers and channels.

Task

4

Converting Files

*T*he tasks in this part walk you through the various processes for saving, converting, and optimizing files. Knowing how to convert files is important; you don't have to work in graphics very long before someone calls to tell you that they can't read the file you just sent them. There are lots of different file formats, ranging from TIFF, JPEG, and EPS down to the obscure formats, such as Amiga HAM and Scitex CT.

File formats have evolved over time in an environment where there were no standards. Therefore, many files are compatible; you'll find that TIFF, PICT, BMP, and other formats are interchangeable as far as pragmatic functionality is concerned. Some systems require specific formats (such as Amiga and Scitex), so you can easily figure out when to employ those options.

Adding to this confusion is the discrepancy between Macintosh and Windows platforms, as well as issues with transferring files between Windows 95, Windows 98, and Windows NT. With all these different systems and platforms, it's a wonder anything gets transferred successfully.

In addition to pure file conversions, it is also important to *optimize* files for use in different capacities, such as prepping files for print or building compact Web files. Optimizing files involves striking a balance between image clarity, proper color modes, and file size.

Fortunately, Photoshop excels in the realm of file conversion. Before it was an image editing program, Photoshop's core technology was in file conversion. That's why there are almost 20 file formats available in the Photoshop **Save As** dialog box. For optimization, you will find the same optimize capabilities in both Photoshop 7 and ImageReady 7. Choosing **File, Save for Web** in Photoshop opens a comparison dialog box that delivers the same kind of optimization control as ImageReady's **Optimize** palette. Unless stated otherwise, the file optimization methods given in these tasks work in either program. ●

How to Save Files in Other Formats

At first glance, changing a file's format can be a confusing and complicated matter, especially if you don't know what all those acronyms stand for. The reality is that it's not as complicated as it first appears. Photoshop provides almost 20 format options from which to choose; all you have to do is know which ones to use.

Begin

1 Choose File, Save As

Regardless of the current format of the file, you change the file format from the **Save As** dialog box. Choose **File, Save As** to open the dialog box.

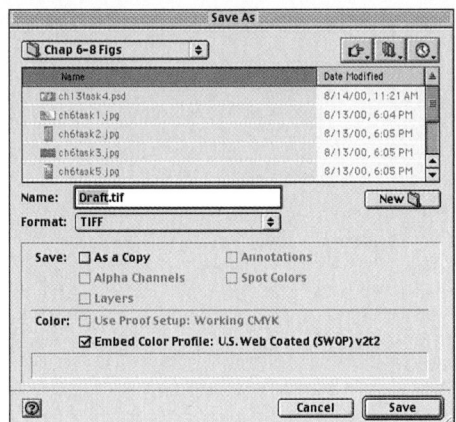

2 Rename File and Select Format

If desired, highlight the current filename in the **Name** list and type a new filename in the **Name** field. Access the **Format** pop-up menu and choose a new file format.

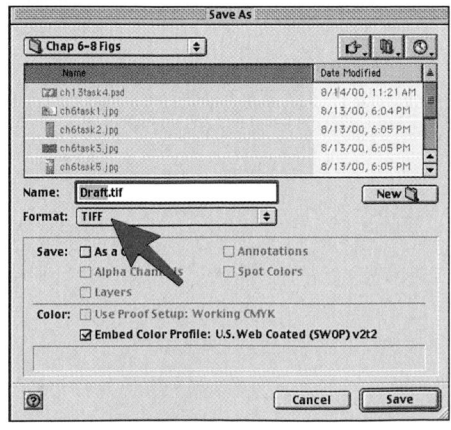

3 Choose File Destination

If desired, use the pop-up menu at the top of the dialog box and navigate to a new destination folder in which you want to store the image.

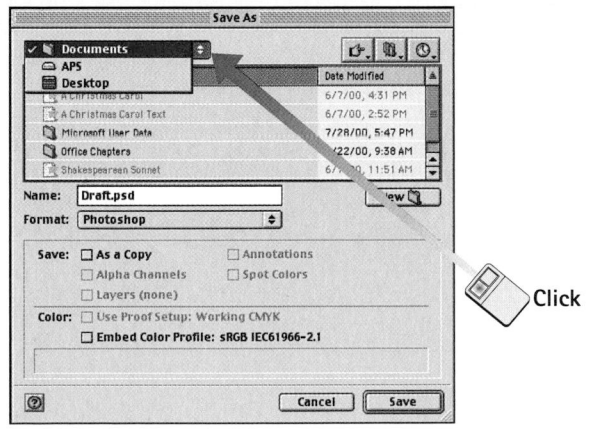

Click

4 Duplicate the File if You Want

In the **Save** section of the **Save As** dialog box, enable the **As a Copy** check box to duplicate the file. The **As a Copy** option ensures that the original file will not be overwritten.

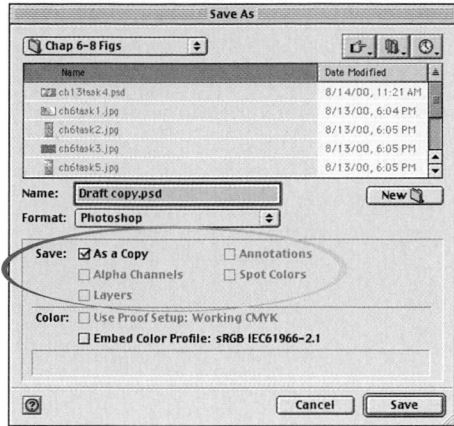

5 To Save as a JPEG

When you choose to save a file in JPEG format, clicking **OK** launches the **JPEG Options** dialog box. Select the appropriate **Image Options** and **Format Options** and click **OK.** For more on these options, see Task 7, "How to Build JPEG Files for the Web," later in this part.

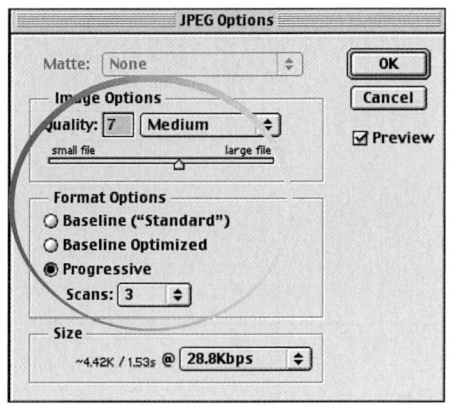

6 To Save as a PDF

When you choose to save a file in Photoshop PDF format, clicking **OK** launches the **PDF Options** dialog box. Select either the **JPEG** or **ZIP** option in the **Encoding** area. If you select **JPEG,** you must also choose a compression rate. Choose any other options that apply and click **OK** to finish.

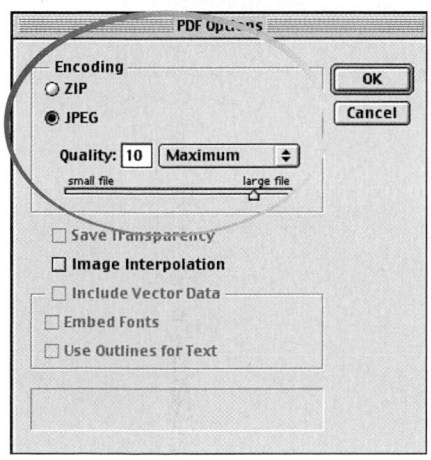

7 To Save as a TIFF

When you choose to save a file as **TIFF,** clicking **OK** in the **Save As** dialog box launches the **TIFF Options** dialog box. Specify whether the file must be compatible with a Mac or PC. In addition, you should almost always enable the **LZW Compression** check box, which dramatically compresses the file size without impacting image quality.

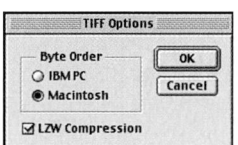

Continues ➔

8 To Preserve the Alpha Channels

When saving a file, it is possible to preserve its associated alpha channels. *Alpha channels* are separate channels used to save selections and to create masks. To preserve the alpha channels, enable the **Alpha Channels** check box in the **Save** section of the **Save As** dialog box. This option is grayed out if there are no alpha channels associated with the file.

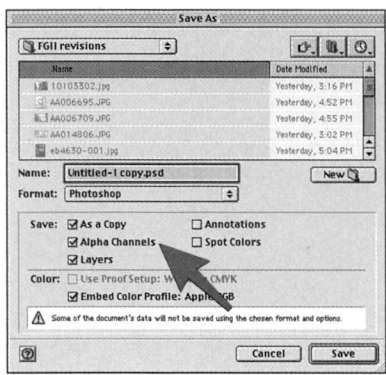

9 To Preserve Layers and Annotations

When saving a file, it is possible to preserve each individual layer and any annotations associated with the file. To preserve the individual layers of a file, enable the **Layers** check box in the **Save** section of the **Save As** dialog box. To preserve any voice or text annotations, enable the **Annotations** check box. These options are grayed out if there are no layers or annotations associated with the file.

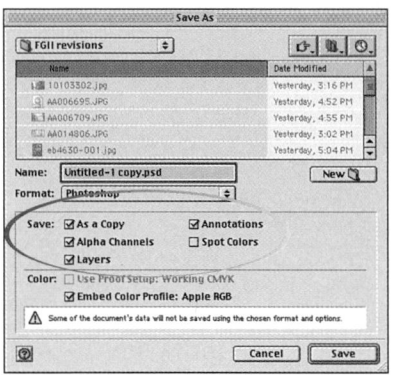

10 To Preserve Spot Colors

When saving a file, it is possible to preserve each individual spot color channel along with the file itself. To preserve a file's spot colors, enable the **Spot Colors** check box in the **Save** section of the **Save As** dialog box. This option is grayed out if there are no spot color channels associated with the file.

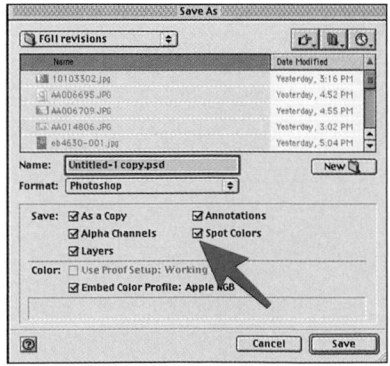

11 To Set the Color Options

When saving a file, it is possible to preserve any color-proofing options along with the file itself. To save the current proofing setup (as specified in **View, Proof Colors**), enable the **Use Proof Setup** check box in the **Color** section of the **Save As** dialog box. To embed the current RGB working space, select the **Embed Color Profile** check box.

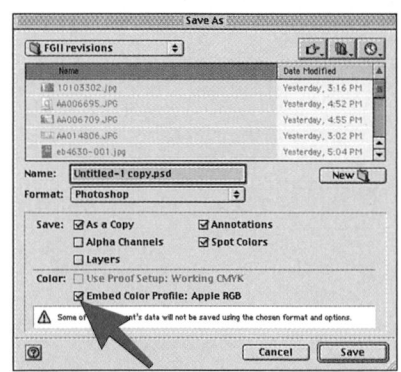

12 Save the File

When you have selected the options you want to use to save the file, click **Save** to close the **Save As** dialog box and save your file.

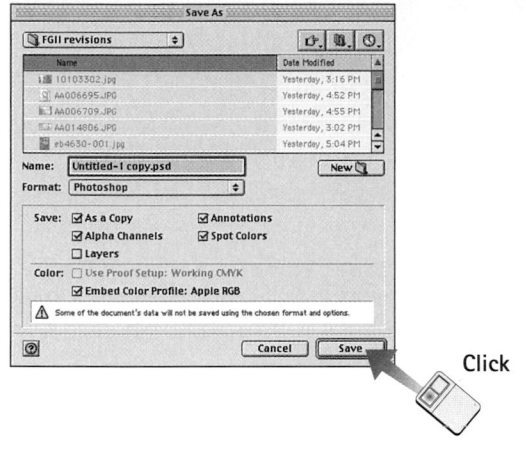

Click

End

How-To Hints

JPEG, PDF, or TIFF?

You save a file in JPEG format if you have a photographic image that must be compressed for onscreen viewing (such as the Web). Choose the PDF format if you have a Web document that you want to keep consistent for layout design and print versions. Save a file in TIFF format if you want to save a clipping path with the file to be used in a program such as Illustrator, PageMaker, or InDesign.

LZW Slows Things Down

Saving a TIFF file as LZW does have its drawbacks—mainly that opening and closing files takes longer because Photoshop has to compress and decompress the data. For smaller files, it's no big deal, but for files that are more than 20MB, you will notice the difference.

Be Careful Saving JPEGs

The image quality of a JPEG file will erode if you repeatedly save the file as JPEG. The compression doesn't just happen one time—it is reapplied with every save. You should convert the file to JPEG only at the very end, when the image editing is complete.

How to Optimize Color Files for Printing

Preparing a file for printing means a lot of different things. It could mean a complicated offset professional color project with film and plates, or it could refer to an inkjet proof or a laser print. For the sake of argument, this task refers to color printing on a press or proofing device. It is important that you check with your printer before prepping files and setting things up because all printers do things a bit differently. What follows are general guidelines for how to optimize a file for printing.

2 Set the Color Settings

Choose **Edit, Color Settings** to open the **Color Settings** dialog box. Select **US Prepress defaults** from the **Settings** menu. In the **Working Spaces** section, select the various profiles and parameters specified by your printer or leave the defaults. In the **Color Management Policies** section, select **Preserve Embedded Profiles** whenever a match or near match is available; otherwise, you must experiment with converting to the appropriate working spaces. See Part 1, Task 8, "How to Specify Photoshop Color Models," for details.

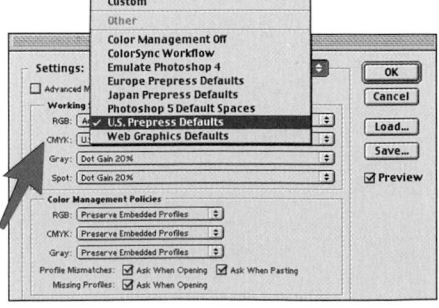

Begin

1 Determine Output Resolution

In most cases, you will print at 300dpi for high-quality images. You can reduce this number slightly for some offset presses (inkjet and color laser printers and copiers are even more forgiving). Open the **Image Size** dialog box by choosing **Image, Image Size.** If you know the resolution requirements required by your printer, type them in the **Resolution** field; if you don't, type **300** as a baseline and select **pixels/ inch.** Make sure that the **Resample Image** check box is not selected to avoid degradation of image quality.

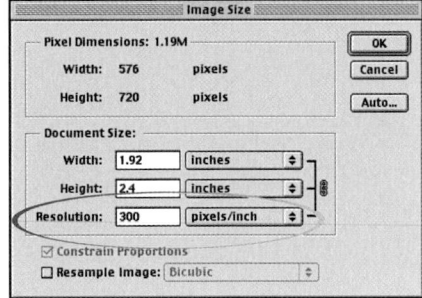

3 Set Page Layout

Select **File, Print with Preview** to launch the **Print** dialog box. In the **Scaled Print Size** area, set the scale percentage as necessary to fit the image on the page size. Use the thumbnail image as a guide for entering the proper new value. If necessary, go to the **Position** area and deselect the **Center Image** check box and drag the thumbnail image to reposition it on the page.

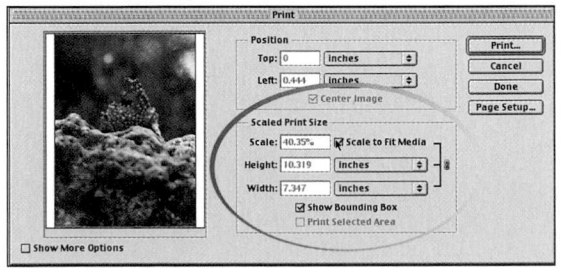

4 Check for Out-of-Gamut Colors

To print in color, you have to convert the color mode for your image to CMYK. Because the CMYK color format allows fewer colors than, say, the RGB format, you could lose some of the colors in your image during the color conversion. Choose **View, Gamut Warning.** The gamut mask points out the areas where colors could be lost in the image so that you can address the problem before the image goes to the printer.

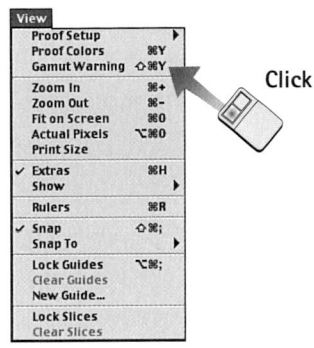

Click

5 Correct Problem Colors

After you identify where the problem colors lie, choose **View, Gamut Warning** again to turn off the gamut mask and then choose **View, Proof Setup, Working CMYK.** Photoshop displays a preview of how the colors will look when they are converted. These color shifts are often subtle, and you may decide you can live with them. If not, edit the colors in your image using any of the color tools. (*Hint:* The **Sponge** tool may soften some saturated colors.)

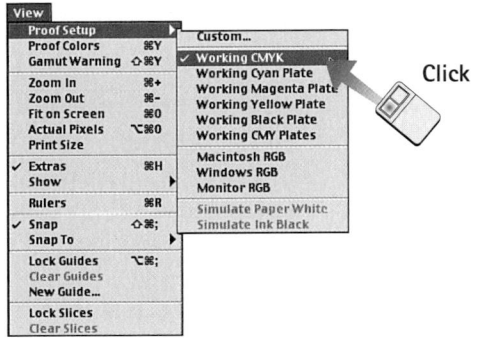

Click

6 Convert File to Proper Color Mode

After you correct any color problems, convert the file to CMYK format. Choose **Image, Mode, CMYK Color** to convert the file.

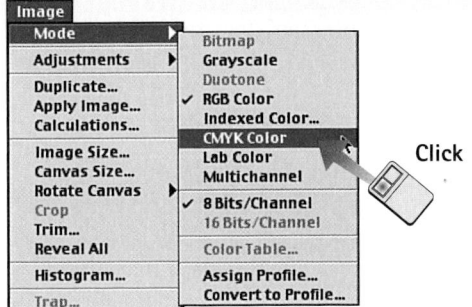

Click

7 Save File in Proper Format

Now save the file in the proper format as specified by your printer: Choose **File, Save As** and then select the desired format from the **Format** menu. If in doubt, save the image as a **Photoshop EPS** file (for a PostScript device) or as a **Basic TIFF** file (for a standard device).

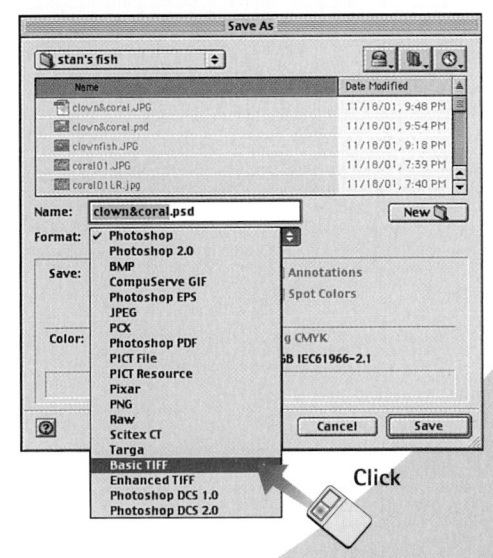

Click

End

How to Move Files from Mac to Windows

There's more to moving a file from a Mac machine to a Windows machine than handing off a file. The same image looks darker in Windows because most Mac monitors are calibrated at a gamma of 1.8; Windows monitors usually are calibrated at 2.2. Moving a file from Mac to Windows can lead to some very muddy results if the image is dark to start with on the Mac. When moving a file from Windows to Mac, the *gamma factor* is less of an issue because of the cross-platform capabilities built into the Macintosh. As long as the **PC Exchange** settings are correct, files should move over without a problem.

Begin

1 Open File in ImageReady

In Photoshop, open the file you want to move from the Mac to Windows. With the file open in Photoshop, you can easily open it in ImageReady by clicking the **Jump to** button at the bottom of the toolbox.

Click

2 Set Preview for Windows Gamma

If you're using a Mac, choose **View, Preview, Standard Windows Color.** If you're using Windows, choose **View, Preview, Standard Macintosh Color.** Observe the image on your screen. This option gives you an accurate preview of what the file will look like on the other platform.

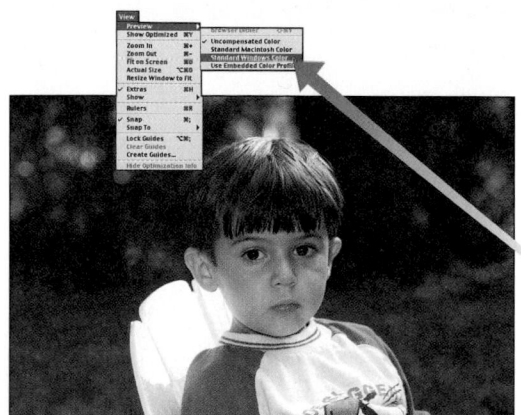

Click

3 Choose Adjust Gamma

Now adjust the image gamma: Choose **Image, Adjustments, Gamma** to open the **Gamma** dialog box. If you're on a Mac, start by clicking the **Macintosh to Windows** button (if you're in Windows, click the **Windows to Macintosh** button); the slider adjusts automatically. Drag the slider to make any further modifications. Toggle the **Preview** check box on and off to check the appearance of the image in both Mac and Windows.

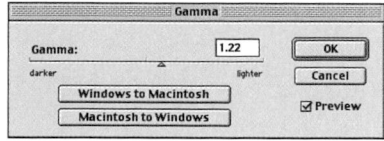

4 Save as Proper Format

From the **Optimize** palette, select the proper file format (either GIF or JPG). Then choose **File, Save Optimized** to save a copy of the file. If you're not sure which file format is best for the image, you can switch between the two and get an idea, in real time, which format will look better and take up less file space. To do so, simply toggle between the two options in the **Optimize** palette.

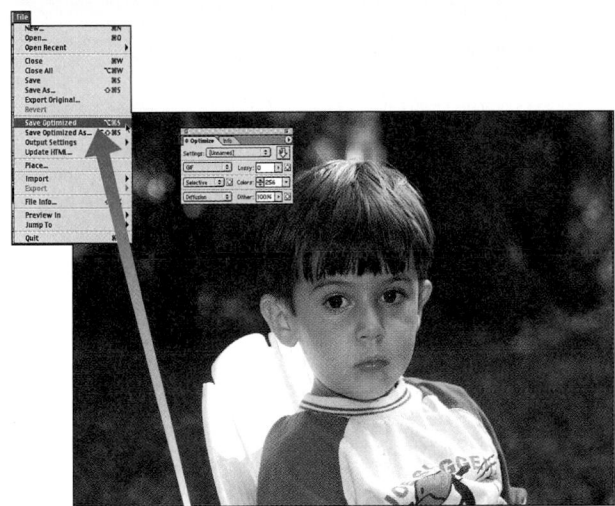

 Click

5 Use a Windows-Compatible Transport Method

When sending the file from Mac to Windows, copy the file to a floppy disk that has been formatted in PC format. If you are sending the file electronically, be sure to zip the file to protect it during transmission.

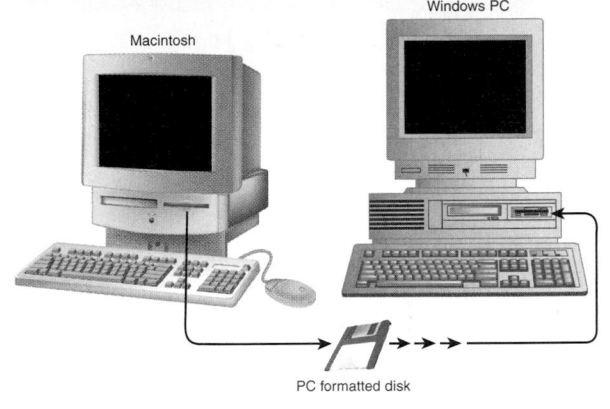

Macintosh

Windows PC

PC formatted disk

End

How-To Hints

Converting in Photoshop

Preparing files for use on another platform (Windows-to-Mac or Mac-to-Windows) works best in ImageReady, although you also can do it from Photoshop. Choose **View, Proof Setup, Windows RGB** to preview how a Mac file will look in Windows. If you're on a Windows machine, you can preview how the Mac gamma will affect an image by choosing **View, Proof Setup, Macintosh RGB.**

Choosing File Formats for the Web

A general rule of thumb is to create GIF files for graphics files and text-heavy images. Use the JPEG format for photographic continuous-tone images in which a little softness will be less noticeable.

How to Build GIF Files for the Web

GIF files are efficient, compact files perfect for use on the Web. As you see in the tasks that follow, GIF files allow you to build in transparency and animation while keeping the file size small. GIF files do not handle photographic images well, however. If you want your photographic images to maintain detail, consider the JPEG file format.

Begin

1 Open and Save File in Photoshop

Open the file you want to convert to GIF format. Choose **File, Save for Web.** The **Save For Web** dialog box opens, and Photoshop creates a duplicate image, leaving the original image untouched.

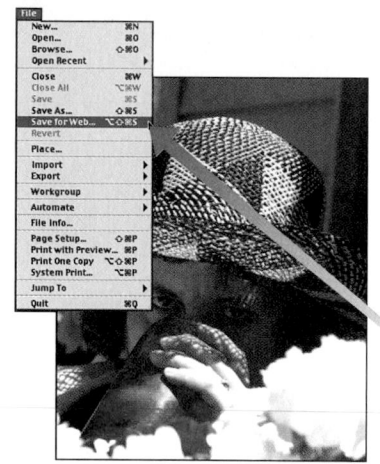

Click

2 Select Optimized File Format

From the first drop-down menu in the dialog box, select **GIF.** Leave the next two options set at **Selective** and **Diffusion** (these options refer to the color conversion and dither patterns).

3 Set Lossy and Dither Sliders

Set the **Lossy** and **Dither** sliders. Start by setting **Lossy** at **100** and **Dither** at **0.** To reduce the file size, keep the **Dither** value as low as possible and the **Lossy** value as high as possible. The image is updated to reflect the changes you make. Watch the image changes to help make a final decision when it comes to applying the various settings.

4 Preview Your Settings

Click the **Optimized** tab to preview the file compression results based on your settings. If the image is too grainy, lower the **Lossy** slider. If it appears solarized and graphic, raise the **Dither** value.

5 Set the Number of Colors

Your next goal is to create a GIF file with as few colors as possible. Shoot for 32 or 64 (some graphics files can use as few as 8 or even 4 colors without compromising the image much). Click and hold the **Colors** drop-down list and select the number of colors. (Alternatively, highlight the number in this field and type the desired value.)

6 Save the File

Click **OK** to close the **Save For Web** dialog box. The **Save Optimized As** dialog box opens. Verify the name and location of the file and click **Save** to save the file.

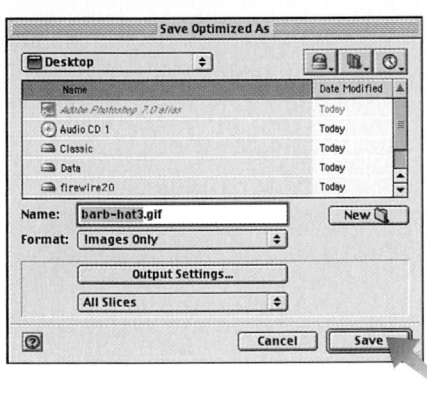

 Click

End

How-To Hints

Using 2-Up or 4-Up Comparison Tables

If you're unclear about multiple compression settings, click the **2-Up** and **4-Up** tabs in the **Save For Web** dialog box. These tabs enable you to compare options side by side.

Previewing in Browsers

If you're unsure about how an image will look in a given browser, use the browser preview feature. While still in the **Save For Web** dialog box, you can either click the **Browser Preview** button or use the **Select Browser** menu to select the desired target browser. Both the button and the menu are at the bottom of the dialog box (in these examples, the button shows the Internet Explorer icon; access the menu by clicking the arrow next to this button).

How to Optimize GIF Color Sets

The more you work with GIF conversion, the more you realize that the most critical step is in mapping the original colors to a minimal yet representative table set. To most people, it sounds inconceivable that 32 colors can replace the thousands of colors in an image. Although you *can* do it, you must be careful about which colors you keep and which you throw away.

1 Open and Save File in Photoshop

In Photoshop, choose **File, Open.** The **Open** dialog box appears. Select the file you want to convert to the GIF format and click **Open.** Choose **File, Save for Web.** The **Save For Web** dialog box opens, and Photoshop creates a duplicate image, leaving the original image untouched.

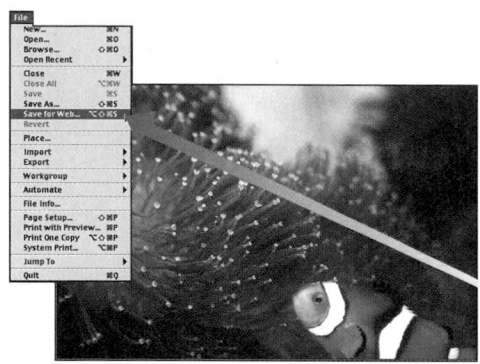

Click

2 Set Basic GIF Settings

Refer to Task 4 and set the compression type (**GIF**) and the **Dither** and **Lossy** settings. From the **Colors** list, select the lowest number of colors while keeping the file's integrity intact. Click the **Optimized** tab to review the results.

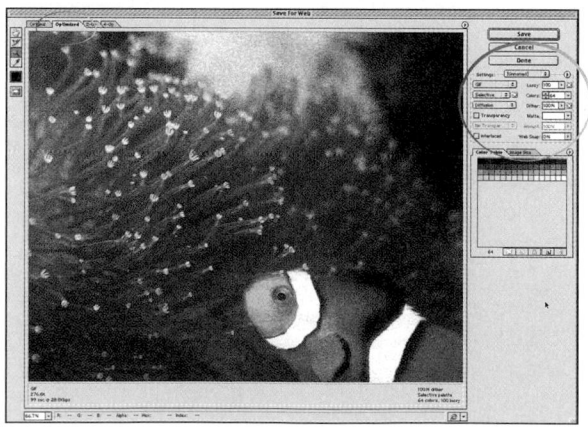

3 Lock Important Colors

Click the **Color Table** tab. Click the **Eyedropper** tool in the **Save For Web** dialog box and click a prominent color in the image. The corresponding color in the Color Table is highlighted. Lock the selected color by clicking the **Lock** button at the bottom of the Color Table. Locking a color prevents it from being removed or dithered. Repeat this step for any critical colors in the image.

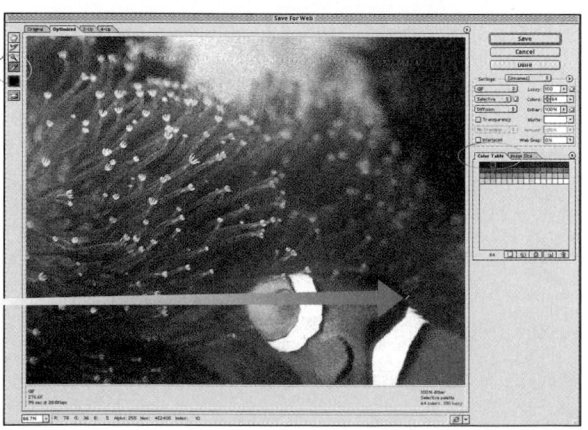

Click

4 Eliminate Close Colors

With the image showing on the **Optimized** tab, choose **Sort by Luminance** from the Color Table palette menu. In the **Color Table,** select a color close to a locked color and choose **Delete Color** from the Color Table palette menu. The screen redraws to delete the selected color from the image. Continue deleting colors until you get a core set that represents the image well.

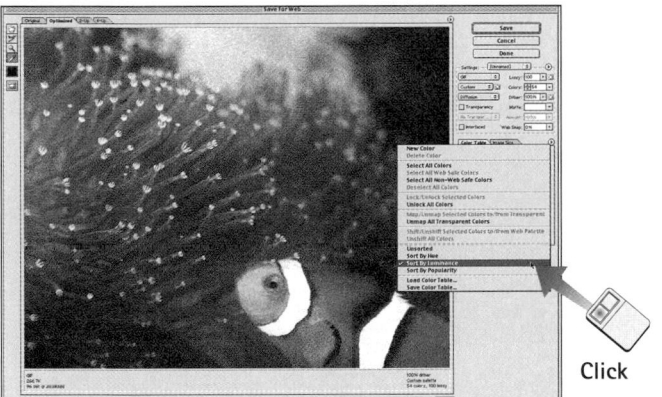

Click

5 Changing Individual Table Colors

With the important colors locked down, determine whether you need to change other colors. To change color swatches, double-click the color in the Color Table; the **Color Picker** dialog box opens. Change the current color, paying close attention to the Web-safe icon in the picker (the 3-sided box icon), which shows you the nearest Web-safe color.

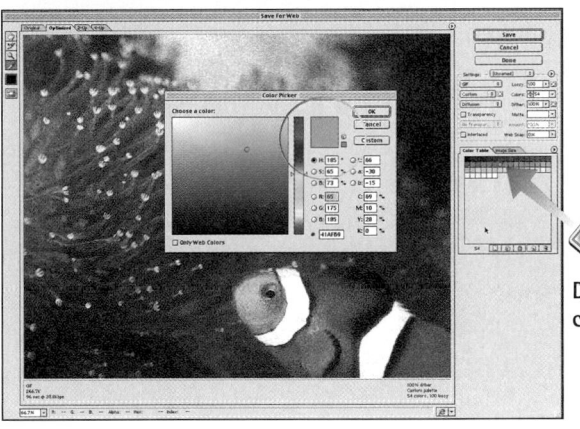

Double-click

6 Save the Color Table

If you're working with the same kind of image, or you want a series of images to use the same color set, save the Color Table you just fine-tuned. Choose **Save Color Table** from the Color Table palette menu. In the **Save As** dialog box that appears, type a name for the color table and click **OK.**

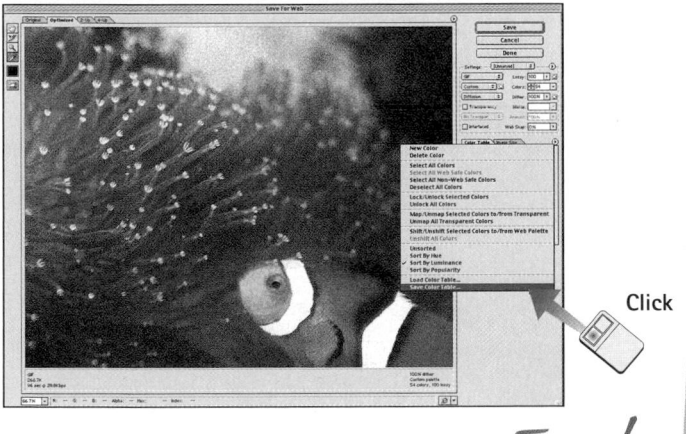

Click

End

How-To Hints

Using a Saved Color Table

To load a saved Color Table profile, open the **Save For Web** dialog box and choose **Load Color Table** from the Color Table palette menu.

Using Web-Safe Colors

Use the **Web Snap** slider in the top-right corner of the **Save For Web** dialog box to convert existing colors to Web-safe colors. Change the slider and monitor the results in the preview. The higher the value in the **Web Snap** slider, the more exactly colors are transformed to the Web-safe palette. The *Web-safe palette* refers to a subset of colors that can be reproduced exactly the same on all platforms and with all browsers. Use these colors to ensure that people who will view your Web graphics see exactly the colors you intended them to see.

How to Create a GIF Transparency

GIF files have an advantage over JPEG files in that they enable you to set certain areas as transparent. This means that you can create silhouette effects to place over Web page backgrounds. The transparent areas in a GIF file are completely invisible. This task uses ImageReady to create the transparency.

Begin

1 Open File in ImageReady

In ImageReady, choose **File, Open.** In the **Open** dialog box, select the file you want to work with and click **Open.**

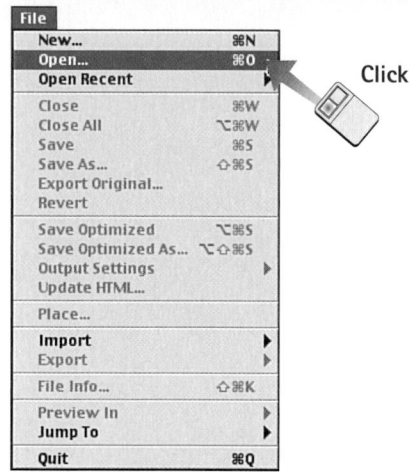

2 Select the Area to Be Transparent

Using any of ImageReady's selection tools (such as the **Magic Wand** tool to select areas of similar color), make a selection representing the area you want to make transparent.

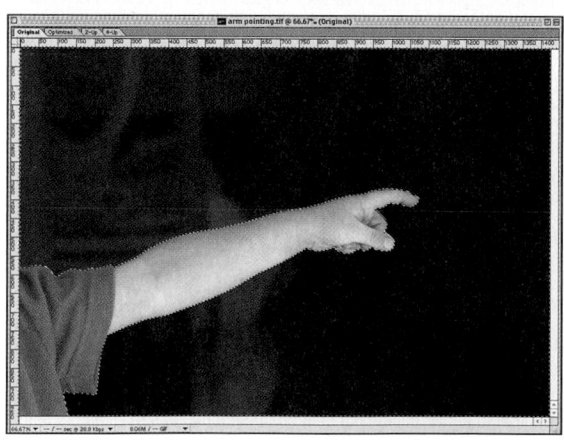

3 Apply a Layer Mask

Open the **Layers** palette by choosing **Window, Layers.** With the selection from Step 2 still active, press and hold the **Option/Alt** key and click the **Add A Mask** button at the bottom of the **Layers** palette. This action "masks out" the selected area, giving you an idea of what the final result will be.

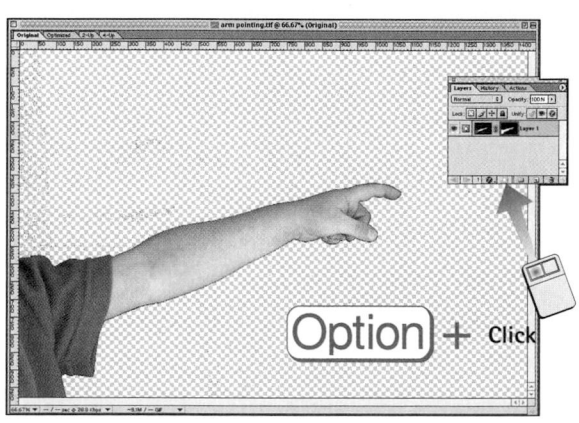

4 Build Optimize Settings

When the transparency is the way you want it, choose **Window, Optimize** to open the **Optimize** palette. Then specify the appropriate settings. (Refer to Task 4, "How to Build GIF Files for the Web," for instructions on setting up a GIF file.)

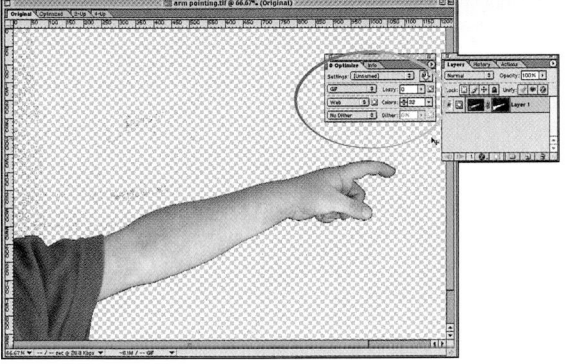

5 Preview in a Browser

Choose **File, Preview In, <selected browser>** or click the **Browser Preview** button in the toolbar to look at the file as it will appear in a browser.

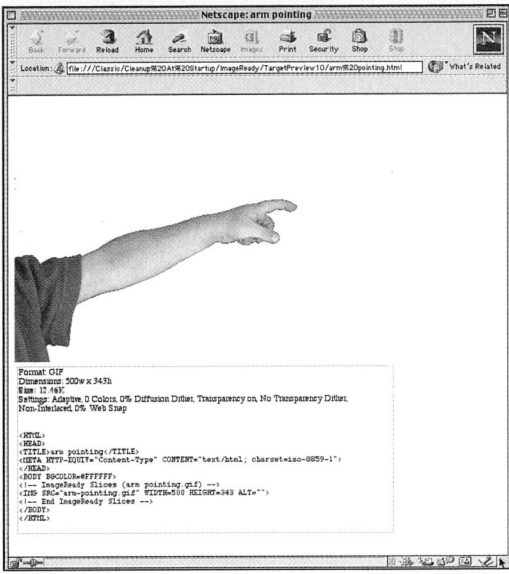

6 Save Optimized File

If the file looks good, close the browser and return to ImageReady. Choose **File, Save Optimized** to save the file using the settings in the **Optimize** palette.

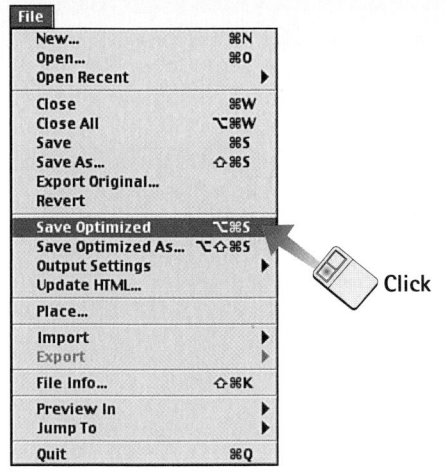

Click

How-To Hints

Fixing the Transparency

If the transparency in the layer mask in Step 3 is not right, click the **Add A Mask** button in the **Layers** palette and paint the transparent selection as you would with any layer mask. (See Part 11, Task 7, "How to Add a Layer Mask," for complete details on layer masks.)

Transparency in Photoshop

You can also set GIF transparencies using Photoshop's **Save For Web** dialog box. Select the color in the color palette and click the **Transparency** icon at the bottom of the palette.

End

How to Build JPEG Files for the Web

The JPEG format works well for continuous-tone images, such as photographs. Even though the compression format creates artifacts that pixelate the image, these snags are hardly visible in photographic-quality images (although they can degrade the quality of hard-edged graphics). Photoshop has a blur function built into the JPEG dialog box that is helpful for many images. You can smooth over many of the artifacts that surface when the quality level gets too low.

Begin

1 Open File in Photoshop

In Photoshop, choose **File, Open.** In the **Open** dialog box, select the file you want to compress with the JPEG format.

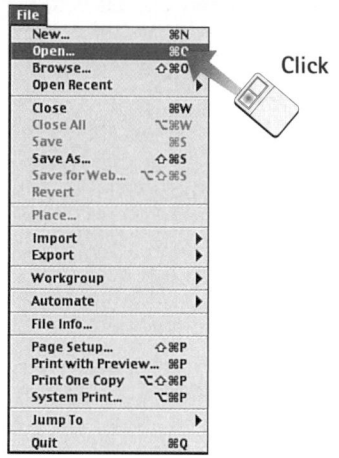

2 Set JPEG Options

Choose **File, Save for Web** to open the **Save For Web** dialog box. From the **Optimized File Format** drop-down list, select **JPEG.** The main control in this section is the **Quality** slider. This setting determines the level of compression in the file, as well as the corresponding quality. Adjust the setting to high, medium, or low, remembering that the higher the quality, the bigger the file size; the lower the quality, the smaller the file size.

3 Select 4-Up to Compare Settings

Click the **4-Up** tab to look at the original image and three variations. This comparison can help you select the setting that creates the highest-quality image combined with the lowest file size.

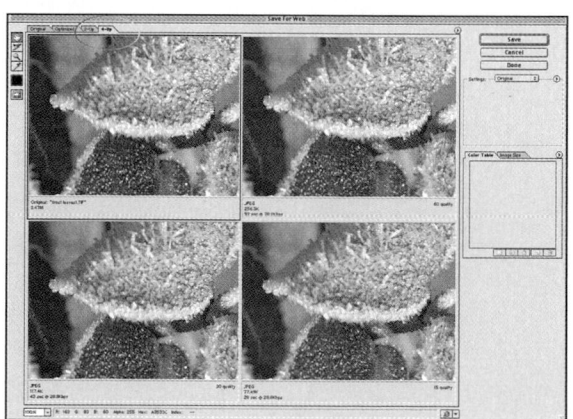

4 Tweak Blur Slider

Click the **Optimized** tab to return to that page and slightly raise the **Blur** slider to see whether this adjustment helps smooth the image. Click **OK** and rename the file to optimize it and save it as a separate file.

5 Reopen File

To check the quality of the image you just created, choose **File, Open.** From the **Open** dialog box, select the optimized file you just created. Check it against the original file to make sure that the detail is solid and that the color is good.

JPEG file

Original TIFF file

6 Test Unsharp Mask Filter

Because JPEG files tend to soften the original image, you may find that a slight **Unsharp Mask** filter helps bring back some detail (the filter also adds to the file size). Choose **Filter, Sharpen, Unsharp Mask.** Start by setting the **Amount** field to **50%** or **100%**; set the **Radius** field between **.7** and **1.0.** If you like the results, click **OK** to apply the mask; if not, click **Cancel.**

How-To Hints

Moving the Image Around

While working in the **Save For Web** dialog box, you can place the mouse cursor over the preview image; when the pointer changes to the hand icon, move the image around so that you can look at specific details in the image. You can also select the magnifying glass tool and zoom in and out of the image to check details.

Keeping Consistent Color

Enable the **ICC Profile** check box in the **Save For Web** dialog box to keep the colors consistent as you compress the image.

End

How to Optimize Files with Variable Compression

Variable compression allows you to alter image compression and quality in different areas of the same image. You can focus more detail around a central character or image while allowing details to erode in unimportant areas, such as the background or flat areas of color. The result is an optimized image that delivers higher quality and lower bandwidth. This task describes the compression process in Photoshop; although you can optimize a file with additional channels in ImageReady following the same process, ImageReady does not add or modify channels.

Begin

1 Open File in Photoshop

The first part of this task involves creating a mask in Photoshop. To do this, open Photoshop and select **File, Open.** From the **Open** dialog box, select the file you want to optimize.

3 Create the Mask

Initially, the new channel will turn the image black. To view the channel and the image as a composite, go to the **Channels** palette and turn on visibility for all channels, including the new channel you just created. In the final compressed image, white areas of the alpha channel will carry the most detail; black areas will have the least detail. With this in mind, paint the channel to emphasize image detail, using any of Photoshop's paint tools. When finished, turn off visibility for the alpha channel in the **Channels** palette.

2 Create a New Channel

Select **Window, Channels** to launch the **Channels** palette. Select **New Channel** from the **Channels** palette menu. Modify any parameters as desired in the **New Channel** dialog box (including mask color and area definition options) and click **OK** to create the new channel.

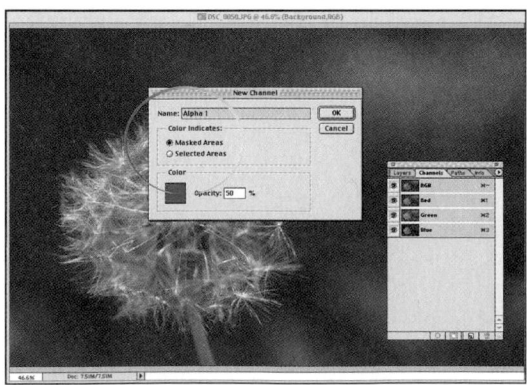

4 Save for the Web

Choose **File, Save for Web** to launch the **Save For Web** dialog box. With the mask in place, you now have the option of opening the file and optimizing it in ImageReady as well.

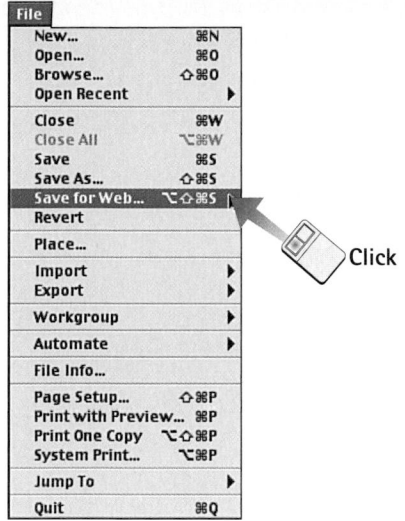

Click

5 For JPEG Files

In the **Save For Web** dialog box, select **JPEG** from the **Optimize File Format** menu. Click the icon next to the **Quality** control to launch the **Modify Quality Setting** dialog box. From the pop-up menu, select the channel created in Step 2. With the **Preview** box checked, adjust the slider to specify the minimum or maximum quality setting to be applied, based on the selected channel. Remember that the pure white channel areas correspond to the maximum settings, and the black areas correspond to the minimum settings. Click **OK**.

Drag

6 For GIF Files

In the **Save For Web** dialog box, select **GIF** from the **Optimize File Format** menu and set the GIF settings as desired. You can use channels to modify the **Dither, Lossy,** and **Colors** settings by clicking the icon next to the associated control to open a dialog box and following the process in the preceding step.

How-To Hints

Feather Masks for Gradual Effects

When building the mask in Photoshop, use the **Blur** filter or the **Airbrush** tool to create soft, graduated areas between light and dark sections of the mask. Doing so reduces the crisp transitions between areas of different quality.

Don't Forget PNG Files

You can also use channels to modify the quality in a PNG-8 file. Use the process outlined in Step 6 to alter the **Dither** and **Colors** settings.

End

Task

Working with Tone

*T*he tasks in this part look at how to work with image tonality. As far as digital images are concerned, *tonality* refers to the grayscale values from 0 to 255 that differentiate the image pixels. Tonality is black and white and shades of gray; tonality is a histogram, a halftone, salt and pepper, the *I Love Lucy* show, and a dark foreboding sky hanging low over the concrete streets of New York.

I'm using this somewhat poetic introduction to emphasize the fact that tonality is one of the most expressive elements of an image. It can establish a full-contrast range, create a feeling of darkness and danger, or obliterate outlines in the form of fog or mist. If you want to create a strong feeling in an image, consider exaggerating the tonality in some way.

In addition to its expressive qualities, tonality also helps to sharpen an image, even as it increases the contrast. Sharp details, rich and complex color, and the look of texture are all created by manipulating black, white, and shades of gray.

The tasks that follow help you to optimize any given file, making it the best it can be. You can take a dark or underexposed image and make it usable with curves and a few filters. Even better, you can take an image that already looks pretty good and make it a real winner. ●

How to Measure and Compare Pixel Values

Knowing how to accurately measure pixel values is an important first step in being able to evaluate and correct digital images. Many times, you have to determine the tonal value of an image area or compare the value of two different areas. It is important to measure these values numerically, because pixel values change from monitor to monitor based on contrast settings, ambient light, and monitor brands. Photoshop uses the **Info** palette to measure pixel values; the **Eyedropper** and **Color Sampler** tools also are helpful aids.

Begin

1 Open the Info Palette

With the image open, choose **Window, Info**. The **Info** palette opens on the desktop.

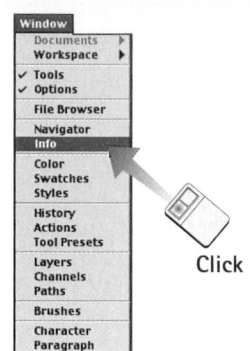

Click

2 Select a Color Model

The top-left section of the **Info** palette represents the actual color value of the currently selected pixel. Click and hold the **Eyedropper** icon to select the color model in which you want the pixel's color specified. (Refer to Part 1, Task 6, "How to Select a Color," for information about color models.) Choose the **Opacity** option to measure the degree of transparency in a given layer.

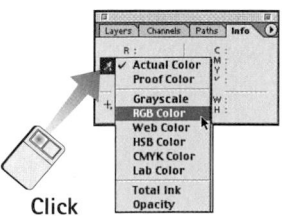

Click

3 Select a Variable Color Model

The top-right section of the **Info** palette tracks a second set of color values, which allows you to compare the same pixel value with two different models. Click and hold the **Eyedropper** icon and select the desired color model from the list. Move the mouse cursor over the image (don't click) and watch the corresponding readings appear in the palette.

4 Enter Coordinate Units

With so many pixels in an image, it can be hard to sample the same one more than once. The pixel coordinates section in the lower-left corner of the **Info** palette tracks the exact cursor position based on the x,y axis. Click and hold the cursor icon to choose the units of measure.

 Click

5 Create Sample Points

To accurately track the same value through the course of your imaging session, you should use eyedropper sample points. Click the **Eyedropper** tool in the toolbox; a submenu of two eyedroppers appears. Select the **Color Sampler** tool (the second tool). Drag the tool over the image and click to place a sample point. A new section is created in the **Info** palette for each sample point you create.

6 Track Sample Values

Drag the sample point to move it; drag the point off the image to delete it. Each image supports up to four sample points. If you want, you can set a color model for each point area in the palette, just as you did in Steps 2 and 3.

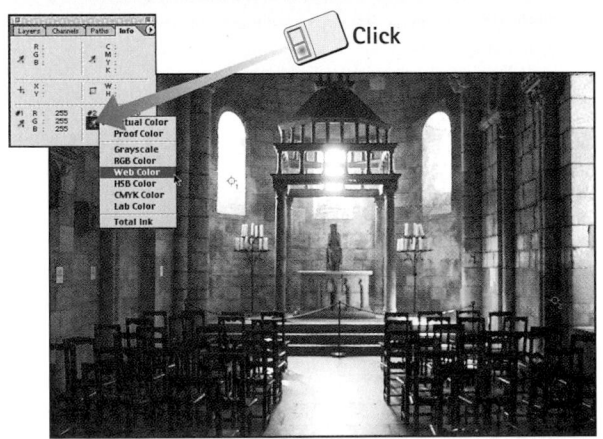

Click

How-To Hints

Selection Dimensions

Use the width/height section in the lower-right corner of the **Info** palette to measure the exact size of an active selection. This capability is especially valuable with the **Marquee** tool, which gives real-time dimensions as you drag. For more information on selections, see Part 3, "Selection Techniques."

End

How to Optimize the Tonal Range

When you capture an image with a digital camera or scanner, chances are that the tonal range in your image is lacking in highlights or shadows. An *optimized tonal range* is one in which the darks are completely black, the highlights are white, and the other tones are well distributed. In Photoshop, you adjust the tonal range of an image with the **Levels** option. Not only does adjusting tone ensure good contrast and detail, it can correct any unwanted color casts. Even if the image looks pretty good to start with, optimizing the tone can improve things even further.

Begin

1 Open the Info Palette

Open the image for which you want to adjust the tonality. Choose **Window, Info** to open the **Info** palette.

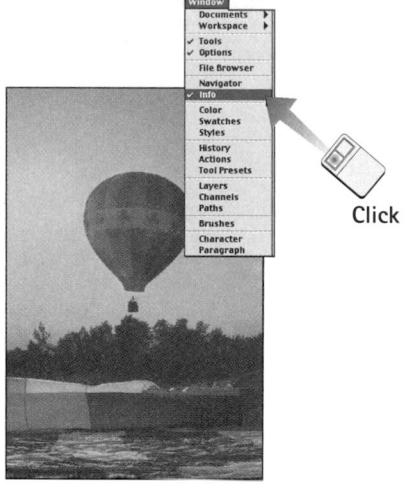
Click

2 Open Levels

Choose **Image, Adjustments, Levels** to open the **Levels** dialog box.

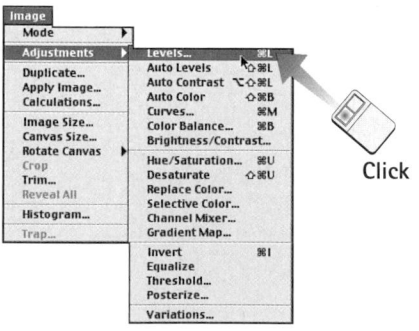
Click

3 Select the Black Point

Click the black **Eyedropper** icon in the lower-right corner of the **Levels** dialog box. Move the cursor over the image; the pointer changes to an eyedropper as it enters the image. Using the readings from the **Info** palette, find the darkest area of the image and click to set the black point.

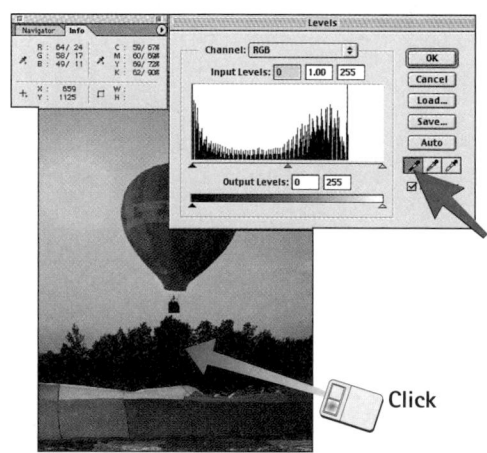
Click

4 Select the White Point

Click the white **Eyedropper** icon in the lower-right corner of the **Levels** dialog box. Move the cursor over the image; the pointer changes to an eyedropper as it enters the image. This time, find the lightest area of the image and click to set the white point.

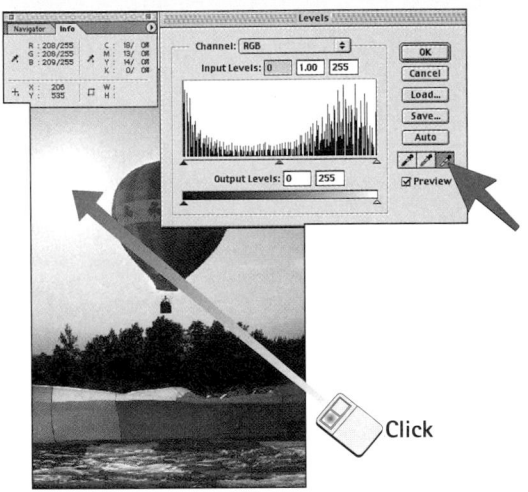

Click

5 Click OK

Click **OK** to apply the effect. By setting the black and white points for the image, you are telling Photoshop what the darkest shadows and brightest highlights in the image are. Doing so establishes the tonal range of the scanned image. You can experiment with setting a black point that is not the darkest area of the image or a white point that is not the brightest area of the image to see what effect this "skewed" tonal range has.

End

How-To Hints

Reselecting the Darkest or Lightest Area

Take your time when looking for the lightest and darkest points in the image. Selecting a pixel that is not close enough to the light or dark point can result in blowing out the highlights or shadows. If you make a mistake, press the **Option** key (Mac users) or the **Alt** key (Windows users) and click the **Reset** button (the **Cancel** button changes to the **Reset** button) to make another attempt.

How to Improve Contrast with Curves

Task 2 showed how to use the **Levels** dialog box to set the white point and the black point of an image, thus optimizing the tonal range for the image. You can use the **Curves** dialog box to increase the contrast in the image, allowing you to selectively enhance image details. If the image seems flat or lacking in contrast, curves can make a dramatic improvement.

Begin

1 Open the Info Palette

Open the image you want to affect. Choose **Window, Info** to open the **Info** palette.

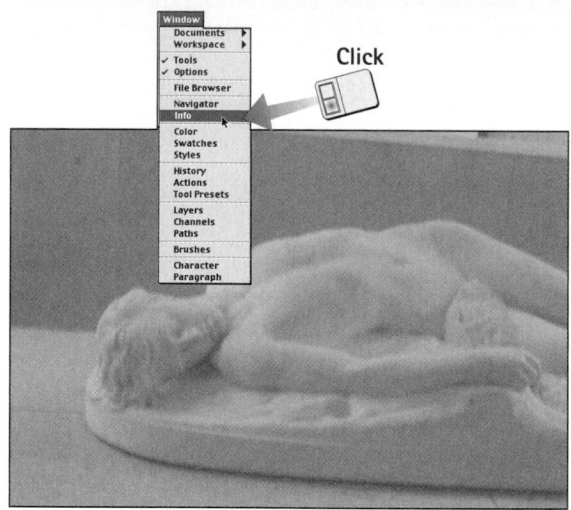

Click

2 Open the Curves Dialog Box

Choose **Image, Adjustments, Curves** to open the **Curves** dialog box.

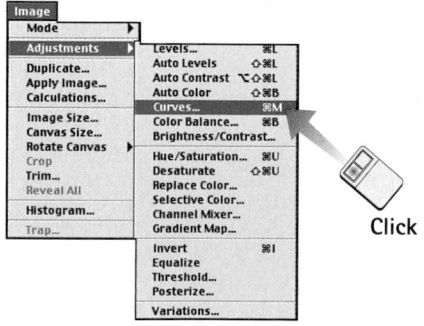

Click

3 Set the Black and White Points

Follow the steps in Task 2 to set the black and white points for the image. Use the **Eyedropper** icons from the **Curves** dialog box rather than those in the **Levels** dialog box.

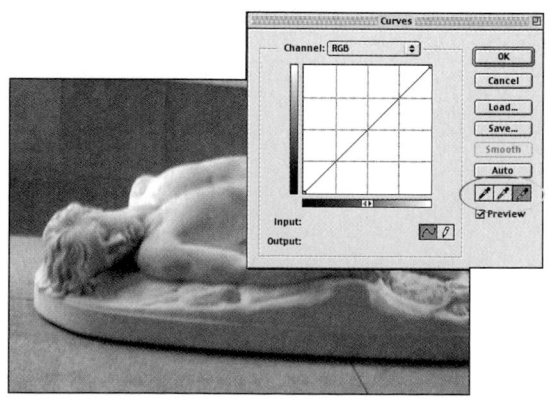

4 Darken Shadows

Click the lower-left portion of the diagonal line in the **Curves** dialog box to place a point on the curve. If necessary, slowly drag the point you placed downward to darken the shadow areas in the image.

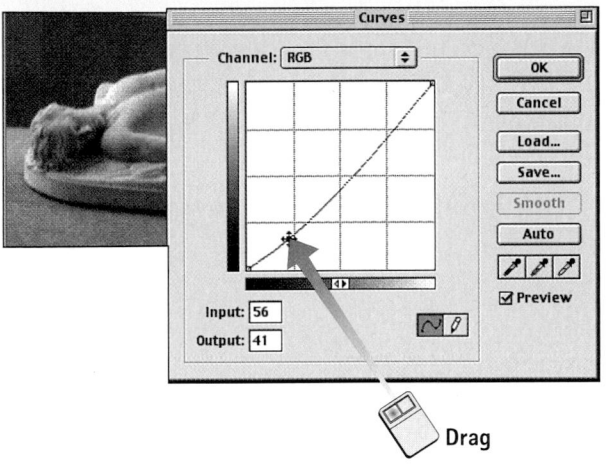

Drag

5 Brighten Highlights

Click the upper-right portion of the diagonal line in the **Curves** dialog box to place a point in the light areas. Slowly drag the point up to lighten the highlights, increasing the overall contrast, especially in the midtones. Click **OK** to apply the effect.

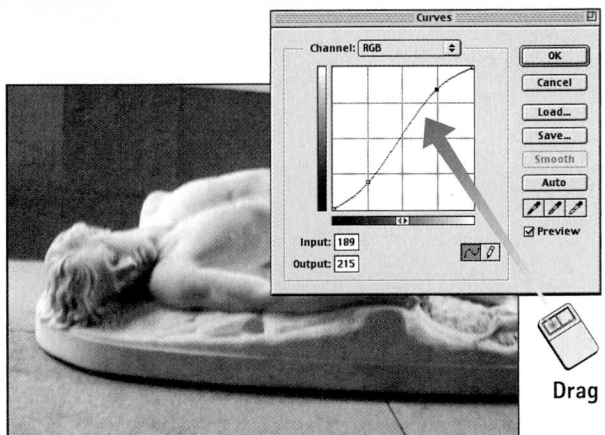

Drag

6 View Results

Compare the final results to the image from Step 1. Notice the improved detail and clarity.

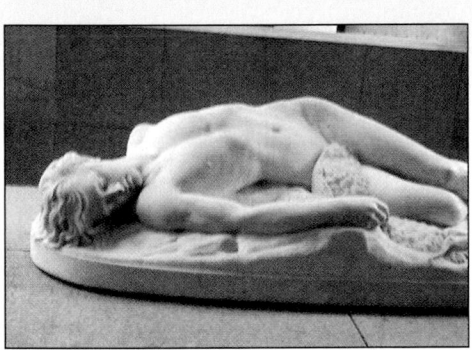

End

How-To Hints

Checking the Input and Output Values

In the **Curves** dialog box, watch the **Input** and **Output** values to understand exactly what changes you're making to the curve. The **Input** value refers to the original pixel values (for example, a midtone value of 128). Clicking at an **Input** value of 128 and dragging up to 160 means that all pixels originally valued at 128 are now a lighter value of 160. In addition, all pixel values around the input value are lightened so that the effect is applied smoothly. Keep the curve shape smooth, and the effect will look natural.

How to Use the Dodge, Burn, and Sponge Tools

At times, you will want to lighten or darken an image only in selected areas. Although you could select an area and make changes only to that area (see Part 3, "Selection Techniques"), you may find the **Dodge, Burn,** and **Sponge** tools more effective. These tools allow you to brush your corrections onto an image: The **Dodge** tool lightens the image, the **Burn** tool darkens it, and the **Sponge** tool lets you saturate or desaturate the color intensity.

1 Select the Proper Tool

Open the image you want to affect. Click and hold the **Dodge** tool in the toolbox. A pop-out menu appears from which you can select the **Dodge, Burn,** or **Sponge** tool. Point to the desired tool and release the mouse button to select it.

Click

2 Set the Options Palette

From the **Options** bar, select **Shadows, Midtones,** or **Highlights** from the **Range** menu, depending on the tonal area of the image you want to modify. For the **Sponge** tool, select **Saturate** or **Desaturate** to increase or decrease the color intensity.

3 Set the Exposure

Exposure refers to the degree of effect applied to the image as you use the selected tool. You also can think of it as intensity or pressure. In the **Options** bar, click and drag to adjust the **Exposure** slider. Select a higher percentage number for a dramatic effect; select a lower number for subtle changes.

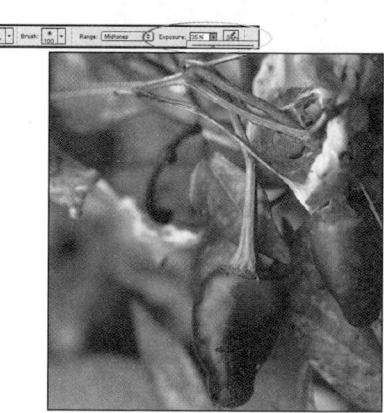

4 Select a Brush

From the **Brushes** palette (located in the palette well on the right end of the **Options** bar), select a suitable brush size for the tool you're working with and the image you're editing. To avoid hard-edged brushstrokes, select a feathered brush.

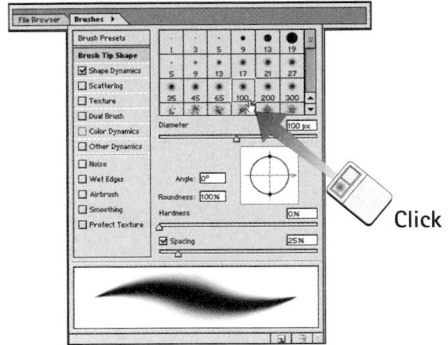

Click

5 Begin Brushing in the Effect

Begin with a very low exposure and a feathered brush that is large enough to cover the desired area in just a few strokes. Repeatedly brush over the area, building up the effect as you go. If a pronounced brushstroke appears, undo the stroke (choose **Edit, Undo**) and lower the exposure. Click and drag lightly to apply the effect, instead of dragging back and forth.

Click

6 Change Brush Size and Exposure

As you work, select a smaller brush size as needed to work into smaller areas. If you change the brush size, consider decreasing the exposure to hide the brushstrokes. This may be necessary because smaller brushstrokes are more visible when repeatedly applied.

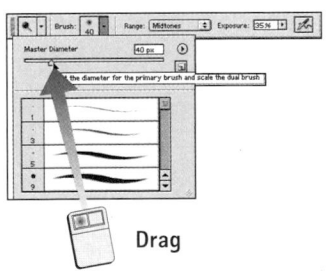

Drag

End

How-To Hints

To Undo the Effect

Because these effects are applied with repeated brushstrokes, choosing **Edit, Undo** does not revert the image to its appearance before you began. Give yourself a safety net by opening the **History** palette and creating a snapshot before you begin. (See Part 2, Task 5, "How to Undo with the History Palette," for more information.) After the effect is applied, click the snapshot to revert to the previous state or to compare the result.

Brushing in a Straight Line

To brush the effect along a straight line, click once at the start of the line, press and hold the **Shift** key, and click at the end of the line. Photoshop applies the effect in a straight line between the two points.

How to Sharpen Images

Sharpening images with Photoshop is a very common and useful task. If your image appears soft or blurry, you can bring back detail, clarity, and contrast with sharpening. Sharpening brings out additional detail in virtually all images except those created on the highest-quality scanners. The best way to add overall sharpness to an image is to use the **Unsharp Mask** filter. Be careful not to oversharpen, which results in an unnatural halo around the objects in the image, flattening the space. If this occurs, choose **Edit, Undo** and reapply the effect.

Begin

1 Select the Unsharp Mask Filter

With the image open, choose **Filter, Sharpen, Unsharp Mask**. The **Unsharp Mask** dialog box opens.

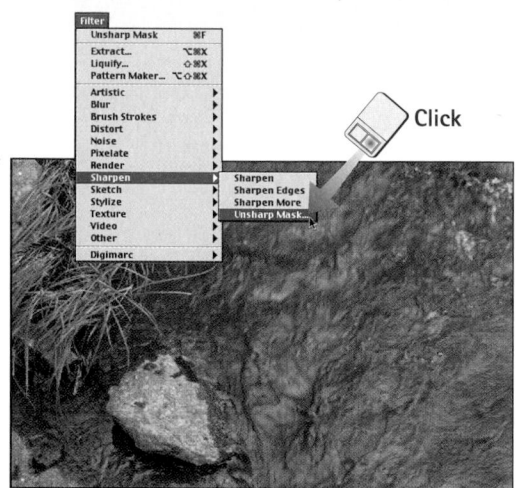

Click

2 Set the Amount Slider

Enable the **Preview** check box and set the thumbnail magnification view to **100** by clicking the **+** or **–** button. The **Amount** slider controls the degree of sharpening applied to the image. Adjust the slider as needed, noting the changes in the preview window in the dialog box.

Drag

3 Set the Radius Slider

The **Radius** control determines whether the effect is applied to a single pixel or to a group of pixels. A higher radius value lowers image detail in exchange for higher overall contrast. For the most naturalistic images, begin by setting this option at **1** and don't let it rise above **3**.

Drag

4 Set the Threshold Slider

The **Threshold** setting excludes a portion of the tonal range from receiving the effect. Leave it at **0** to apply the effect globally; move it higher to exclude tones from dark to light. For all practical purposes, you do not typically change this setting.

5 Apply the Effect

To zoom in on the image window, select **View, Zoom In** as many times as needed. If the image is larger than the image window, you can use the scrollbars to scroll to different areas in the image. Check the image carefully to ensure that all areas are sharpened to the proper level. When you are satisfied with the image, click **OK** to apply the effect.

Click

6 Fade the Result as Necessary

Choose **Edit, Fade Unsharp Mask.** After the **Fade** dialog box opens, move the **Opacity** slider to the left to gradually decrease the sharpen effect as necessary. If you decide to soften the effect, set the slider accordingly and click **OK,** leaving the **Mode** setting at **Normal** (see Part 13, Task 1, "How to use Blending Modes," for details on other mode options). If you determine that the initial effect is acceptable, click **Cancel** to close the dialog box and leave the image unchanged.

Drag

End

How-To Hints

Don't Forget About Color

Although this task uses a black and white image, sharpening an image is as much about color as it is about tone. Be sure to color balance your images to maximize overall contrast and color vibrancy.

Unsharp Mask Does It All

Notice that Adobe lists other sharpening filters in the **Filter, Sharpen** submenu. These options are all rolled into the **Unsharp Mask** dialog box, which you can use to apply all the other filters. Don't waste your time with the other filter options—**Unsharp Mask** is all you need.

How to Use Blur to Sharpen

Although it may sound paradoxical, you actually can use the **Blur** filter to *sharpen* an image. Specifically, you can blur one area of your image to make the other area look sharper. In this task, you intentionally soften the background areas of an image, making the subject appear sharper in comparison. This is a good approach for images that are too soft to be remedied using the **Unsharp Mask** filter alone.

Begin

1 Open the File in Photoshop

Choose **File, Open** and select the file you want to modify.

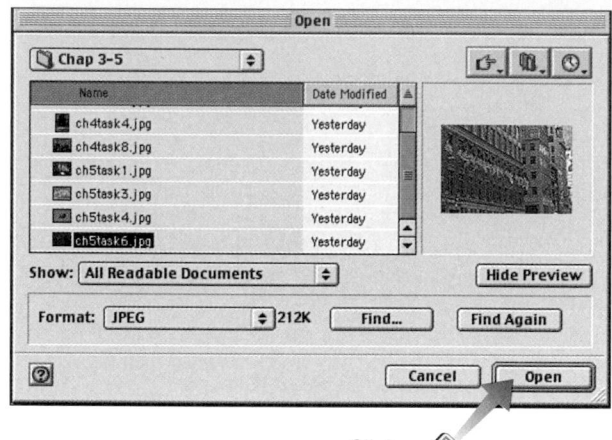

Click

2 Apply an Unsharp Mask

Begin by sharpening the image as much as you can. Choose **Filter, Sharpen, Unsharp Mask** and follow the directions in Task 5 to sharpen the image.

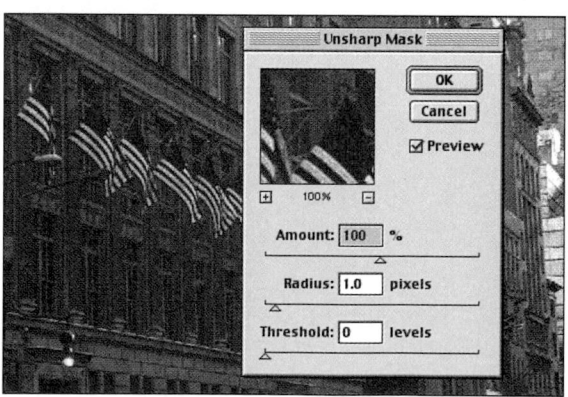

3 Select the Background

Using Photoshop's selection tools, select the area to which you want to apply the blur. For more on making selections in Photoshop, see Part 3, "Selection Techniques." In this example, I've selected the buildings on the right side of the image.

4 Feather the Selection

Feathering softens the edges of a selection, helping it to blend with unselected areas. Choose **Select, Feather**. In the **Feather Selection** dialog box, specify the desired pixel value. The amount of feathering you choose depends on the overall resolution of the image and the subject matter. Click **OK** to apply the effect.

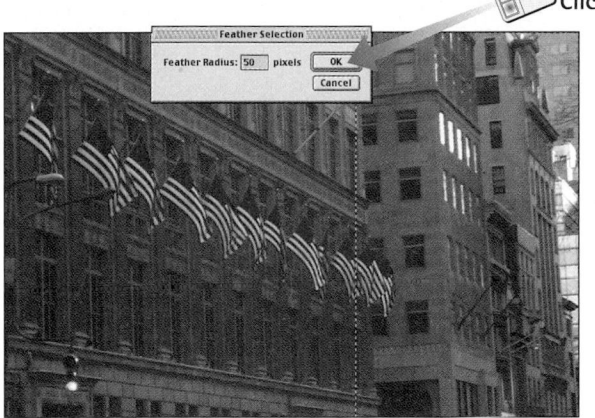

5 Apply Gaussian Blur

Choose **Filter, Blur, Gaussian Blur** to open the **Gaussian Blur** dialog box. (Gauss was a mathematician; the Gaussian blur effect is based on his mathematical formulas.) Adjust the **Radius** slider until the proper blur amount appears in the window. Click **OK**.

6 Touch Up with the Blur Tool

After deselecting the selection (press ⌘+D or **Ctrl+D**), select the **Blur** tool from the toolbox and brush in the smaller areas to complete the blur transition.

End

How-To Hints

Don't Overdo It

The blur effect works best when it is subtle and subliminal. Resist the urge to knock the background way out of focus.

Building Up the Blur Effect

In the **Options** bar for the **Blur** tool, keep the **Pressure** setting relatively low so that you can build the effect with multiple brushstrokes. This will give you more control and accuracy.

How to Convert Images to Grayscale

If you are going to print a color image in black and white, it's a good idea to convert a copy of it to grayscale first. At first glance, converting an image to grayscale seems like an easy task: You choose **Image, Adjust, Desaturate** to remove all the color (or better yet, let the printer force the image to gray). What could be easier? The problem with this approach is that the proper tonal range for all image areas may not be emphasized. In this task, you optimize the tones so that there is detail everywhere, ensuring that the central subject is well represented.

Begin

1 Open the File in Photoshop

Choose **File, Open** to open the desired color image.

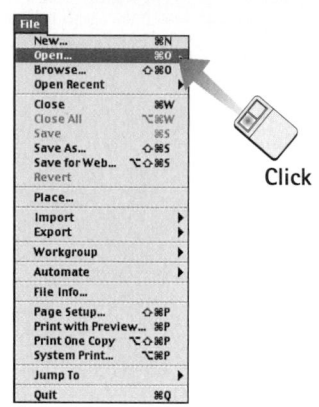

Click

2 Convert to Lab Color

Choose **Image, Mode, Lab Color** to convert the image to the Lab color space. Lab color maintains a better range of tones in the image than does any of the other color models.

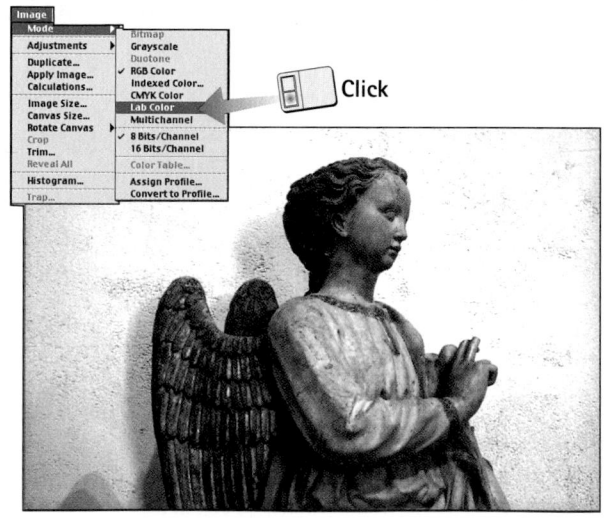

Click

3 Open Channels

Choose **Window, Channels** to open the **Channels** palette. Click the visibility icons (the eye icons) for the **a** and **b** channels to turn them off. Only the **Lightness** channel should be visible.

4 Modify with Curves

Choose **Image, Adjust Curves** to open the **Curves** dialog box. Modify the curves as described in Task 3 to enhance the contrast and range for your image as necessary.

5 Duplicate Channel

With the **Lightness** channel still selected, open the **Channels** palette menu and choose **Duplicate Channel.** In the dialog box that appears, name the new file and choose **New** from the **Destination** pop-up menu. This action saves the **Lightness** channel to a new file that you can modify further.

Click

6 Close the Original File

Close the original file by choosing **File, Close.** Select **Don't Save** in the dialog box that appears to leave the original file untouched.

Click

End

How-To Hints

Another Approach

As an alternative to converting the file to Lab color as explained here, you can keep the file in RGB mode. In this approach, click each channel in the **Channels** palette to view a grayscale rendition of each channel. You will see a wide range of grayscale variations based on the color in the image. If you see one with the tone and contrast you like, select and copy the grayscale channel and paste it in a new file.

Task

Working with Color

*F*or some people, color corrections are very intimidating. They see the RGB or CMYK conversion curves and tables, talk to prepress guys who harp over perfect flesh-tone balance, and decide that color correction is something to be left to the "experts."

Although it's true that you can mess up the color in an image, it's also true that you can do quite a bit on your own. This is especially the case if you're designing for the Web as opposed to print: The monitor is much more representative of the way the final image will look on the Web as opposed to its appearance on paper.

The tasks in this part explain the basics of color correction and show what a huge difference color can make in an image. Although you won't be a prepress expert, you should learn to trust your eye a bit more and to have confidence in correcting the color in your own images. ●

How to Work with Color Variations

If you're not familiar with color correction and color theory, variations is the place to start. The **Variations** dialog box is an intuitive color-correction tool that lets you correct color visually instead of using sliders, curves, and numbers. The dialog box features thumbnails of your image, with visual previews of how various color and tone corrections will look. The thumbnails are arranged to follow the standard color wheel, with primary colors opposite each other. As you work in this mode, notice how adding one color subtracts from the opposite color. For example, adding red subtracts from cyan.

Begin

1 Open the Variations Dialog Box

With the image file you want to affect open, choose **Image, Adjustments, Variations** to launch the **Variations** dialog box. At the top left of the box are two images; they help you compare your original image and the current variation you have created. At the beginning, these images are identical, but they will deviate from each other as you work.

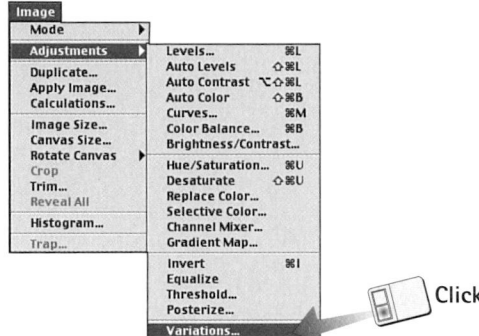

Click

2 Select a Tonal Area

Although all the controls in the **Variations** dialog box modify the entire image to some extent, the controls allow you to focus on one area of the tonal range at a time. Click the **Highlights, Midtones, Shadows,** or **Saturation** radio button to focus the correction on this one area.

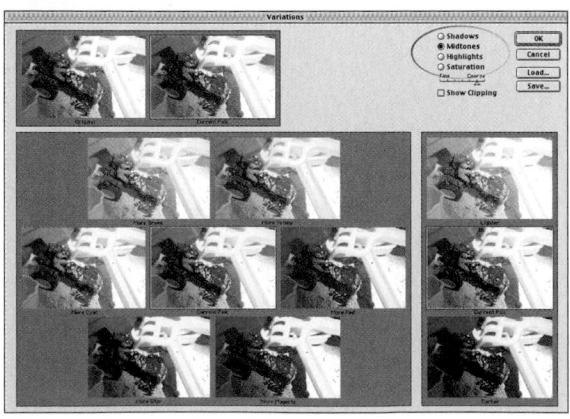

3 Modify the Color

Click any of the thumbnail images in the color wheel array of thumbnails to add the corresponding color to the original image. As you do, notice that the original image takes on the selected color cast; all the surrounding thumbnails reorient themselves to the new current image. As you continue clicking thumbnails, the color corrections continue to be applied in an additive way.

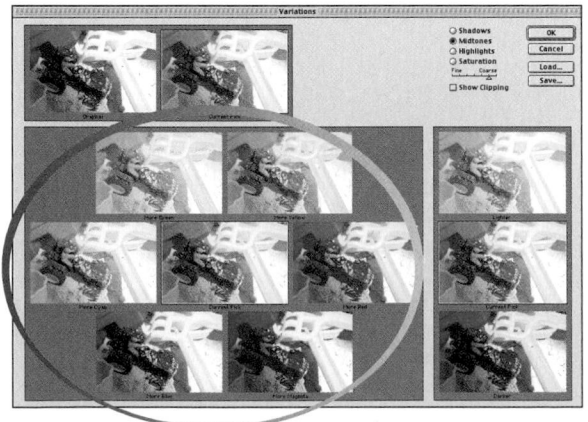

4 Modify the Coarseness Slider

As you get closer to the desired color, you may find that the variations between color choices are too broad. You may want to add a red that's somewhere between the current shade of the image and the **More Red** thumbnail. To create more subtle color shifts, move the **Coarseness** slider toward the **Fine** end of the scale. This adjustment makes all the color variations more subtle, allowing you to select the variation that looks the best.

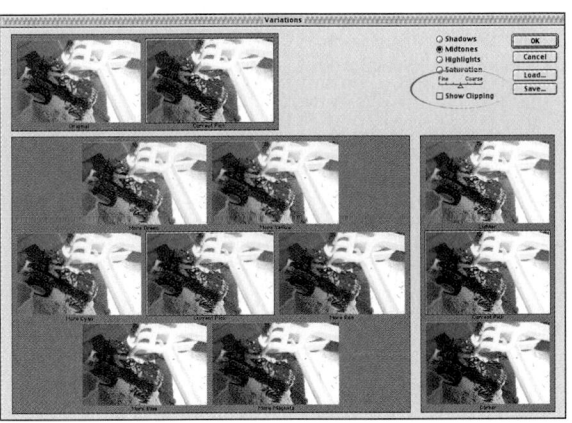

5 Modify the Tone

The three thumbnails on the right of the dialog box control the overall tone of the image. Click the top thumbnail to lighten the image; click the dark thumbnail to darken the image.

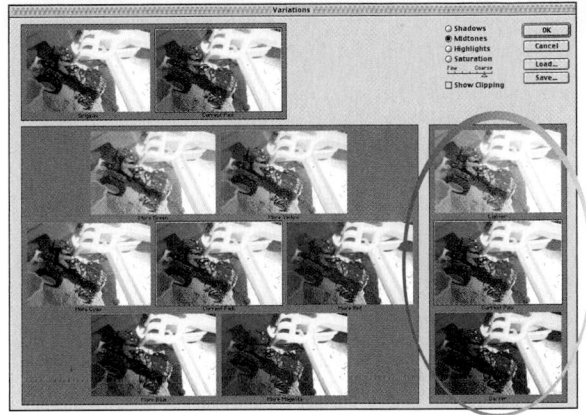

6 Save Settings

If you are working with a group of similar images, you may want to save your settings so that you can reload them at a later time with one mouse click. Click the **Save** button. When the **Save** dialog box opens, type a name for the settings file you are creating and click **Save**.

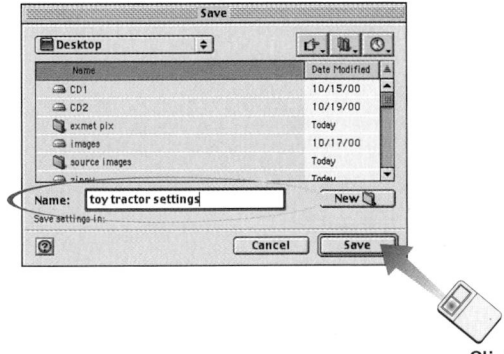

Click

7 Apply the Color Correction

To reload the saved settings, open the image, open the **Variations** dialog box, click the **Load** button, and select the desired settings file. Click **OK** to apply the correction to the image.

End

How-To Hints

Checking the Clipping

If you enable the **Show Clipping** check box in the **Variations** dialog box, Photoshop applies a mask to areas of the image that will not convert to CMYK. This mask lets you monitor whether your corrections will work for print.

How to Make Global Color Corrections

Global color corrections can fix an image that appears to have a color cast or overall tint. This color cast could have been caused by an input device (such as a scanner or digital camera) or by a light source (such as fluorescent lighting). This task shows you how to correct the tint of an image so that the image appears natural to the eye. You can apply this technique to images of natural subjects (such as trees and sky) as well as to more abstract projects.

Begin

1 Open the File

Choose **File, Open** and select the image file you want to edit.

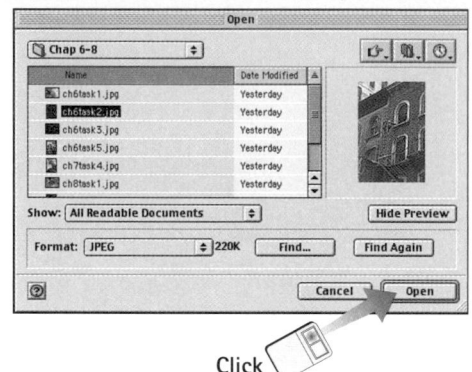

Click

2 Open the Info Palette

Choose **Window, Info** to display the **Info** palette.

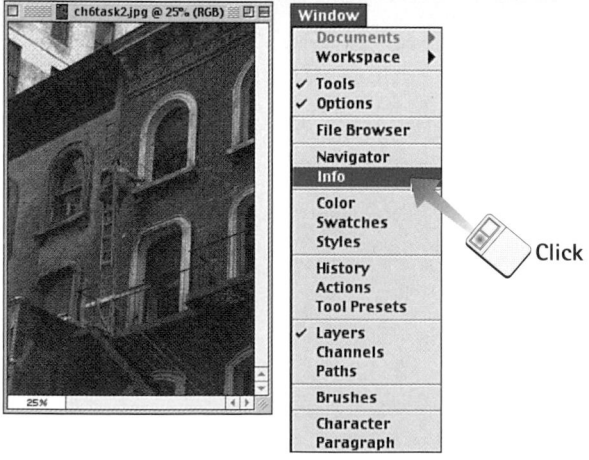

Click

3 Set the Black and White Points

If you haven't done so already, set the black point and white point, as explained in Part 5, Task 3, "How to Improve Contrast with Curves." In brief, open the **Curves** dialog box by selecting **Image, Adjustments, Curves** and use the black and white eyedroppers in the **Curves** dialog box to set the points. Click **OK** to apply the effect.

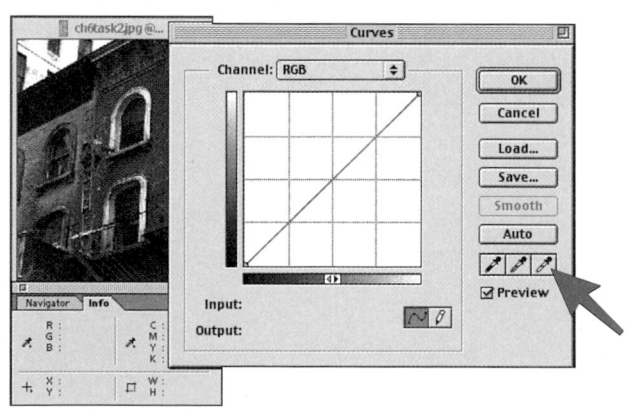

4 Measure Values

Look at the image onscreen and search for areas that appear to have a color cast. A cast is especially evident in parts of the image that you know are supposed to be white or gray. With the **Curves** dialog box still open, move your mouse pointer over these areas and measure the results in the **Info** palette.

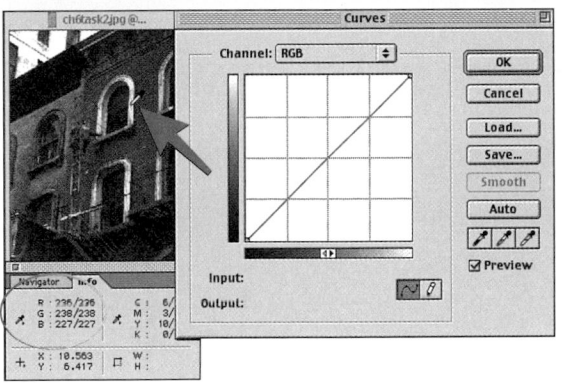

5 Evaluate the Results

In comparing the numbers, look for a number that is much higher or lower than the other two. In this case, the red and green are close in value, but the blue is low, indicating that the sample area is a bit yellow (the inverse of blue). If a number is low, its inverse is dominant; you must add the low color to balance the color cast. (Red's inverse is cyan, green's inverse is magenta, and blue's inverse is yellow.)

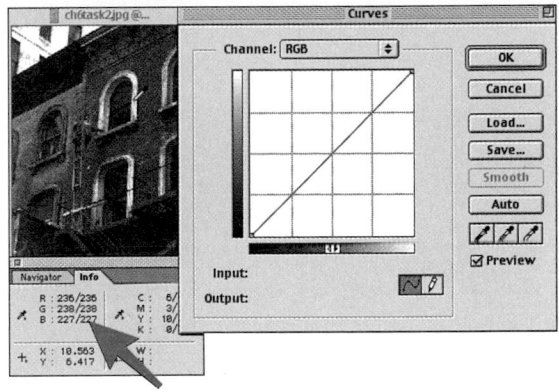

6 Select a Channel Color

This step corrects a specific color channel based on the evaluations made in the previous step. In the **Curves** dialog box, click the arrow next to the **Channel** box and select the color you want to modify, based on your readings in Steps 4 and 5. This action launches a curve that corresponds to that color channel only.

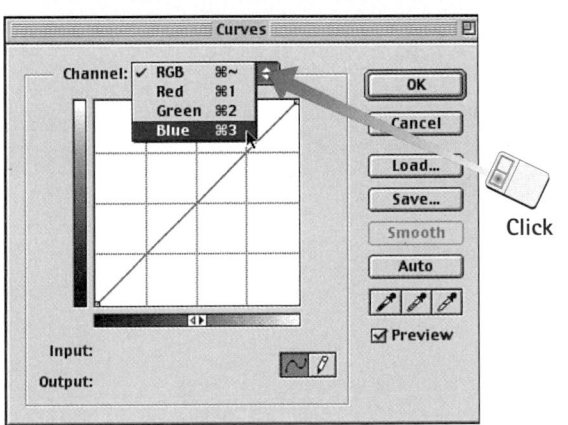

Click

7 Modify the Color

Click and drag the curve up or down, adding or subtracting the target color to eliminate the color cast from the image. Click **OK** to apply the change.

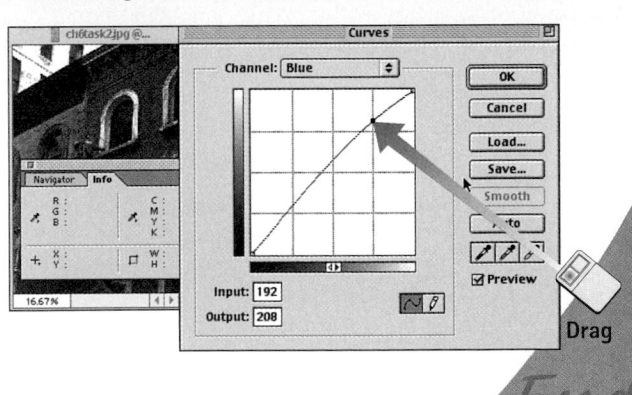

Drag

End

How to Correct a Range of Colors

At times, you may want to change a range of colors within an object or area. You may want to make a red ball yellow, for example, or a blue car green. This involves changing more than just one color shade because numerous values represent the highlights and shadows across the form. At the same time, you don't want to change any areas outside the desired object. Photoshop offers the perfect set of tools for making these kinds of changes: the **Select Color Range** and the **Hue Saturation** controls. This task shows you how to specify a range of colors and globally change them to another color.

Begin

1 Open the File

Choose **File, Open** and select the image file you want to modify.

2 Select Color Range

Choose **Select, Color Range** to launch the **Color Range** dialog box. From the **Select** drop-down list box, choose **Sampled Colors** so that you can select the colors in the image that you want to change.

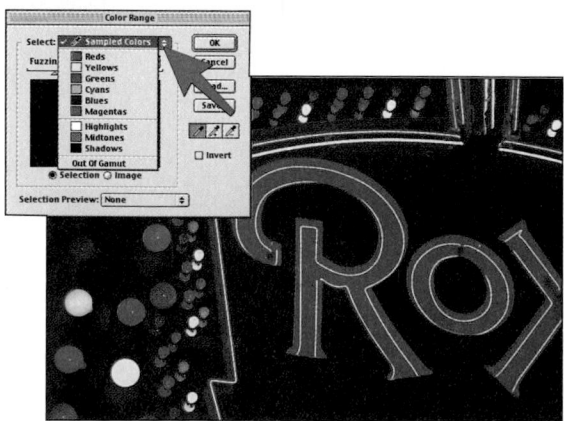

3 Sample the Color Range

The **Eyedropper** icon should be selected by default. If it's not, click it in the dialog box and then click in the thumbnail or main image to choose a color. Select **White Matte** from the **Selection Preview** pop-up menu to preview the colors selected against a white background within the main image window. The selected color is shown in the main image window against a white background so that you can see exactly what is included in the sampling. Drag the **Fuzziness** slider to increase or decrease the range of colors selected. Click **OK** to create a selection of the color range as shown.

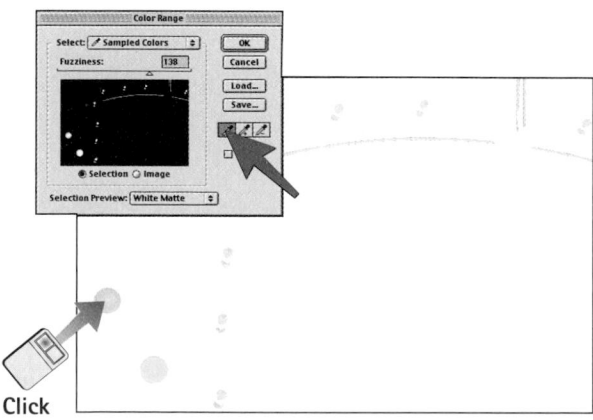

Click

4 Change the Hue

Choose **Image, Adjustments, Hue/Saturation** to launch the **Hue/Saturation** dialog box. Drag the **Hue** slider to shift the color range as desired.

Drag

5 Check the Brightness

If the color range selected is very dark or very light, you may find that moving the **Hue** slider does not change anything. In this case, drag the **Lightness** slider and then modify the **Hue** slider as needed to achieve the desired effect.

Drag

End

How-To Hints

Using the Photoshop Controls

Although ImageReady offers a **Hue/Saturation** dialog box, use the Photoshop version if possible. Photoshop's Hue/Saturation controls offer a more interactive interface, showing you what things will look like *as you move* the slider instead of forcing you to click **OK** before you can see the results.

Checking Colorize

If you want the selected area to change to all one hue, enable the **Colorize** check box in the **Hue/Saturation** dialog box. This option lets you select a single hue for the selected range by moving just the **Hue** slider.

Selecting a Target Area First

As you specify a color range, it is normal for stray pixels from other areas, such as the background, to creep in and add "noise" to the image. To keep stray pixels to a minimum, select the object with any of Photoshop's selection tools before you sample a color range (see Part 3, "Selection Techniques"). You also can use the **Image, Adjustments, Color Balance** command to apply this same kind of effect.

How to Make Subtle Color Changes

All of Photoshop's color tools let you make subtle tweaks to the image, but the **Color Balance** command offers more control than the other tools—especially if you're changing the image globally. This approach lets you gradually shift the colors, isolating changes in the **Highlight, Midtone**, or **Shadow** areas. The effect is similar to adding a warming filter to a camera lens: Colors are enhanced rather than completely changed.

Begin

1 Open the File

Choose **File, Open** and launch the image file you want to modify.

2 Select Color Balance

Choose **Image, Adjustments, Color Balance** to launch the **Color Balance** dialog box. Enable the **Preview** check box to make sure that the changes are updated in the main window as changes are made.

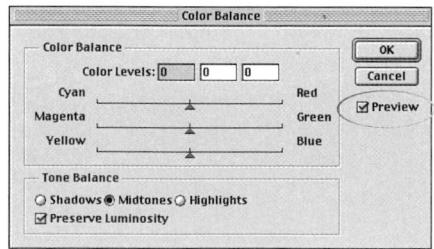

3 Target a Tonal Range

Target the primary tonal area to be modified. Should the color shift be applied primarily to the shadows, midtones, or highlights? In this example, you'll start with the midtones and work into the shadows. Select the corresponding option to target that specific area.

4 Shift the Color

Move one of the three color sliders toward the color you want to add to the selected tonal range. In this example, drag the **Cyan/Red** slider toward **Red** and notice the changes in the midtones of the angel image.

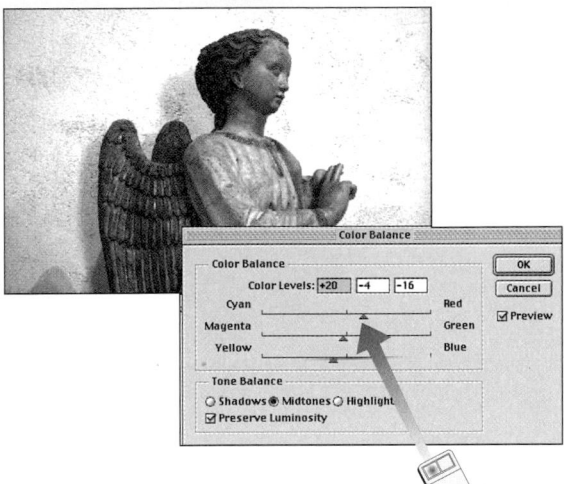

Drag

5 Check Other Tonal Ranges

Click the two remaining tonal range buttons and add color in those areas as well. This step is necessary, especially if you want to apply a color correction globally across the entire range of the image. When finished, click **OK** to apply the effect.

End

How-To Hints

Changing the Range to Which You Are Applying Color

The **Color Balance** tool isolates the color changes in specific areas in the tonal range (shadows, midtones, or highlights). If a given correction is not having the desired effect, switch tonal ranges.

Preserving Luminosity

When working with RGB images, select the **Preserve Luminosity** check box in the **Color Balance** dialog box to prevent changing the luminosity values in the image while changing the color. This option maintains the overall tonal range in the image as changes are made.

How to Build Duotones for the Web

Duotones are grayscale images that are tinted for a graphic effect. Although they originally were designed to push the tonal range of standard grayscale images, designers have embraced duotones for their graphic look and feel. This task shows you how to set up a pseudo-duotone effect for the Web, adding a second color to tint a grayscale image. Task 6 addresses setting up actual duotone plates for print.

Begin

1 Open the File

Select **File, Open** to launch the desired image. Open the **Layers** palette by selecting **Window, Layers.**

2 Create a New Adjustment Layer

Select **Layer, New Adjustment Layer, Gradient Map** to create a new adjustment layer that will generate the duotone effect. If you want, change any of the settings in the **New Layer** dialog box and click **OK** to create the new layer. You can also make these modifications from the **Layers** palette at any time.

3 Launch the Gradient Editor

After you click **OK** in the **New Layer** dialog box, the **Gradient Map** dialog box opens, showing the default black and white gradient. With the **Preview** check box enabled, click the gradient to launch the **Gradient Editor.**

Click

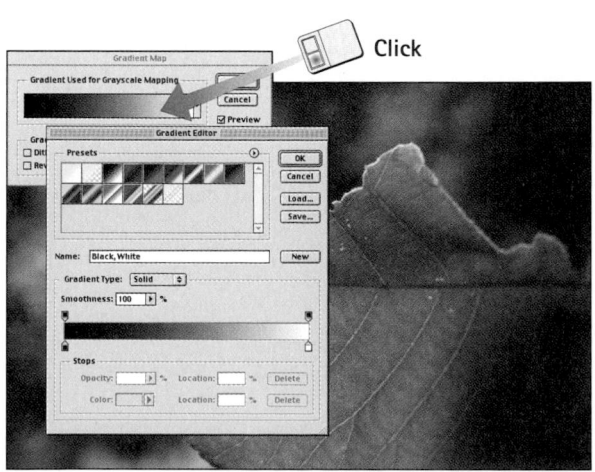

4 Select the Duotone Colors

Click the color stop on the lower-left of the gradient to select it, and then click the **Color** swatch to launch the **Color Picker.** From the **Color Picker,** choose the first color you want to use in the duotone and then close the **Color Picker.** Repeat this step with the color stop on the lower-right of the gradient to select the second color in the duotone.

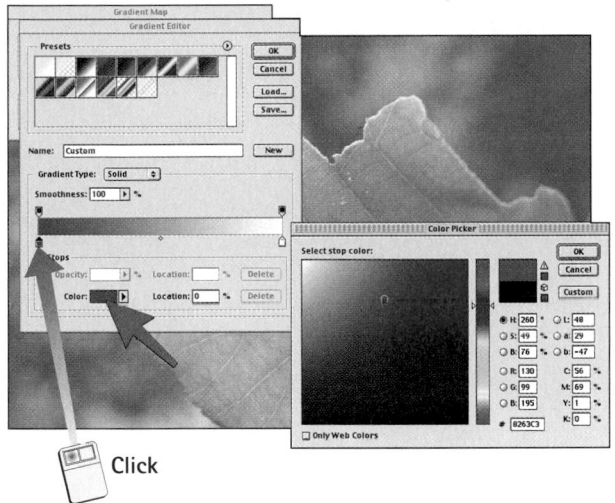

Click

5 Add Tritone and Quadtone Colors

To create a tritone image, click anywhere in the color stop row, just below the gradient bar, to create a third color stop. Click the **Color** swatch to select the color from the **Color Picker,** and drag the stop to the left or right to control where the third color is applied to the image. To create a quadtone image, repeat this step to add a fourth color.

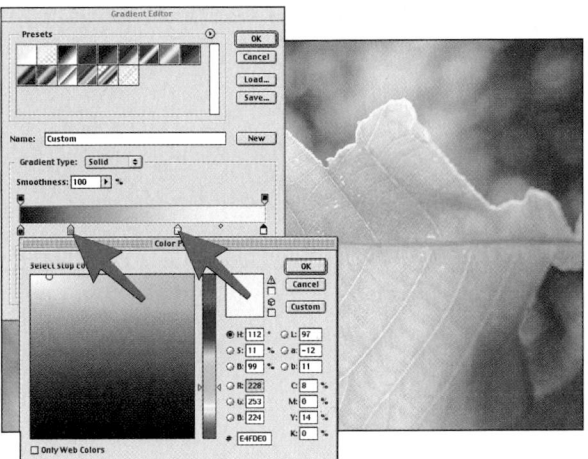

6 Save the Gradient

Move the cursor into the gradient swatch palette at the top of the **Gradient Editor** window and click to add the gradient to the palette for future use (use the **Name** field to provide an appropriate name for the swatch). Click **OK** in the **Gradient Editor** window and again in the **Gradient Map** dialog box to complete the effect.

How-To Hints

Electric Color Effects

Change the gradient to a **Noise** gradient to shake things up even more. In the **Gradient Editor** window, select **Noise** from the **Gradient Type** menu. Change any of the RGB sliders or even select the **Randomize** option to experiment with different effects.

Reversing the Effect

Close the **Gradient Editor** window and click the **Reverse** check box in the **Gradient Map** dialog box to reverse the color mapping and create a negative effect.

End

How to Build Duotones, Tritones, and Quadtones for Print

Where a duotone adds one color to the black plate, a *tritone* adds two colors to the black plate, and a *quadtone* adds three colors to the black plate (for totals of three and four colors, respectively). Work closely with your printer to create a plan for setting percentages and proofing the image before printing. This task shows you how to apply the settings and set up the file for the printer; your printer should help you define the settings.

Begin

1 Open the File

Choose **File, Open** and launch the image file you want to modify. If you worked with an image in Task 5 to create a duotone for the Web, note that you should use the *original* image for this task, not the already converted image.

2 Convert to Grayscale

If you started with a color image, choose **Image, Mode, Grayscale** to convert the color model from its original color set to a true grayscale image.

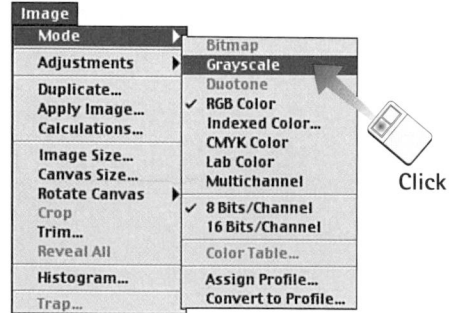

Click

3 Optimize the Tonal Range

Set the white and black points as explained in Part 5, Task 2, "How to Optimize the Tonal Range": Select **Image, Adjust, Curves** and select the black or white eyedropper from the **Curves** dialog box to set the black or white point and optimize the tonal range. Click **OK** to close the dialog box. Now you have an optimized black-and-white monotone image with which to work.

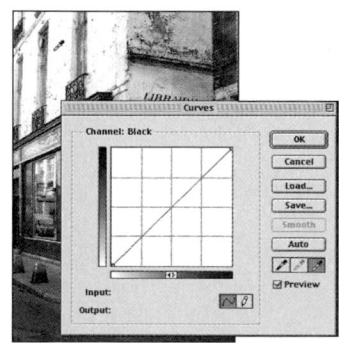

4 Open the Duotones Dialog Box

Choose **Image, Mode, Duotone** to open the **Duotone Options** dialog box. This dialog box does not open unless you are using a grayscale image. Click the **Type** pop-up menu and select **Duotone.**

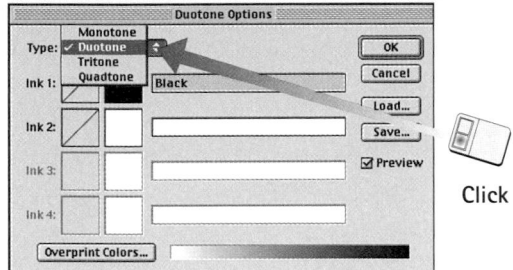

Click

5 Apply the Color

Click the color swatch below the black color swatch to launch the **Custom Colors** dialog box, which defaults to the **Pantone Coated** standard. (You can select a different color set from the list if you want.) Scroll through the colors and click a swatch to see it applied to your image. After you find the color you want, click **OK** to return to the **Duotone Options** dialog box. (You can also select a color other than black. To do this, click the black color swatch and choose a color.)

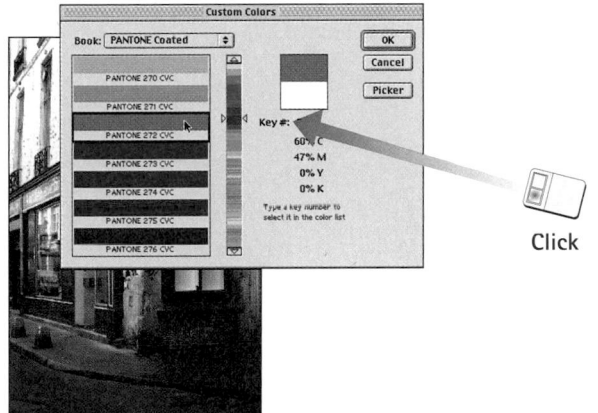

Click

6 Set the Tonal Curve

The *tonal curve* determines which areas in the image are affected by the second color. Click the **Curve** button next to the **Ink 2** label to launch the **Duotone Curve** dialog box. Click the diagonal line in the curve grid and drag it up or down to add or subtract the color in that area. The image updates as you do this, so trust your eyes more than the numbers unless you are following required specs from your printer. Remember that you can also change the curve for the black plate, represented by the **Ink 1** label.

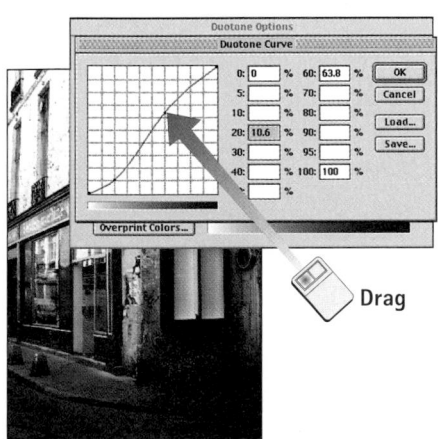

Drag

7 Add Additional Colors

If you select **Tritone** or **Quadtone** from the **Type** box in the **Duotone Options** dialog box in Step 4, Photoshop creates one or two additional ink sets. Select colors and set the curves as described in Steps 5 and 6 for each of the ink sets. Click **OK** to apply the effect.

End

Task

7

Image Editing Basics

The tasks in this part of the book look at the basic skills you need to modify and process most kinds of images. It is inevitable that you will need to resize, rotate, flip, or silhouette almost every image with which you work. These basic tasks are important because you must know how to do them before you can apply more advanced processing. In addition, if you do not properly perform tasks such as silhouetting and resizing, you may destroy image resolution or create less-than-desirable results.

These tasks sometimes are referred to as *preprocessing tasks* or *image prep tasks* because they are a precursor or requisite step before more serious work can begin. A better way to look at the process is to consider these tasks as fundamental skills that every Photoshop user must master. Exercising these skills with speed and precision will bring a high level of consistency and quality to all your work.

An area you should pay special attention to is resizing images safely to minimize loss of image quality. Images are made up of small building blocks called *pixels*; the number of pixels in an image's width and height determines the image's resolution. Consider an image that is 500 pixels high and 700 pixels wide. If you ask Photoshop to increase the image size to 700 high by 900 wide, you are asking it to add pixels. Where do these pixels come from? Photoshop makes them up, using a process called *interpolation*.

When adding a new pixel, Photoshop looks at the surrounding pixels to determine the value of the pixel it will add. When Photoshop interpolates an image, it can use one of three methods: Bicubic, Bilinear, and Nearest Neighbor. With the Bicubic method, Photoshop looks at the pixels on all four sides as well as on all diagonals and makes a guess at what the new value should be. With the Bilinear method, Photoshop looks only at pixels vertically and horizontally. With the Nearest Neighbor method, Photoshop looks only from side to side to make the decision of what the new pixel should be. As you can imagine, the Bicubic method delivers the highest level of quality for most photographic images—although it takes the longest to process. And, although the Nearest Neighbor method generally provides the lowest quality for photos, it does a great job on hard-edge, graphic shapes and is also the fastest method of interpolation. ●

How to Resize Images

The size of a Photoshop image is measured in width and height, combined with a resolution value expressed as *pixels* or *dots per inch (dpi)*. For example, you could have a 4×5-inch image at 300dpi. When resizing images, it is important to understand your minimum target resolution and to never go below it. (For example, in the print world, 300dpi is generally a target resolution.)

Begin

1 Open the Image in Photoshop

Choose **File, Open** and select the image file with which you want to work.

2 Check the Image Size

Choose **Image, Image Size** to open the **Image Size** dialog box. Make sure that the **Constrain Proportions** check box is enabled. This option ensures that the width-to-height ratios are maintained and prevents you from distorting the image as you resize it.

Click

3 Deselect Resample Image

Make sure that the **Resample Image** check box is disabled. Deselecting this option keeps you from accidentally degrading image quality, especially if you plan to enlarge the image. Resampling works well when you want to resize and shrink the image, but resampling can be disastrous when you're trying to increase the dimensions.

Image Size		
Pixel Dimensions: 4.5M		OK
Width: 1024 pixels		Cancel
Height: 1536 pixels		Auto...
Document Size:		
Width: 14.222 inches		
Height: 21.333 inches		
Resolution: 72 pixels/inch		
☑ Constrain Proportions		
☐ Resample Image: Bicubic		

4 Enter Target Resolution

Resolution refers to the number of dots per inch (dpi) or pixels per inch (ppi). For print, you want the image resolution to be between 225dpi and 300dpi; in contrast, the Web needs only 72dpi. Type the target resolution for this image in the **Resolution** field. As you do this, the dimensions (the **Height** and **Width** fields in the **Document Size** area) change, ensuring that image quality is not sacrificed. In this case, typing **300** in the **Resolution** field changed the dimensions from 14×21 to approximately 3×5.

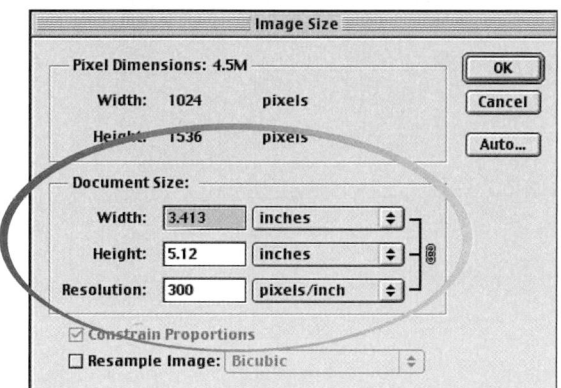

5 Enter Target Dimensions

Because resolution is tied to image dimension, changing the dimension values modifies the target resolution you entered in Step 4. To change dimensions without altering resolution, enable the **Resample Image** check box and select **Bicubic** as the interpolation method. If you are designing for the Web, enter the dimension size in the fields in the **Pixel Dimensions** area; if you are designing for print, use the **Document Size** section. Specify the units of measurement in the pop-up menus (remember that image quality degrades if you enable the **Resample Image** check box), and then increase the image dimensions. Enter the desired dimensions and click **OK** to resize the image.

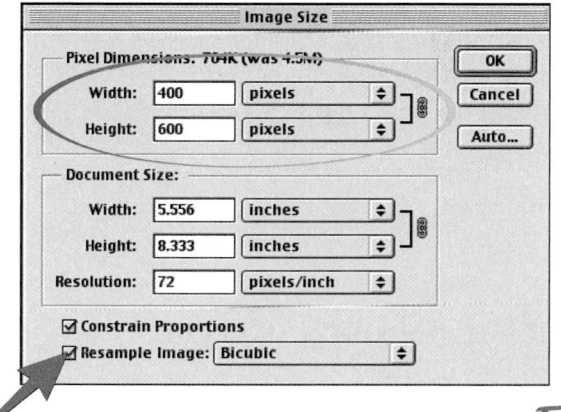

End

How-To Hints

Resizing Graphics

When resizing graphics with hard edges and flat color, you may get better results by choosing **Nearest Neighbor** from the **Resample Image** pop-up menu rather than **Bicubic**. Nearest Neighbor creates very crisp lines and hard edges, preserving more of the original look of the design.

Enlarging Size and Reducing Resolution

You should avoid enlarging an image without decreasing resolution. For example, to enlarge a 4×5 image at 600dpi to 5×7, you should reduce the resolution to approximately 425dpi. This precaution keeps you from interpolating the image and losing detail. If you deactivate the **Resample Image** check box in the **Image Size** dialog box, Photoshop automatically makes these adjustments for you.

How to Add Canvas

Task 1 looked at how to scale an image up or down by increasing the resolution or dimensions of the image itself. In contrast, this task explains how to keep the image the same size and just add more workspace around it. Photoshop calls this extra workspace *canvas* and enables you to specify exactly how much is added. Adding canvas is important when adding and combining images, adding flat color for text, or any time you need to increase the image dimensions without enlarging the image data.

Begin

1 Open the Image

Choose **File, Open** and select the image file with which you want to work.

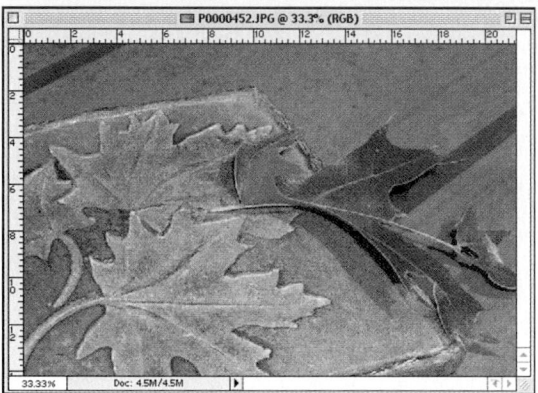

2 Set the Background Color

When you add canvas to an image, the canvas is filled automatically with the current background color. Click the **Background** color swatch in the toolbox. The **Color Picker** dialog box opens; use this dialog box to select a color for the background of the canvas you will add. Or, you can move the cursor into the image area to sample a color from the image itself. Alternatively, you can leave the background set to white.

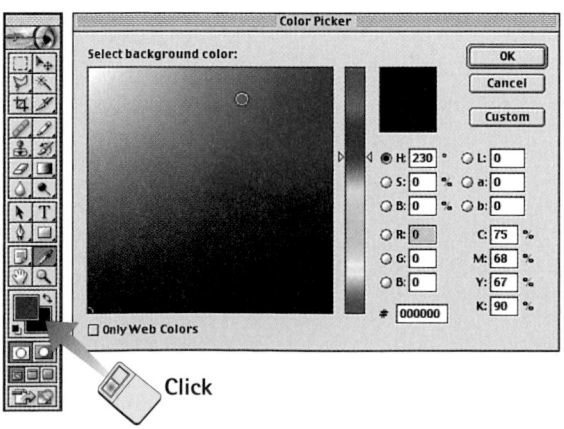

Click

3 Open the Canvas Size Dialog Box

Choose **Image, Canvas Size** to open the **Canvas Size** dialog box.

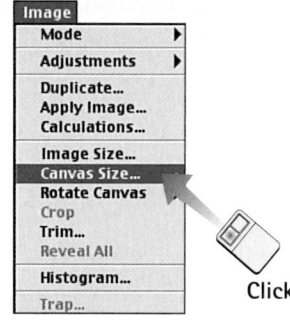

Click

4 Specify Anchor Placement

The **Anchor** diagram lets you specify where the extra canvas is added. The darkened box represents the current image; the remaining grid represents the canvas to be added. Click in the diagram to move the dark box and control where the extra canvas will be placed.

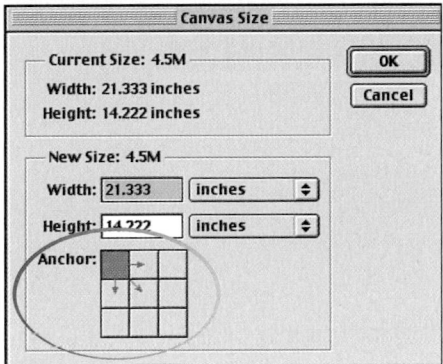

5 Specify Dimensions

Note the current size of the image at the top of the dialog box. Type values for the new image size in the **Width** and **Height** fields in the **New Size** area. Use the drop-down menus to specify units of measurement if necessary. Click **OK** to apply the effect.

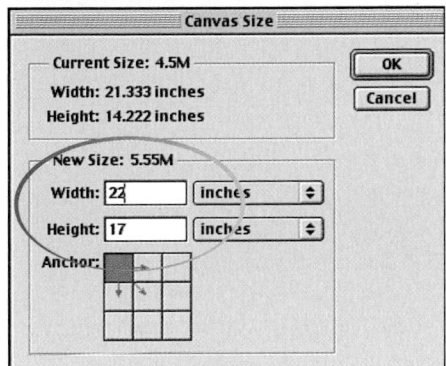

6 Observe the Results

This example shows the canvas that was added when I moved the **Anchor** box to the upper-left corner of the grid and increased the width of the image from 21.333 inches to 22 inches and the height of the image from 14.222 inches to 17 inches. Notice that the extra space appears as blank canvas around the original image.

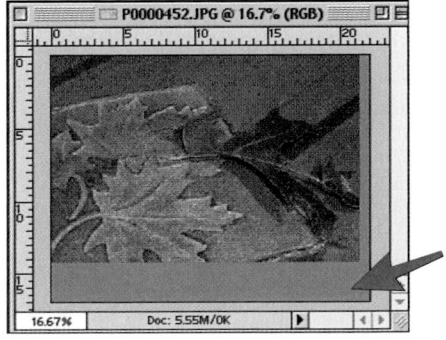

End

How-To Hints

Transparent Background

When a multi-layered image has no background layer, adding canvas always places transparent canvas rather than canvas that has the background color. To force the added canvas to have a white background, choose **Flatten Image** from the **Layers** palette menu. You also can fill the canvas to force the added canvas to white, or fill it by using the **Paint Bucket** tool, as explained in Part 8, Task 8, "How to Fill with the Paint Bucket."

How to Crop an Image

Cropping an image involves cutting an image down to a specific square or rectangular section, excluding all other unwanted areas. You may want to crop an image to fit it to a specific dimension or to enhance the composition. Sometimes cropping involves trimming away a little detail around the edges. At other times, you may isolate a small component of an image and discard everything else. Cropping an image does not change the resolution or image quality; it only shrinks the canvas size as unwanted areas are eliminated.

Begin

1 Open the Image

Choose **File, Open** and select the desired image file.

2 Select the Crop Tool

Select the **Crop** tool from the toolbox.

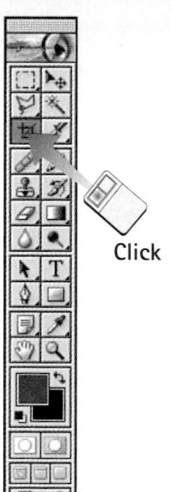

Click

3 Define the Crop Area

Click and drag the **Crop** tool over the image to specify the area to be cropped. A dotted line appears, showing what has been selected; if **Shield Cropped Area** is selected in the **Options** bar, the area outside the crop area is covered with a mask color. If the selection is wrong, click the × button in the **Options** bar to deselect and then drag again to specify the area. Everything outside the dotted rectangular area *will not* appear in the finished image area.

Drag

4 Modify the Crop Area

Notice that the crop area has handles at the corners and on the sides. To modify the crop area by extending a side, drag a side handle. To extend the crop area from two adjoining sides, drag a corner handle. To move the entire crop area, click inside the selected crop area and drag the box to a new position.

 Drag

5 Rotate the Crop Area

You can even rotate the crop area. To do this, position the cursor outside of a corner handle until it changes to a rotate icon. Click and drag to rotate the crop box.

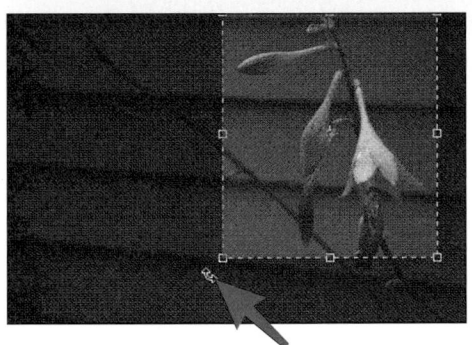

6 Crop the Image

When the rotated crop selection is where you want it, double-click in the selection to crop the image, or click the check mark button in the **Options** bar. The image window is resized to display the new image with some blank canvas around it. The additional canvas represents the amount needed to "square off" the canvas area. If no rotation has been done, the crop will square off as previewed.

How-To Hints

Crop Perspective

To create an angled, perspectival crop effect, check the **Perspective** box in the **Options** bar for the **Crop** tool. As you move the cursor into the image area, it changes to an arrow icon, indicating that the perspective option is active. You can then click and drag each crop handle independently. As you can guess, this option also lets you create crops that aren't rectangular, whether or not the crops create accurate perspective.

End

How to Flip and Rotate an Image

You may have to reverse the orientation of an image for compositional or aesthetic reasons. This is relatively simple to do in Photoshop (provided that there is no text that would be reversed). In addition to reversing an image, you may want to rotate the entire image canvas, reorienting it to a new position. This is a common requirement for optimizing scans that were set up in the wrong direction. This process is similar to the **Free Transform** command discussed in Part 11, Task 5, "How to Transform Layers." The main difference is that **Free Transform** operates on individual layers rather than the entire image (so your text, on a separate layer, won't be affected).

Begin

1 Open the File

Choose **File, Open** and select the desired image file.

2 Rotate the Image

Select **Image, Rotate Canvas**. From the submenu, choose **90° CW** (clockwise), **90° CCW** (counterclockwise), or **180°**. In this example, I choose **90° CW**. The command is executed as soon as you select it from the menu.

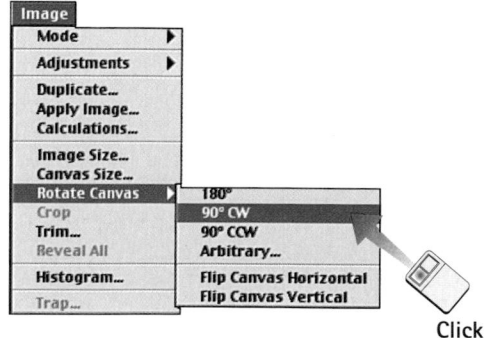

Click

3 Apply Arbitrary Rotation

Choose **Image, Rotate Canvas, Arbitrary** to open the **Rotate Canvas** dialog box. You can use this dialog box to specify the precise degree and direction of rotation. In this example, I want to rotate the image an additional **19°** clockwise (**CW**). Click **OK** to rotate the canvas, which enlarges to accommodate the angled image.

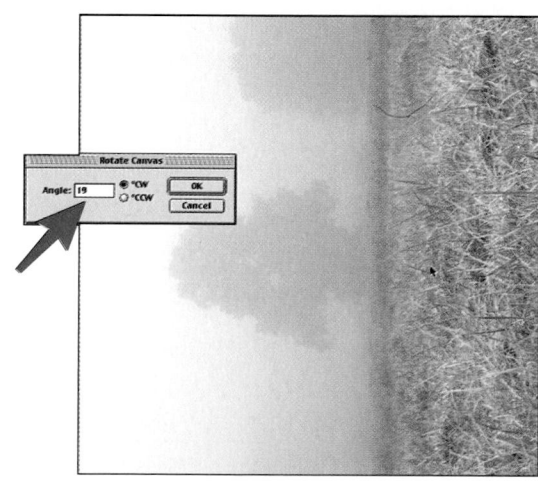

4 Flip the Image Horizontally

Choose **Image, Rotate Canvas, Flip Canvas Horizontal** to flip the image horizontally.

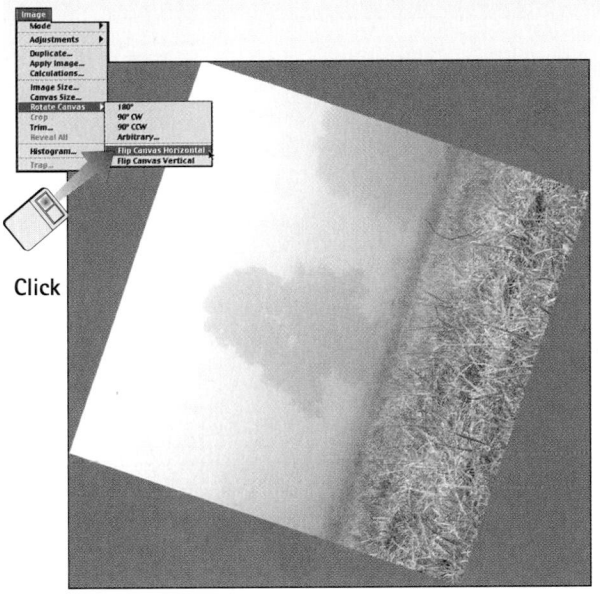

Click

5 Flip the Image Vertically

Choose **Image, Rotate Canvas, Flip Canvas Vertical** to flip the image vertically.

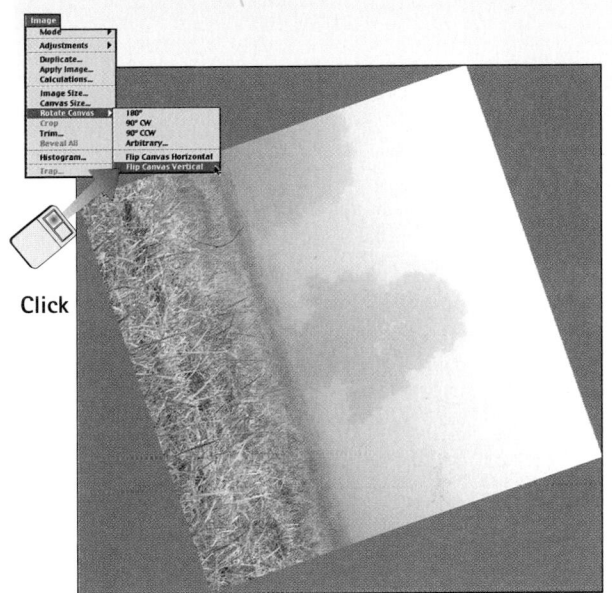

Click

6 Observe the Results

As you can see, rotating and flipping an image can greatly affect how the image is perceived. Although you haven't really changed anything about the image other than the way it is presented to the viewer, you can see that presentation is important.

How-To Hints

Rotating and Flipping

When you *rotate* an image, it's as if you place a print of the image on the desktop and spin it—nothing about the image changes except the orientation. When you *flip* an image, however, it's as if you created a mirror image. Any lettering is now backwards and left hands look like right hands. When you flip an image, make sure that there is no text, cars on a road, or other tell-tale signs that could give this manipulation away.

End

How to Silhouette an Image

Silhouetting an image refers to isolating part of an image against a white background, cutting it out from the rest of the frame. This task uses the **Extract** command to silhouette an image cleanly and easily. The **Extract** command asks you to define the edge of the object and then cuts it away from the background. Then you can smooth and modify the silhouette edges endlessly before you accept the final result.

Begin

1 Open the File

Choose **File, Open** and open the desired image file. Then choose **Filter, Extract** to open the **Extract** dialog box.

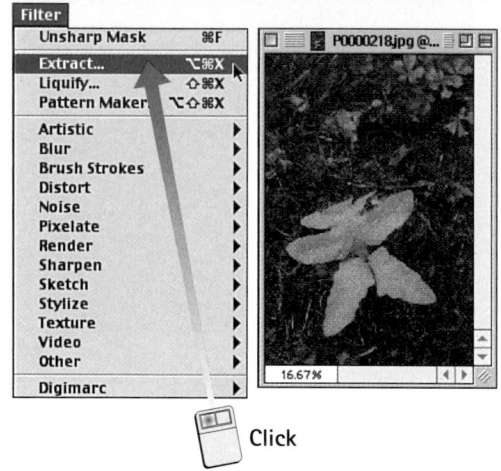

Click

2 Select the Edge Highlighter Tool

In the **Extract** dialog box, select the **Edge Highlighter** tool from the mini-toolbox on the left. In the **Tool Options** area, drag the **Brush Size** slider to set an appropriate brush size. (Use a smaller brush size to define sharper edges more accurately; use a larger brush to highlight wispy, intricate edges, such as hair or trees.) Then select highlight and fill colors from the pop-up menus, choosing colors that give a clear view of both the mask and the underlying image.

3 Define a Silhouette Edge

Leave the **Smooth** setting at **0** and drag along the edge between the object and the part of the image to be erased. Be sure that the line over-laps both the object and the background. Don't be concerned with other object areas that touch the edge of the image you're tracing around.

 Drag

4 Fill the Object

Select the **Paint Bucket** tool and click in the outlined image area to fill the object.

Click

5 Preview the Result

Click the **Preview** button to process a preview of the silhouette. Use the **Show** drop-down list to switch between previews of the **Original** and **Extracted** images.

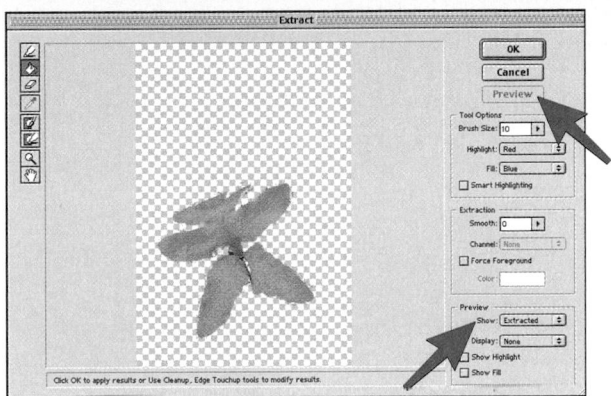

6 Modify the Preview

If artifacts appear in the background, increase the **Smooth** slider to remove them. (In this example, notice that the dark bit of grass at the upper-right edge of the leaf is minimized as the **Smooth** slider is adjusted.) You also can use the **Eraser** and **Paint Bucket** tools in the **Extract** dialog box to adjust the outline and fill as necessary. When the preview is accurate, click **OK** to extract the image. If necessary, you can now use the **Background Eraser** and **Magic Eraser** tools from the main toolbox to clean up any stray pixels and remaining artifacts.

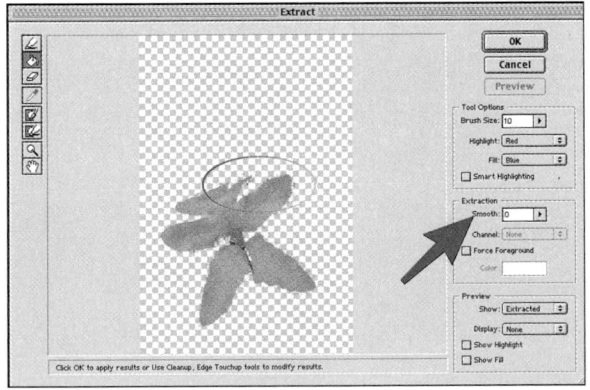

How-To Hints

Forcing the Foreground

If a single, flat color dominates the object, sample it with the **Eyedropper** tool from the **Extract** dialog box and enable the **Force Foreground** check box in the **Extraction** section of the **Extract** dialog box. This action selects all pixels matching the selected foreground color.

Other Methods

Although the **Background Eraser** and **Magic Eraser** tools do similar things as the **Extract** command (see Part 8, Task 3, "How to Erase a Background"), the **Extract** command is especially suited for problem areas, such as smoke and fine-hair details.

End

How to Use the Heal Brush

The new **Heal Brush** is built on the concept and functionality of the **Clone** tool, in that it paints using sampled data from a user-specified point. Instead of just moving the pixel info from one spot to the other as the **Clone** tool does, however, the **Heal Brush** actually blends the two data sets together, blurring information and smoothing the results. The **Heal Brush** does a great job of eliminating spots and scratches from scanned photographs, and is also superb at touching up blemishes and wrinkles on faces. If you work with portraiture or photo restoration, you'll use this new tool a lot.

Begin

1 Open the Image

Select **File, Open** to open the desired image.

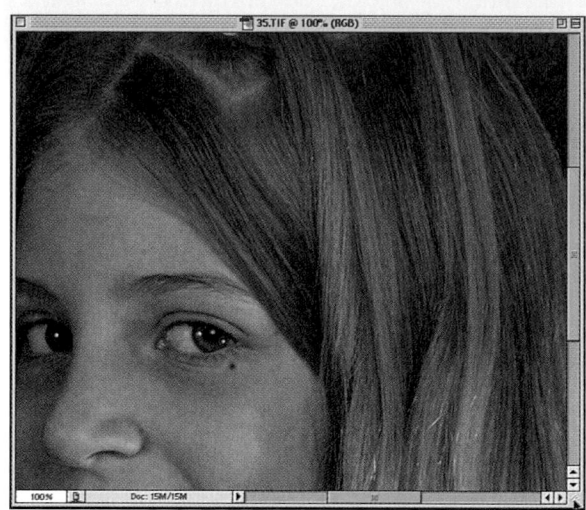

2 Select the Heal Brush Tool

Select the **Heal Brush** tool from the toolbox. If necessary, click and hold the **Patch** tool and select the **Heal Brush** from the pop-out menu that appears.

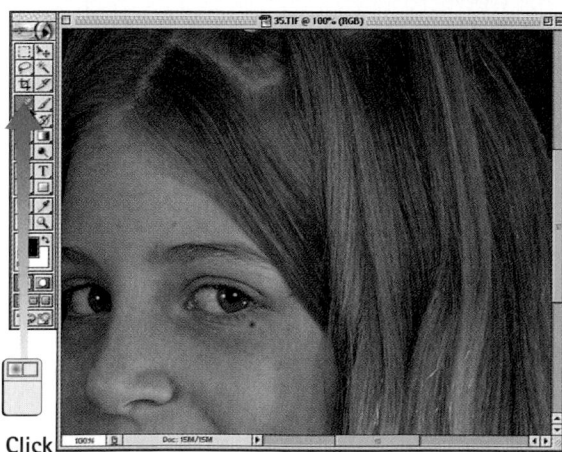

Click

3 Set the Tool Parameters

In the **Options** bar for the **Heal Brush**, set the brush size and blending mode. For the **Source**, choose either **Sampled** or a preset **Pattern**. If you want the source point to move as you move the cursor, enable the **Align** check box.

4 Set the Sample Point

Hold down the **Option** key (Mac users) or **Alt** key (Windows users) and click to set the source point for the brush. If your goal is to smooth a blemish or scratch, choose a source point that resembles the area you want to repair.

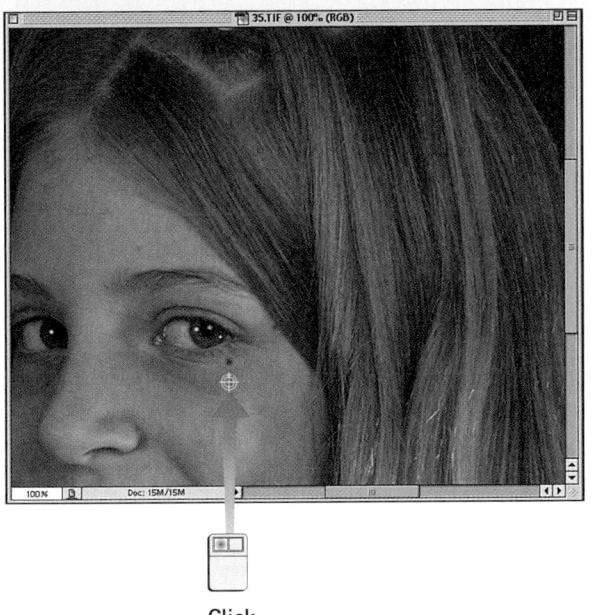

Click

5 Paint the Corrections

Position the cursor over the area to be repaired, and click to paint the corrections. Photoshop briefly flashes the sampled data as it is being applied, and then it paints the correction.

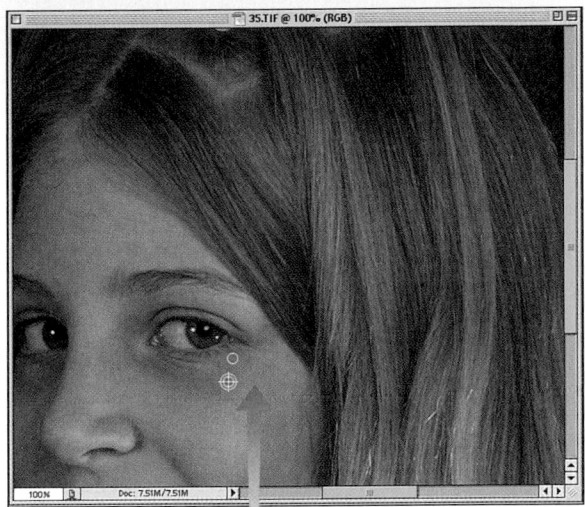

Click

End

How-To Hints

Using the Blending Modes

Remember to use the blending modes to your advantage whenever necessary. For example, if you're trying to clean up darker blotches on an otherwise solid background, use the **Lighten** mode and sample the same color and values as the background. These options will correct the dark spots without altering the background.

Task

PART 8

Drawing, Painting, and Filling with Color

Considering that Photoshop is often called a "paint" program, it's surprising how seldom the paint tools are used. Typical users will resize images, color correct, or apply a filter, but few people focus on the drawing or painting functions of the program.

Handled properly, the drawing and painting tools can yield predictable and acceptable results—even if your drawing skills are limited. Touching up images, spotting photographs, and erasing an area of a photo all involve the drawing and painting techniques described in the tasks in this part.

The underlying skill for almost all these tasks is the ability to effectively use a brush to apply the effects. When using a brush, the basic rule of thumb is to move from big and light strokes to small and heavy strokes. This means that you should start with the largest possible feathered brush set to the lightest possible setting. As you build up the effect, reduce the size of the brush to concentrate the results and slightly increase the pressure by increasing the **Opacity** slider. The one instance when this rule does not hold true is when you are doing line drawings and you want to put down a clean brushstroke.

The tasks in this part also look at filling areas with color or gradients. Although "filling" is certainly not the same as "brushing in" an effect, it does create a graphic effect that many people associate with digital drawing. ●

How to Paint an Image

Painting an image in Photoshop involves selecting a brush and applying an effect to an image. This task outlines the basic procedure for working with any of Photoshop's painting tools, regardless of the effect you are applying or the kind of file to which you're applying it. Photoshop makes available the **Airbrush**, **Paintbrush**, **Rubber Stamp**, **History/Art History Brush**, **Eraser**, **Pencil/Line**, and **Sharpen/Blur** painting tools and the **Dodge/Burn/Sponge** tools.

Begin

1 Select the Brush Tool

Open an image file. Click the **Paintbrush** tool in the Photoshop toolbox.

Click

2 Choose a Blending Mode

With the **Paintbrush** tool selected, choose **Normal** from the **Mode** menu in the **Options** bar.

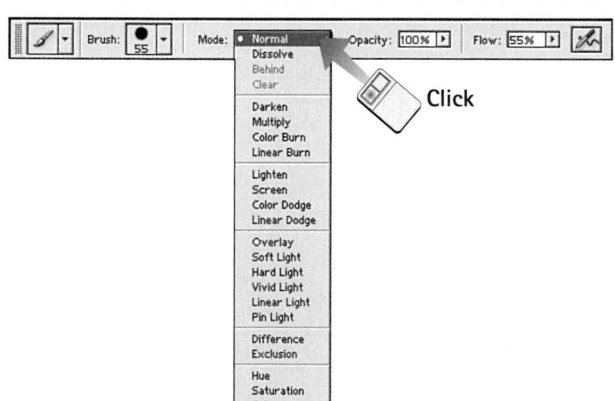

Click

3 Set the Opacity

The **Opacity** slider controls the density of the brushstrokes applied by the tool. Click and drag the slider to a lower setting for more transparent effects; leave it at 100% to paint with a completely opaque stroke. The **Flow** slider controls the feather of the brush. Combine **Flow** and **Opacity** to create the proper balance of transparency and soft brush strokes.

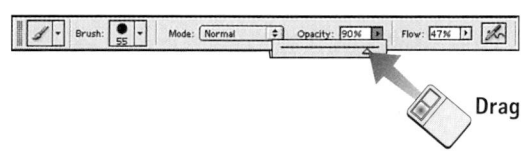

Drag

4 Choose a Brush

Click the small arrow next to the **Brush** icon in the **Options** bar to open the brush palette. Move the **Master Diameter** slider to set the brush size, or select a preset from the list. To avoid painting the image when you click, try clicking in an empty space in the **Options** bar.

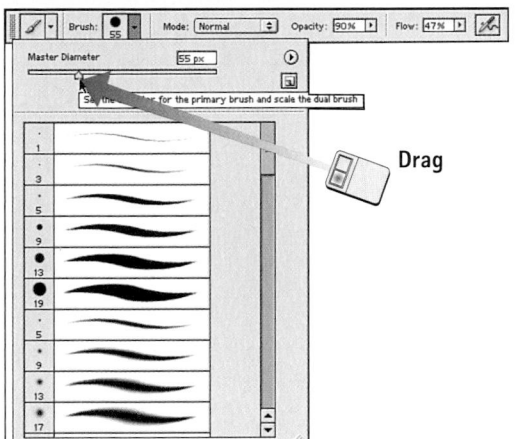

Drag

5 Paint the Image

To apply the paint effect, move the cursor into the image window and click and drag.

Drag

End

How-To Hints

Grouping Similar Palettes Together

You can group similar palettes together by clicking and dragging the palette tab and moving one palette onto another. You can also drag palettes to the palette well on the right side of the **Options** bar.

Tapping in Big Brushes

To modify a large area without leaving telltale brushstrokes, use a large brush with a light **Opacity** setting. Instead of dragging, position the brush over the area and lightly click the mouse. Click repeatedly while moving the mouse slightly to build up a gradual effect.

Setting Brush Size Preferences

You can set the **Paintbrush** cursor so that it appears as the currently selected brush size rather than as a tool icon or a set of crosshairs. This way, you know exactly how large the brush is (its circle icon shows you) in relation to the resolution of the image; you have a better sense of where you will paint the effect. Choose **Edit, Preferences, Displays & Cursors** and click the **Brush Size** button in the **Painting Cursors** section of the dialog box.

TASK 2

How to Erase an Image

Erasing an image is the opposite of painting in the sense that it removes the current pixel values in the image window, based on the brushstrokes. When you erase, consider which Eraser tool you should use and what you want to erase. The **Eraser Options** bar offers three Eraser tool options: **Brush**, **Block**, and **Pencil**. The **Brush** eraser lets you erase using a brush preset, as described in Part 2, Task 6, "How to Create Custom Tool Presets." The **Block** eraser offers a flat, geometric effect that's perfect for hard-edged erasures, and the **Pencil** eraser lets you erase a single pixel at a time.

1 Select the Erase Tool

With the image you want to modify open onscreen, click the **Eraser** tool in the toolbox and drag to select the desired tool. Choose from the **Eraser**, **Background Eraser**, or **Magic Eraser** tool.

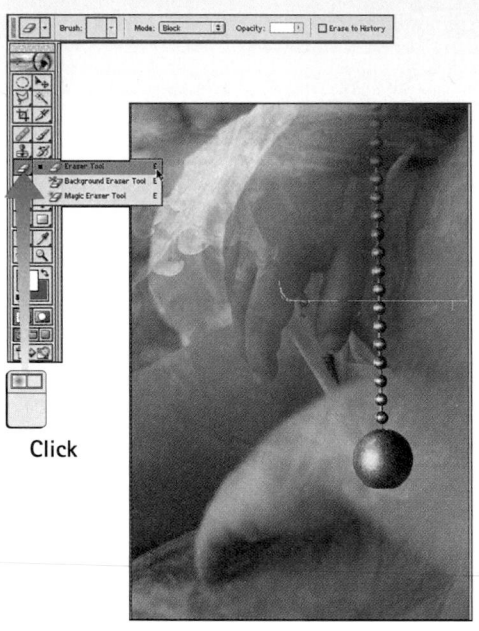

Click

2 Choose an Eraser Type

From the **Mode** menu in the **Options** bar, select the desired eraser type. Your options are **Brush**, **Pencil**, and **Block**.

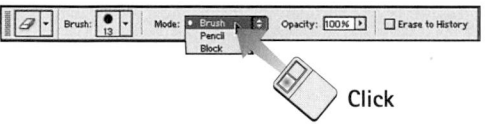

Click

3 Set the Pressure If Necessary

For all brush types except **Block**, click and drag the **Opacity** slider to set the desired opacity of the erasure effect. A lower value creates transparency; a high value erases the image more completely. If you want to soften an image rather than erase it, set a low value and brush over it several times.

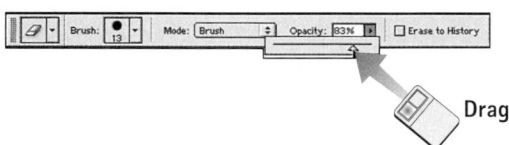

Drag

4 Choose a Brush Size

For all eraser types except **Block**, select the desired brush size from the menu in the **Options** bar. Select from a preset, or drag the **Master Diameter** slider to set the brush size. When using the **Block** eraser, select the **Magnify** tool and click to zoom in (to zoom out, Mac users can press the **Option** key, Windows users can press **Alt** key, and click again); this action creates the desired brush size relative to the image.

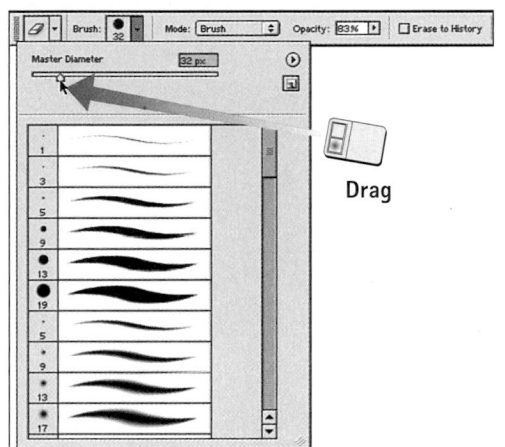

Drag

5 Erase the Image

Move the cursor into the image window and click and drag to erase the image. If you're using the **Block** eraser, you can click once to erase a clean square corresponding to the **Block** eraser size.

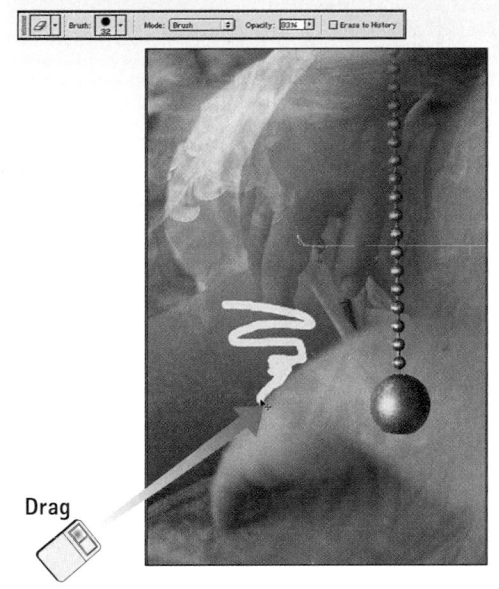

Drag

End

How-To Hints

Zooming for the Block Eraser

Although you cannot select smaller brush sizes for the **Block** eraser, you can click the **Magnify** tool in the toolbox and zoom in to erase tight areas.

Erasing to History

Enable the **Erase to History** check box in the **Eraser Options** bar to erase the image back to the **History** palette state, as specified by the **History Brush** selection setting. See Task 4, "How to Use the History Brush," for more information on using the **History Brush**.

How to Erase a Background

Photoshop offers two ways to erase a background: the **Background Eraser** and the **Magic Eraser**. This task looks at how to use both tools, highlighting the differences between them. The **Background Eraser** erases an image area selectively, based on a pixel's value. It remembers the first pixel value you click and then erases only that value, ignoring other values. This initial value is referred to as a *sample point* because the value of the pixel is used as a sample to determine how the eraser interacts with the image. You use the **Tolerance** slider to determine whether the brush erases the exact value sampled or a range of values based on the sample.

Begin

1 Select Background Eraser

With the image you want to modify open onscreen, select the **Background Eraser** from the toolbox. If necessary, click and hold the active **Eraser** tool and drag to select the **Background Eraser** from the pop-out menu that appears.

Click

2 Protect Foreground Color

It's possible to protect a specified image color from being erased, making it easier to delete the background. To do this, select the **Eyedropper** tool and sample the color you want to "protect." With the desired color as the current foreground color, select **Protect Foreground Color** in the **Options** bar.

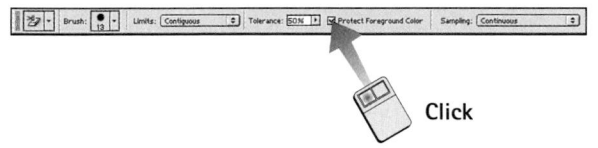

Click

3 Select the Eraser Type

From the **Limits** menu in the **Options** bar, select the **Find Edges** option. This option erases adjacent pixels while maintaining strong edges—the perfect choice for eliminating the area behind the boy's head. The **Contiguous** and **Discontiguous** options do not keep as crisp an edge as **Find Edges** and do not work as well for this image.

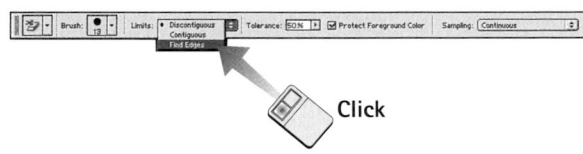

Click

4 Estimate the Tolerance Setting

Always start with a low tolerance value and increase as you erase to keep a crisp edge to the image. The higher the **Tolerance** setting, the more the tool erases. Therefore, if there is high contrast between the background and object, set the **Tolerance** slider to a higher setting. The result will be a fast and clean erasure with a crisp edge. If the background and object are similar in contrast, use a low **Tolerance** setting and erase the area several times, perhaps using a smaller brush. Each image is unique; you'll have to experiment to find the right settings. To set the tolerance, drag the **Tolerance** slider in the **Options** bar.

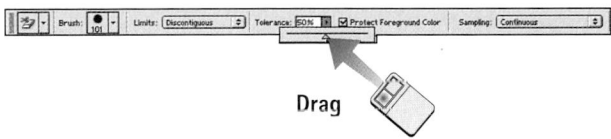

Drag

5 Set the Sampling Option

Click the arrow next to the **Sampling** drop-down list and select **Once**, **Continuous**, or **Background Swatch**. The **Once** option samples only the pixels read when you first click the eraser on the image. As you continue to drag the eraser, only the initial pixel value is erased. The **Continuous** option samples continuously, allowing you to erase adjacent background areas of different colors. You can cover a wider range of pixels—although you run the risk of erasing the image edge. The **Background Swatch** option erases only the active color in the background swatch in the toolbox. With this option, you can select a background color, and the eraser erases only that specific color.

Click

6 Erase the Background

Move the cursor into the image window and click and drag to erase the background. The exact erasure result depends on the sampling option you chose in Step 5.

Drag

Continues

How to Erase a Background Continued

At this point, let's start over with the same image and use the **Magic Eraser** instead of the **Background Eraser** to get the job done. The **Magic Eraser** eliminates broad areas of the background with a single mouse click, in much the same way that the **Magic Wand** tool selects broad areas. When you click in the image, the **Magic Eraser** measures the pixel value you clicked and erases all adjoining pixels as well. For example, if you have a large flat area of solid color, a single click erases the entire area.

In these next steps, you use the **Tolerance** slider in the **Options** bar to specify how wide or narrow your erasure range will be. Increase the **Tolerance** setting to erase the full area in spite of slight variations in pixel values. Decrease the **Tolerance** setting to erase a more narrow range of pixel values. It helps to examine the image carefully and click the "best" spot to select the color you want to erase.

7 Select the Magic Eraser

Select the **Magic Eraser** from the toolbox. If necessary, click and hold the active **Eraser** tool and select the **Magic Eraser** from the pop-out menu that appears.

Click

8 Enable the Anti-Aliased Option

In the **Options** bar, enable the **Anti-aliased** check box to create a smooth erasure edge. Enable the **Use All Layers** check box to erase across all visible layers. Enable the **Contiguous** check box to erase all adjoining pixels; leave this option disabled to erase the pixel value wherever it appears in the image.

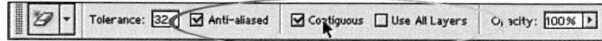

9 Erase the Image

Click in the image window to erase a range of pixels. If you don't like the result, choose **Edit, Undo**, revise the **Tolerance** setting, and try again. Continue clicking to delete the desired area.

Click

End

How-To Hints

Switching Tools

To switch quickly among the **Eraser**, **Magic Eraser**, and **Background Eraser** tools, press **Shift+E**.

Adjusting Tolerance Often

Keep an eye on the areas you are erasing and adjust the **Tolerance** setting up or down to optimize the amount of background being erased. Using a low **Tolerance** setting may require you to sample often, erasing the background a chunk at a time. This may be necessary to keep a clean line of separation between the subject and background.

Protecting the Foreground Color

When using the **Background Eraser,** select the **Eyedropper** tool from the toolbox and sample the color in an image, making it the active foreground color swatch. Then enable the **Protect Foreground Color** check box in the **Options** bar for the **Background Eraser**. Now, when you use the **Background Eraser** on the image, the tool won't delete pixels of the selected foreground color. Also remember to adjust the **Tolerance** slider to get the exact edge effect you're after.

How to Use the History Brush

The **History Brush** allows you to selectively paint an iteration of an image from a previous state, as displayed in the **History** palette. Recall that as you work on an image, previous image states are recorded in the **History** palette. The **History Brush** lets you access these previous states as a source file, brushing them back into an image. The **History** palette stores only a limited number of states as specified with the **General Preferences** box (select **Edit, Preferences, General**). As you add states to the palette, you can convert a state to a snapshot to preserve that state. The basic rules of working with the **History** palette are outlined in Part 2, Task 5, "How to Undo with the History Palette."

Begin

1 Select the History Brush Tool

With the image file you want to modify open onscreen, select the **History Brush** tool from the toolbox. Note that all history states are erased when a file is closed; for this task, make sure that you are working with a file that has been modified from its original state since it was opened.

Click

2 Set the Opacity

In the **Options** bar, set the **Opacity** slider to determine the transparency or opacity of the brushstroke. For example, set the **Opacity** slider to **100** to add the history state as a solid area. Lower the value on the **Opacity** slider to increase the transparency of the brushstroke.

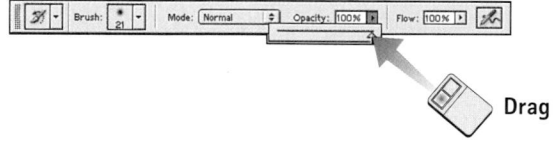

Drag

3 Select a Brush

Select a brush size and a feathered effect from the **Brush** menu in the **Options** bar.

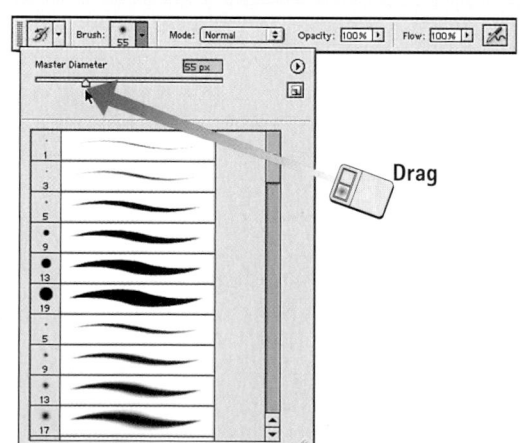

Drag

4 Set the Source

Choose **Window, History** to open the History palette. Compare the various available history states and snapshots, and click the left column to place the source icon (a paintbrush) next to the state or snapshot you want to use as a source.

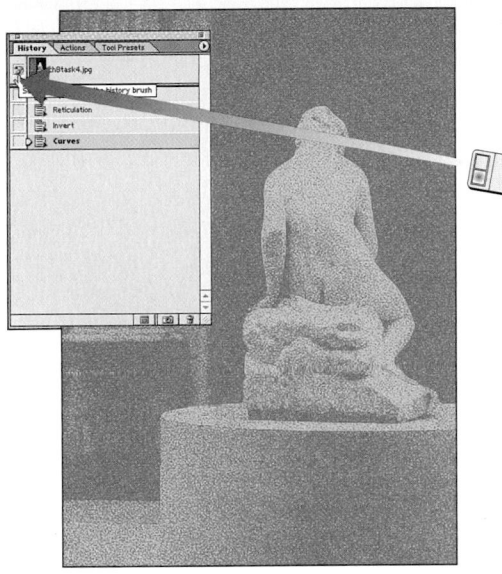

Click

5 Paint the Image

Move the cursor into the image window and click and drag to paint in the source image as it exists in the state you selected from the **History** palette in Step 4.

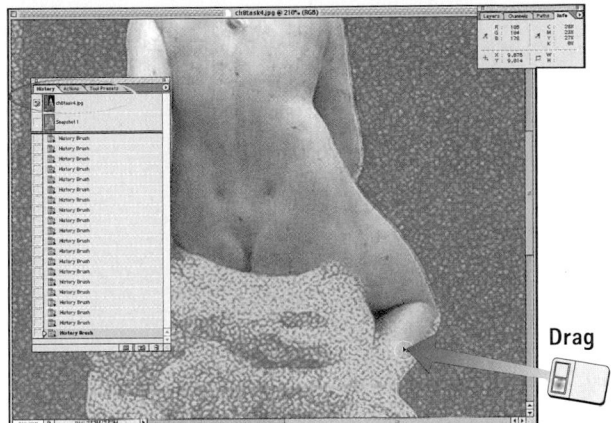

Drag

6 Look at the Results

In this example, the image was modified with a filter; the original image was used as the source to paint back the figure of the statue. The before and after images are shown here side by side so that you can see the differences.

End

How-To Hints

Painting in Corrections

The **History Brush** is a great tool for brushing color corrections into an image. Apply any of Photoshop's color-correction commands and then select the previous state from the **History** palette, undoing the effect. While still in the **History** palette, click in the left column next to one of the color-correction commands to set the **History Brush** source icon, as described in Step 4 (even though the tile is grayed out, you still can set the icon). Select the **History Brush** and brush the correction into the exact areas you want within the image.

As a wild alternative, you can paint a history state back in with the **Art History** brush. Located in the **History Brush** pop-out menu, this tool paints with expressive brush-stroke patterns that echo the initial history state. With the **Art History** brush selected, modify **Style, Fidelity, Area,** and **Spacing** options to create a wide range of effects.

How to Use the Clone Stamp

The **Clone Stamp** tool (also called the **Rubber Stamp** tool) "clones" one area of an image, enabling you to paint it into another area. It can be useful for filling in an open area with a pattern or a color or for duplicating or repeating an object. The basic process for using the **Clone Stamp** tool requires you to set a *source point* (the point from which the pixel values come) in the image and then to paint that value into another area of the image.

Begin

1 Select the Clone Stamp Tool

Open the image file you want to modify and select the **Clone Stamp** tool from the toolbox.

Click

2 Set the Opacity

In the **Options** bar for the **Clone Stamp** tool, click and drag the **Opacity** slider to set the transparency of the effect. For example, if you want to select a part of the image and apply it to another area on the image at the same intensity as the original, set the **Opacity** slider to **100**. Set the slider to **50** if you want the copied area to appear more transparent (lighter) than the original area.

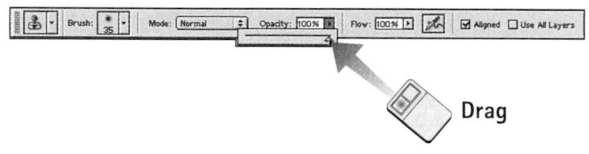

Drag

3 Set the Aligned Option

Enable the **Aligned** check box if you want the reference point to move when you move the brush. For example, if you place the reference point to the left and down 50 pixels from the current brush position, the reference point will always be to the left and down 50 pixels as you paint with the brush. Leave this option disabled if you want the reference point to sample the same area every time you click the brush (the size of the area depends on the brush size you select).

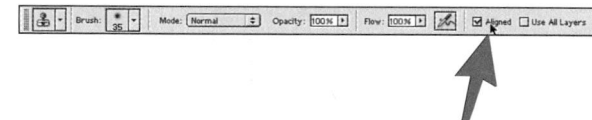

4 Select a Brush

Select a brush size and feather appropriate for the image. For the angel image example, you want to clone the entire face. A medium-sized brush with a slight feathered edge is your best choice for copying the face while blending it into the background. To set the feather, modify the **Flow** slider.

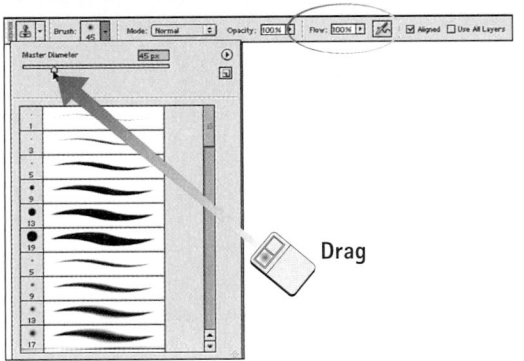

Drag

5 Set the Reference Point

Move the brush into the image window and position it at the desired reference point. Press and hold the **Option** key (Mac users) or the **Alt** key (Windows users) and click to set the reference point. The reference point is the starting point for the area you will clone.

Alt + Click
Option + Click

6 Stamp the Image

With the reference point set, click and drag in a new location (away from the original area) in the image. Notice that a crosshair (the reference point) effectively paints a copy of the original area in the new location. If the **Aligned** check box was not enabled, the specific area you referenced in Step 5 is the starting point, regardless of where you click.

Drag

How-To Hints

Sampling All Layers

Enable the **Use All Layers** check box on the **Options** bar for the **Clone Stamp** tool if you want the tool to sample all the layers as it paints. This is a good way to selectively consolidate material from multiple layers into one layer.

Pattern Stamping

You can also paint a predefined pattern into an image with the **Pattern Stamp** tool, located in the **Clone Stamp** pop-out menu. With the **Pattern Stamp** tool selected, choose a pattern from the **Pattern** palette in the **Options** bar, select a brush size and other paint options, and paint the pattern into the image.

End

How to Draw Graphic Shapes

When you are editing images, there are many times when you might want to draw a flat geometric shape, such as a box or circle. Whether you want to create a screened area to add text, build a Web interface, or create an image composite, graphic shapes play a central role in the process. Adobe has made this function even more useful in Photoshop 7 because you can now draw and edit graphics in the image as if they were vector objects.

Begin

1 Open File

Choose **File, Open** and select the file you want to modify with a graphic shape.

2 Choose Shape Color

Click the **Foreground** color swatch in the toolbox to open the **Color Picker**. Select the color you want for the shape you will draw and click **OK**.

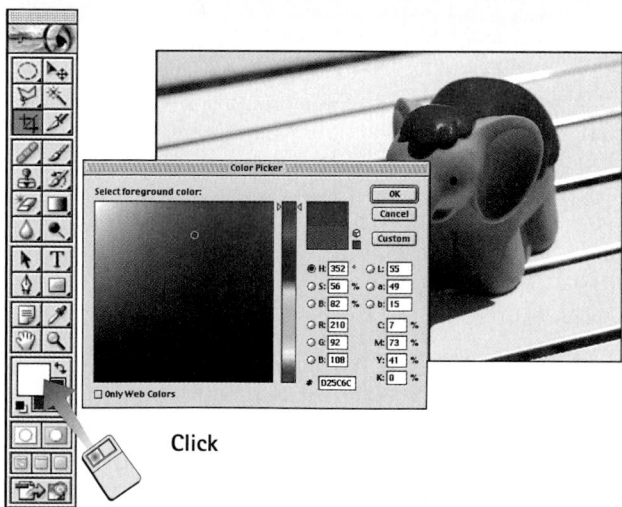

Click

3 Select the Shape Tool

Choose the desired shape tool from the toolbox. Click and hold the graphic shape button to see a menu of all the shape options: **Rectangle**, **Ellipse**, **Polygon**, **Line**, and **Custom**. When you drag the selected shape, remember that the **Shift** key constrains rectangles and ellipses into squares and circles.

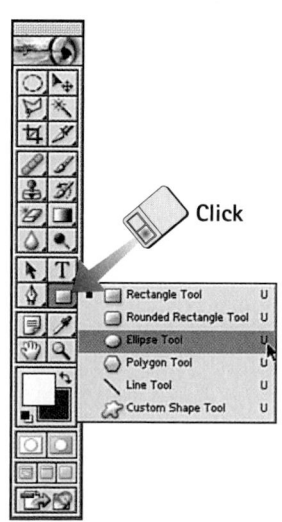

Click

4 Set the Shape Type

In the **Options** bar for the selected shape tool, select the method for drawing the shape. Choose the **Fill Pixels** icon to create a flat filled region on the current active layer. The **Paths** icon creates a separate shape layer with a clipping path. The **Shape Layers** icon creates an unfilled work path.

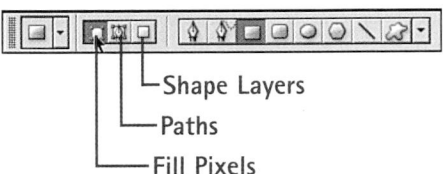

└─ Shape Layers
└─ Paths
└─ Fill Pixels

5 Draw the Shape

Click and drag in the image to draw the desired shape. Remember to use the **Opacity** slider and blending modes in the **Options** bar if necessary. If you selected the **Paths** option in Step 4, a new layer will appear in the **Layers** palette. If you selected the **Shape Layers** option, an active path will appear onscreen.

Drag

6 Edit the Shape

If you started with the **Paths** or **Shape Layers** option in Step 4, you can edit the shape you've drawn; after you draw the first shape, the edit options are activated, which allow you to add to, subtract from, restrict, or invert the path. Drag subsequent shapes using these options.

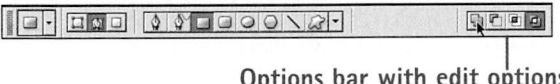

Options bar with edit options

End

How-To Hints

Setting Shape Options

Each shape tool includes a menu of shape options for specifying how the shapes are drawn. Click the arrow at the end of the second group of icons in the **Options** bar to open the **Geometry Options** menu; select from parameters such as rounded corners and fixed shape sizes.

Using the Custom Shape Tool

The **Custom Shape** tool allows you to draw unique shapes as selected from a predefined shapes palette. To create a custom shape, create a shape using the path or shape tools. Choose **Edit, Define Custom Shape** and enter a name for the shape. It will now appear in the list of shapes in the **Options** bar. Be sure to select **Fixed Size** in the **Geometry Options** menu of the **Options** bar to draw the shape with its original proportions.

How to Build a Custom Brush

Photoshop 7 makes tremendous improvements to its painting and custom brush capabilities. Photoshop 7 provides the capability to create custom brushes that feature advanced texture and color control, random stroke variation, pressure sensitivity controls, and much more. These options are controlled through the **Brushes** palette. In the **Brushes** palette, brush presets are displayed on the right, above the **Master Diameter** slider. The full list of settings options appears on the left.

Begin

1 Create a New Scratchpad File

Select **File**, **New** to create a new file. Set the background to white and set the parameters as desired in the dialog box that appears. You will use this file to test the results as you build your custom brush.

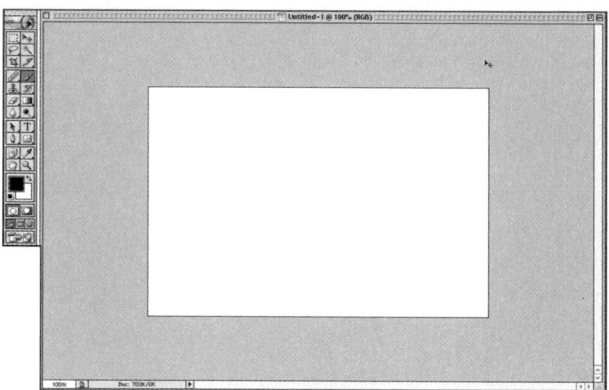

2 Open the Brushes Palette

By default, Photoshop places the **Brushes** palette in the palette well. Click the **Brushes** tab to open the palette, or select **Window**, **Brushes**.

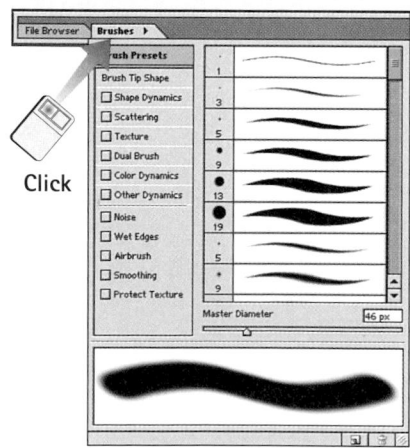

Click

3 Set the Brush Shape

Select the **Brush Tip Shape** option in the left column to load the brush shape options. Adjust the **Diameter** slider to specify the overall brush size in pixels. Specify **Angle**, **Roundness**, and **Hardness** settings as desired, evaluating the results in the preview field at the bottom of the palette. You can also set brush angle and roundness by dragging components of the crosshairs icon. Click and drag the black dots to set the roundness; click and drag the arrowhead to set the angle. Paint in the sample file to fine-tune your results.

Drag

4 Set Shape Dynamics

Back in the **Brushes** palette, choose **Shape Dynamics** from the list on the left to load the shape dynamics options. Shape dynamics provide control over variations within brushstrokes, which are referred to as *jitter*. You can set **Size**, **Angle**, and **Roundness** variations using the associated sliders. The **Control** menu below each slider allows you to set the method for controlling the variation, such as a tablet or stroke fade. You can also specify the brush's minimum diameter and roundness percentage. Paint in the sample file to fine-tune your results.

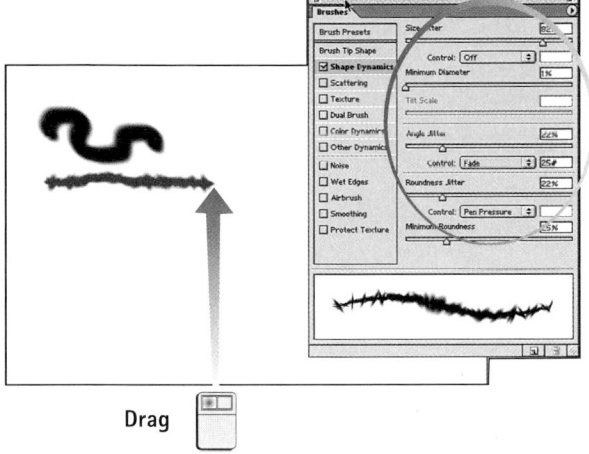

Drag

5 Set Scatter

Select the **Scattering** option in the **Brushes** palette to load the scatter options. *Scatter* refers to the way the brush stroke spreads out from the line drawn by the mouse or pen. By default, the main **Scatter** slider sets a vertical percentage variation; enable the **Both Axis** check box to set both vertical and horizontal variation. The **Count** slider controls the density or flow of the marks, and the **Count Jitter** slider controls variations within the flow. Use the **Control** menus below the sliders to set the controlling method. Paint in the sample file to fine-tune your results.

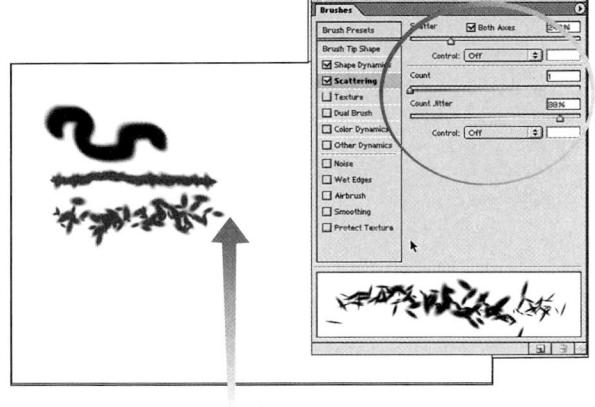

Drag

6 Set Texture Capabilities

Select the **Texture** option in the **Brushes** palette to load the texture options. Click the swatch to select a texture from the **Pattern Picker** that opens. You can also set the size, blending mode, depth, and depth variation. Paint in the sample file to fine-tune your results.

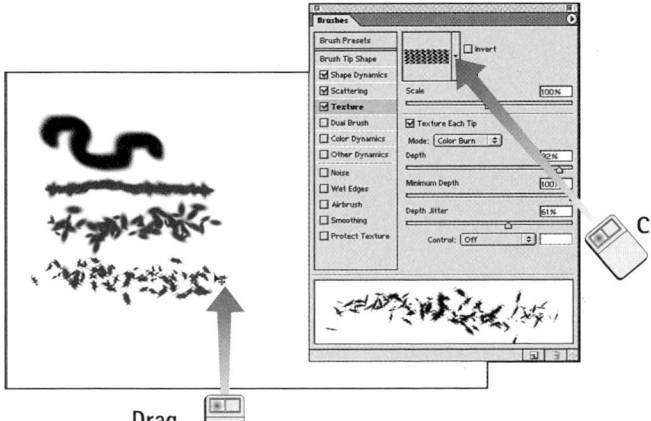

Click

Drag

Continues

7 Set Dual Brush Capabilities

Select the **Dual Brush** option in the **Brushes** palette to create a brush with multiple brush tips in the same stroke. First set the mode and brush shape for the second brush tip using the **Blend Mode** menu and the **Shapes Preset** palette. Then modify diameter, spacing, scatter, and count to complete the effect. Remember that these settings affect only the second brush tip shape. Photoshop combines these options with the current settings for the first brush. Paint in the sample file to fine-tune your results.

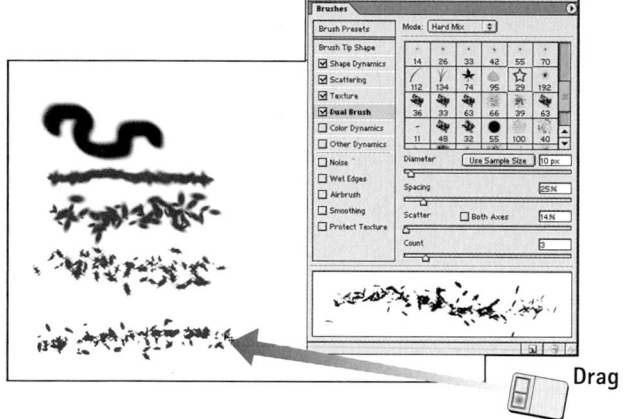

Drag

8 Set Color Dynamics

Select the **Color Dynamics** option in the **Brushes** palette to control color variation within the brush stroke. Settings allow you to blend the foreground and background colors within the stroke and to set variation in hue, saturation, brightness, and color purity. Paint in the sample file to fine-tune your results.

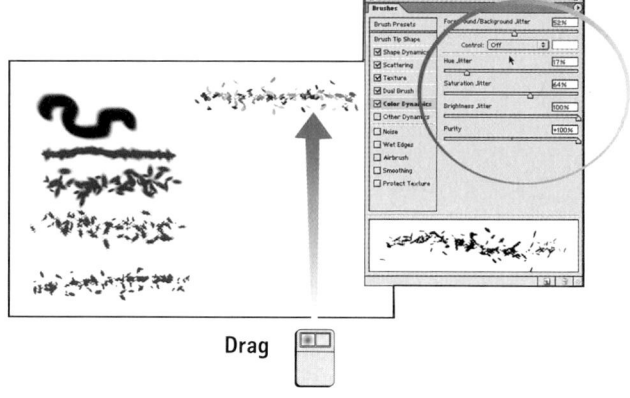

Drag

9 Set Other Dynamics

Select the **Other Dynamics** option in the **Brushes** palette to control the opacity and flow of the brush stroke. Adjust the sliders as needed, and paint in the sample file to fine-tune your results.

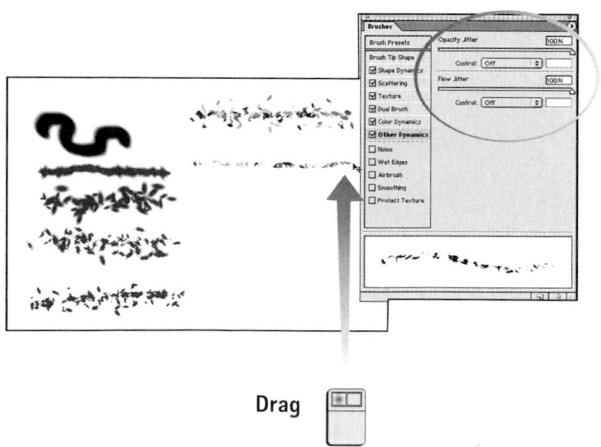

Drag

10 Set Paint Characteristics

The paint characteristics check boxes at the bottom of the list of options on the left side of the **Brushes** palette allow you to enable or disable **Noise, Wet Edges, Airbrush, Smoothing,** and **Protect Texture** features.

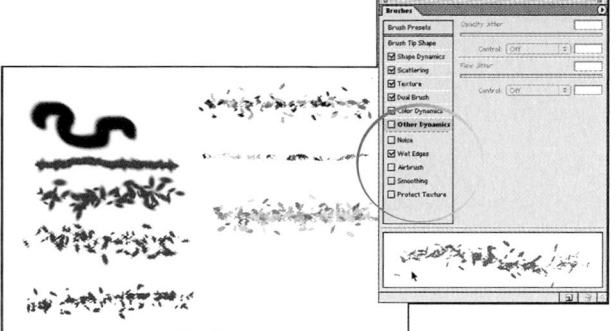

11 Use the Brush

Close the **Brushes** palette and use the customized brush in your work. If you want to save the custom brush for later use, you can save the custom brush as a tool preset.

End

How-To Hints

Setting Up for Pressure-Sensitive Drawing Tablets

Remember to set the associated **Control** menus to **Pen Pressure, Tilt,** or **Thumbwheel** if you're using an input device that supports these features.

Using Custom Brushes with Tool Presets

Remember to save specific settings as a brush preset (refer to Part 2, Task 6, "How to Create Custom Tool Presets"). Also, keep in mind that certain brush settings and options may vary depending on the paint tool that is currently selected.

How to Fill with the Paint Bucket

The **Paint Bucket** tool follows the same basic principle as the **Magic Eraser** you used in Task 3. The difference is that instead of erasing continuous pixels, the **Paint Bucket** tool changes the pixels to a single color. As with the **Magic Eraser**, you apply the **Paint Bucket** effect with a single mouse click. The **Tolerance** setting plays a big role in the final result.

Begin

1 Select the Foreground Color

With the image file you want to modify open, click the **Foreground** color swatch in the toolbox. The **Color Picker** opens. Select the fill color you want to use with the **Paint Bucket**. (With the **Color Picker** open, you also can select the foreground color by clicking in the image window itself.)

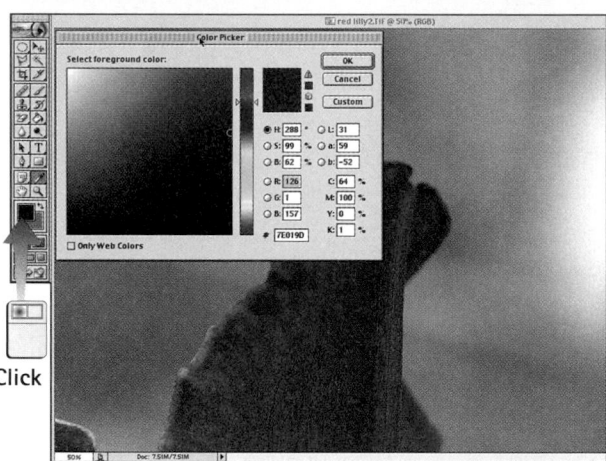

Click

2 Select the Paint Bucket Tool

Select the **Paint Bucket** tool from the toolbox. If it is not visible, click and hold the **Gradient** tool and select the **Paint Bucket** tool from the pop-out menu that appears.

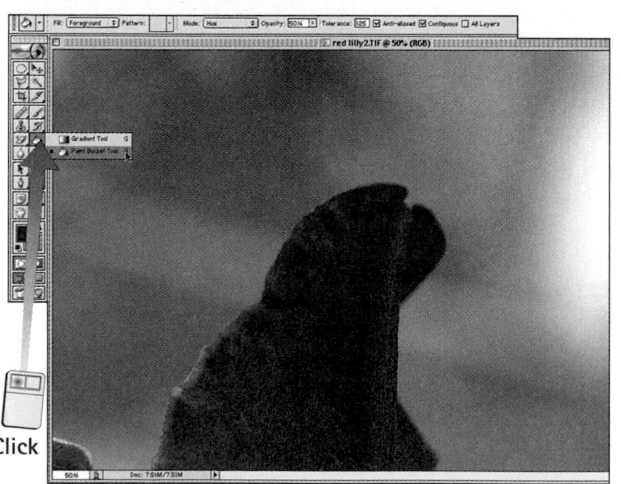

Click

3 Set the Opacity and Fill Type

In the **Options** bar, drag the **Opacity** slider to modify the transparency of the effect. Set the opacity to less than **100** to fill the area with a transparent color. Always set the **Fill** menu to **Foreground** unless you want to fill with a saved pattern. If no pattern is saved, the **Pattern** menu is grayed out.

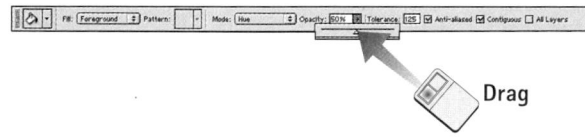

Drag

4 Set Tolerance

The **Tolerance** option determines how adjoining pixels are changed by the **Paint Bucket** tool. Type a high value in the **Tolerance** box to spread the fill color across a wider tonal area. Type a low value to change a narrow color range.

5 Fill the Area

Click in the image window to fill an area with the specified color. By default, the effect is confined to an area on a single layer, based on the **Tolerance** setting. You can target the entire image by enabling the **All Layers** check box in the **Options** bar for the **Paint Bucket** tool.

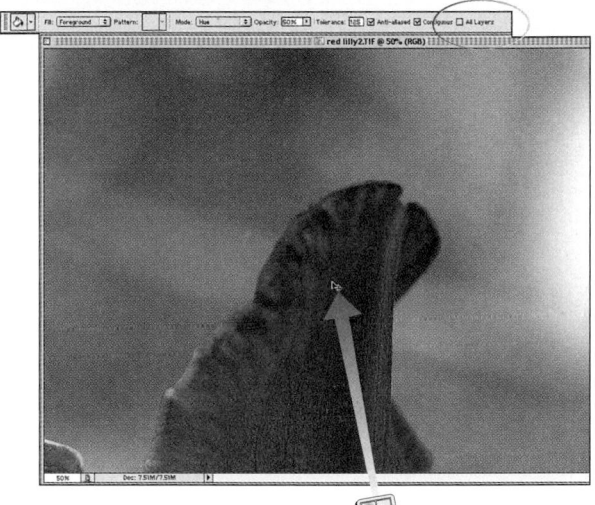

 Click

6 Undo If Necessary

If the effect is too broad or narrow, undo it by choosing **Edit, Undo Paint Bucket** or by using the **History** palette. Alternatively, adjust the **Tolerance** slider in the **Options** bar for the **Paint Bucket** tool and reapply the effect.

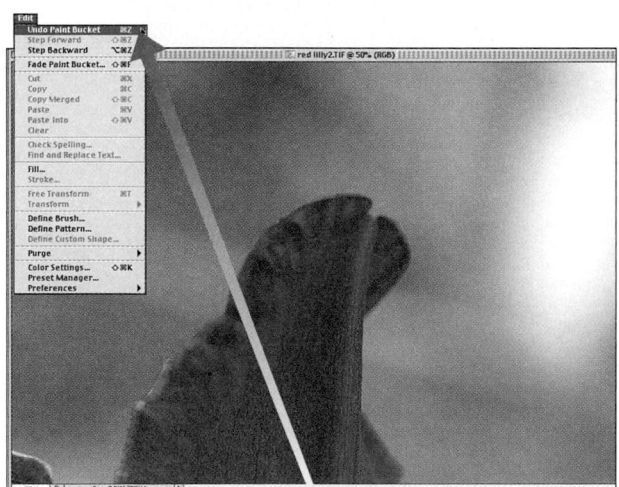

 Click

How-To Hints

Changing All Values

By default, the **Paint Bucket** tool applies its effect to adjoining pixels of similar color. You can change *all* pixels of a similar value by deselecting the **Contiguous** check box in the **Options** bar. For example, with **Contiguous** deselected, if the foreground color is red and you click a yellow pixel, all yellow pixels in the entire image will change to red, regardless of whether they adjoin or not.

End

TASK 9

How to Use the Pattern Maker

The **Pattern Maker** generates random patterns that can be applied to an image or saved as a preset. This tool goes beyond simply allowing you to save patterns; it assists you in creating custom tiles that can be used to develop amazing abstract patterns and backgrounds.

1 Open the Image

You can use any image to generate patterns. Select **File, Open** to launch the desired file. To explain how the **Pattern Maker** works, I will use an image with a single text character.

2 Set the Sample Area

Choose **Filter, Pattern Maker** to launch the **Pattern Maker** window. Select the **Rectangular Marquee** tool in the upper-left corner of the window and drag to draw a sample area to be used as a starting point for pattern generation.

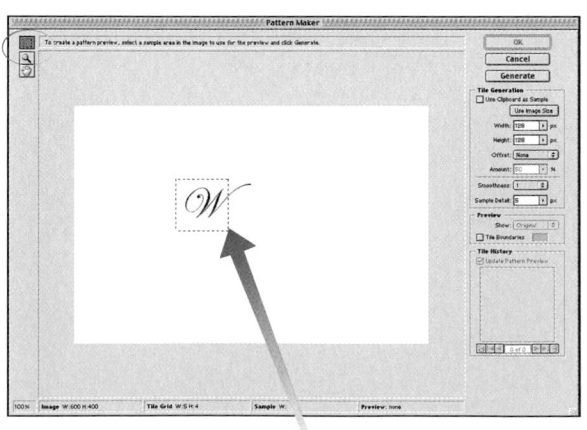

Drag

3 Generate the First Variation

Click the **Generate** button to create the first pattern design. **Pattern Maker** automatically fills the screen with a random design generated from the sampled area. Click **Generate Again** to create additional variations of the pattern.

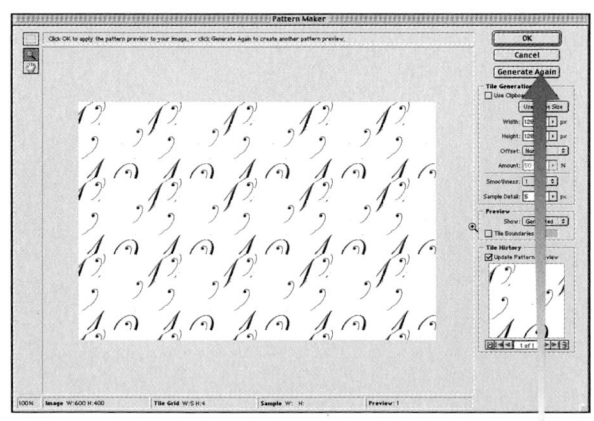

Click

4 Modify Tile Size and Offset

In the **Tile Generation** section of the **Pattern Maker** window, enter alternative values in the **Height** and **Width** fields to change the tile proportions in the pattern. To offset the tile alignment, use the **Offset** pop-up menu. Select a vertical or horizontal offset and enter an offset percentage in the **Amount** field. Click **Generate Again** to create a new pattern.

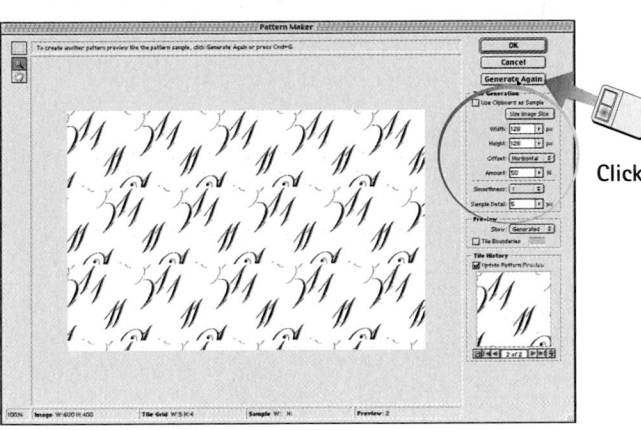

Click

5 Set Smoothness

To modify the smoothness of the rendering, set the **Smoothness** pop-up menu to **1**, **2**, or **3**. To control how much detail is present in the pattern, set a pixel value in the **Sample Detail** field. Click **Generate Again** to create another pattern that reflects these changes.

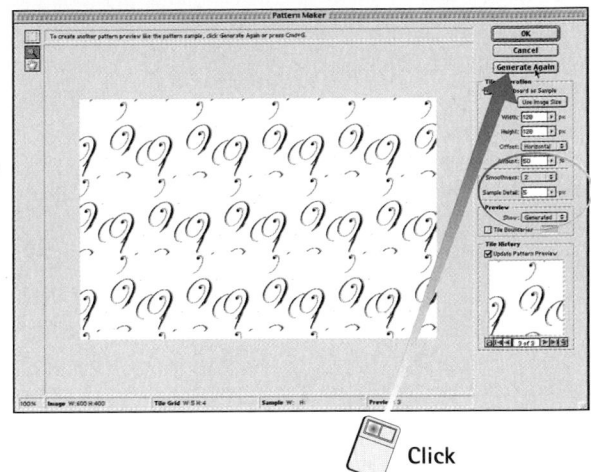

Click

6 Apply or Save Pattern

Click **OK** to apply the pattern to the current image. You can also click the **Save Preset Pattern** icon at the bottom of the **Tile History** section to save the tile as a pattern preset.

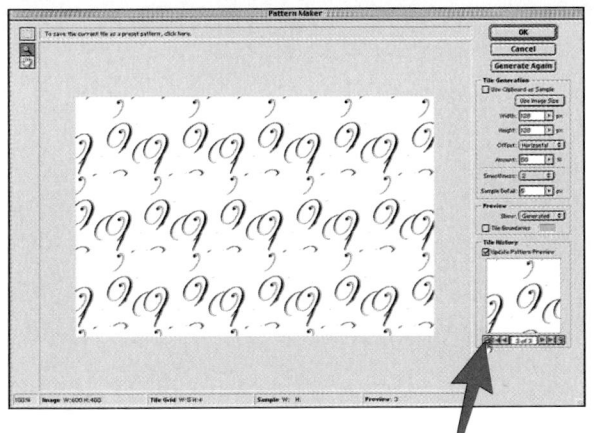

End

How-To Hints

Using the Clipboard as a Sample

You can use any image data saved to the Clipboard as a source for a pattern. To do this, copy any image content and select the **Use Clipboard as Sample** check box in the **Tile Generation** section of the **Pattern Maker** window. Click **Generate** to view the results.

Previews and Navigation

All tiles generated in a given session are saved in the **Tile History** section for review and evaluation. Use the forward and back arrows to browse the various iterations of the pattern, which you can save or apply to the image.

How to Apply Gradients

A *gradient* is a fill that gradually blends two or more colors together. These color blends can be applied in circular-shaped, diamond-shaped, and cone-shaped gradients, as well as standard linear and bar shapes. When you apply a gradient, it expands to fill the entire selected area. Gradients are useful as background fills behind an object and in layer masks to fade out an image (see Part 11, Task 7 for details on layer masks).

Begin

1 Select the Fill Area

Open the image file with which you want to work. If necessary, select the area to be filled with the gradient. If no area is selected, Photoshop fills the entire image with the gradient effect.

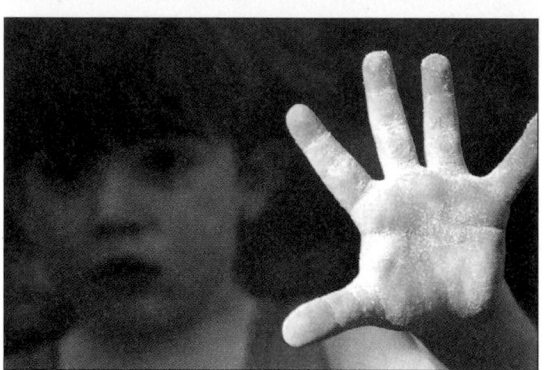

2 Select Gradient Type

Select the **Gradient** tool from the toolbox. If it is not visible, click and hold the **Paint Bucket** tool and select the **Gradient** tool from the pop-out menu. In the **Options** bar, select the **Linear**, **Radial**, **Angle**, **Reflected**, or **Diamond Gradient** tool.

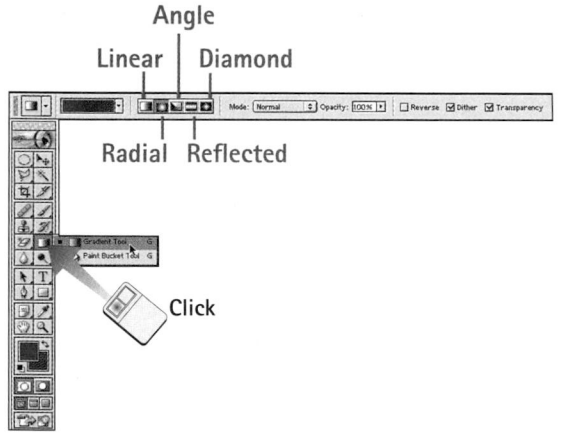

Angle

Linear | Diamond

Radial | Reflected

Click

3 Set Foreground/Background Colors

The colors in the gradient will be applied using the foreground and background colors specified in this step. In the toolbox, click the **Foreground** and **Background** color swatches and select the desired gradient colors from the **Color Picker** dialog box that appears.

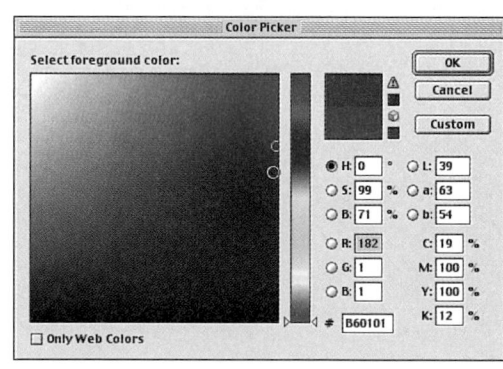

Click

4 Set the Gradient Colors

In the **Options** bar, click the gradient swatch (the first icon) to open the **Gradient Editor** dialog box. Click to select the first swatch in the palette. The gradient sample displayed will now reflect the colors you selected in Step 3. Click **OK** to close the dialog box.

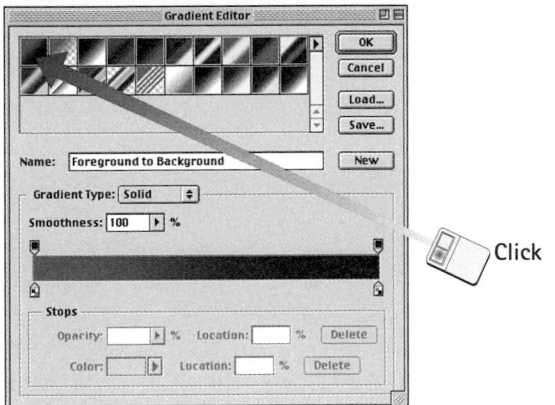

Click

5 Set Options

In the **Options** bar for the **Gradient** tool, set the **Opacity** slider as desired, choosing a setting of less than **100** to create a transparent gradient. If you want, you can also select a different gradient type by clicking one of the icons in the bar. Leave the **Transparency** check box disabled and enable the **Dither** check box if you want to reduce banding in the gradient. Finally, enable the **Reverse** check box if you want to switch the colors in the gradient.

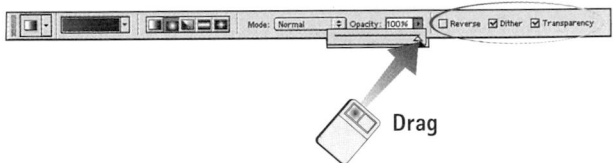

Drag

6 Apply the Effect

Position the cursor in the image where you want the gradient to start. Click and drag, releasing the mouse to apply the effect. Remember that the gradient will cover the entire image; the point at which you release the mouse determines the end of the gradient transition from the foreground color to the background color you selected.

Drag

End

How-To Hints

Applying Gradients in Their Own Layers

For full flexibility, apply gradients in their own layers. Doing so allows you to go back and adjust transparency, blending modes, and positioning as needed. You can also use layer masks to control the visibility of the gradient.

Tweaking a Gradient

If you are not satisfied with the angle or tone break, drag again to reapply the gradient, overwriting the previous attempt. This works only if the **Mode** option in the **Options** bar is set to **Normal** *and* if the **Opacity** slider is set to **100**.

How to Create Custom Gradients

Building a custom gradient in Photoshop involves defining the number of colors in the gradient, as well specifying as how they fade and transition between each other. It also is possible to build transparency into the gradient, which allows the layers below the current layer to show through the gradient. Gradients are similar to custom brushes in that you can customize them for each image. Photoshop lets you create and save custom gradients and add them to the preset list for easy access. After you create a gradient, you can use it with any of the gradient shapes selected from the **Options** bar.

Begin

1 Select a Gradient Tool

Select the **Gradient** tool from the toolbox. In the **Options** bar, click the gradient swatch to launch the **Gradient Editor** dialog box.

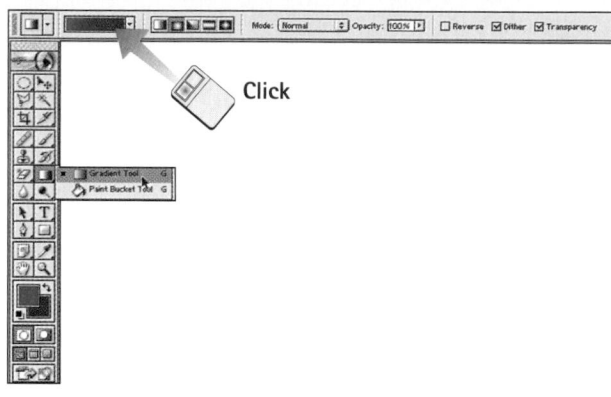

2 Select a Preset

From the palette at the top of the dialog box, select one of the existing gradient presets if you want to use it as a starting point. Selecting a preset is a good idea if you want to predefine many of the parameters (such as color choices and color stops).

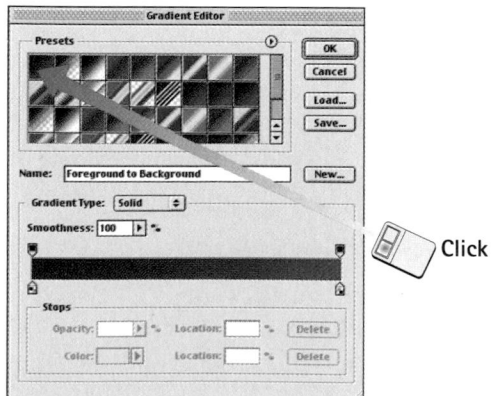

3 Select the Starting Color

Double-click the left color stop in the gradient bar in the **Gradient Editor** dialog box to open the **Color Picker**. Select a color you want to use in the gradient you are creating and click **OK** to close the **Color Picker**. The new color appears on the left end of the gradient bar, and the gradient is updated.

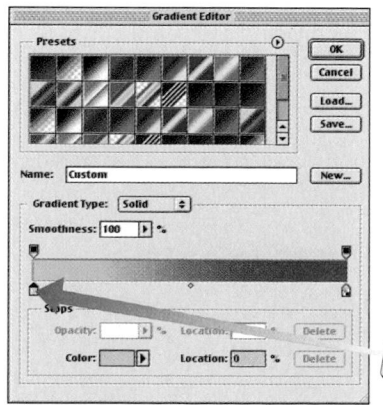

4 Select the Ending Color

Double-click the right color stop in the gradient bar in the **Gradient Editor** dialog box to open the **Color Picker**. Select another color you want to use in the gradient you are creating and click **OK** to close the **Color Picker**. The new color appears at the right end of the gradient bar, and the gradient is updated.

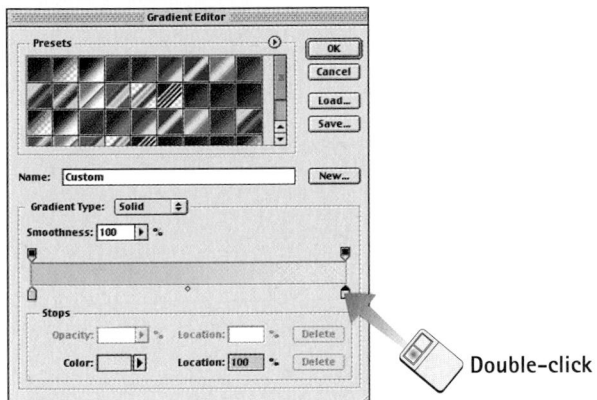

Double-click

5 Set the Break

The *break* in a gradient determines where a 50% mix of the two colors occurs. By default, the break is in the middle of the gradient, but you can adjust the placement by dragging the diamond that appears below the gradient bar. By adjusting the break point, you can designate a dominant color for the gradient.

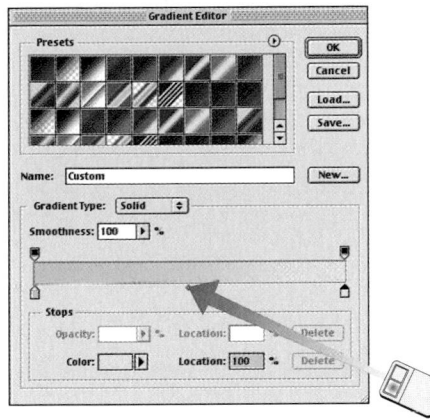

Drag

6 Add Additional Colors

Double-click in the color stop section below the gradient bar to add a third color stop. This action opens the **Color Picker**. Select the third color you want to add to the gradient, click **OK** to close the **Color Picker**, and add the color to the gradient. Drag the new color stop as necessary to control the color placement in the gradient. Notice that a new diamond is placed between each color to control the breaks between colors.

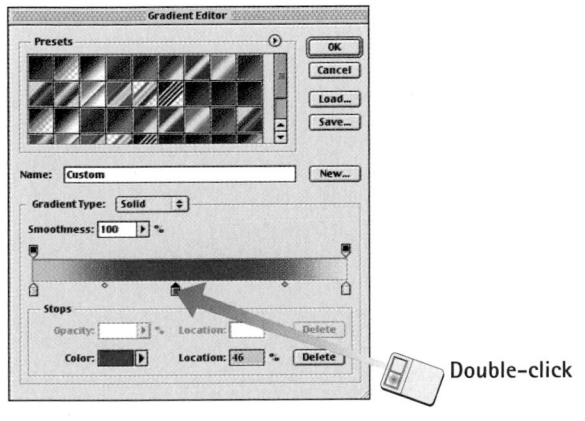

Double-click

7 Save the Gradient

Click **New** to save the gradient and add its swatch to the gradient palette. Click **OK** close the **Gradient Editor**. If you want, you can click the **Save** button to save the gradient as a separate file to be loaded later. When you do this, a **Save As** dialog box opens for you to name the gradient file and specify where it goes.

End

How-To Hints

Using Transparency

You can build transparency into a gradient to allow lower layers to show through. Photoshop includes opacity stops along the top of the gradient preview in the **Gradient Type** section. Select a stop and enter a value in the **Opacity** field. Move the stop to control how the transparency transitions through the effect.

Task

Using Type

There was a time when using text in Photoshop was a pretty bad idea. In the pre-version 2.5 days, there were no layers, History brushes, or multiple undos, so when you placed text on an image, it was there permanently. Kerning or leading was out of the question—and heaven forbid if you had a typo! Unless you were very brave or very stupid, text was the domain of illustration and layout programs.

This began to change as Adobe added layers with version 3. Then an enhanced text tool, vertical type, and kerning controls hit the scene. One of the biggest enhancements has been Photoshop's capability to keep text as an editable item at all times. When text was placed as a bitmap, if you misspelled the word, you were out of luck. With editable text, however, you just reopen the dialog box and make the correction.

The tasks in this part profile the primary features for working with type in Photoshop. As a general rule, you still will not want to set large amounts of type in Photoshop (the bitmap nature of the program will hurt readability when compared with vector-based or text-based applications). Keep your use of text to headlines and a few paragraphs, and you'll find that Photoshop's text capabilities are a full-featured option that was well worth the wait. ●

How to Add Type to an Image

When you add text to an image in Photoshop, it is placed on a separate layer. It remains editable at all times—unless you intentionally convert the image to pixels for further editing (as you must if you want to apply filters that work only on raster layers) or integration. When text is added, a new layer is created. The text is the only element in the layer; all other areas are transparent. Photoshop can access all fonts in your system and makes them available through the **Type Tool** dialog box.

Begin

1 Select the Type Tool and Orientation

With the image you want to work with open, click the **Type** tool in the Photoshop toolbar. In the **Options** bar, click the **Horizontal Orientation** icon (the T with a horizontal arrow).

2 Place the Text Starting Point

Move the mouse pointer into the image area and click to set the text entry point.

Click

3 Select the Font

From the **Font** menu in the **Options** bar, choose a typeface. From the **Font Style** menu, select a typestyle (bold, oblique/italic, and so on). You can also select the font size, alignment, and anti-aliasing method.

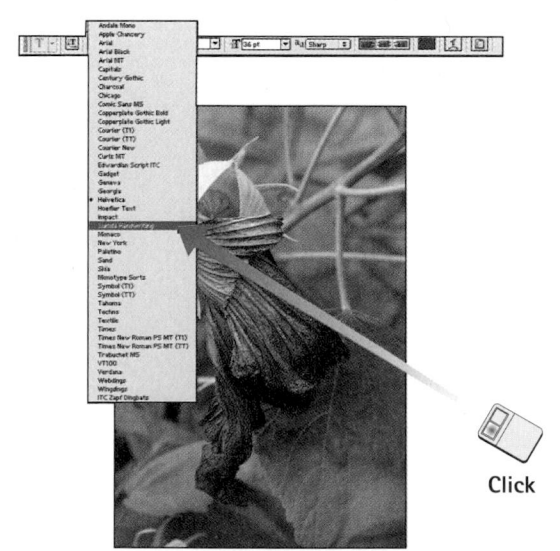

Click

4 Set Parameters

Click the **Palettes** button in the **Options** bar to launch the **Paragraph** and **Character** palettes. In the **Character** palette, set the *kerning* (the spacing between individual pairs of letters), *tracking* (spacing between entire lines of letters), *leading* (whether the letters sit on an invisible baseline or "float" above or below it), horizontal or vertical scale, and type color. You can also change the font from this palette. In the **Paragraph** palette, you can align the text to the left, center, or right (in relation to the entry point), and you can set justification parameters, paragraph indentation, and hyphenation.

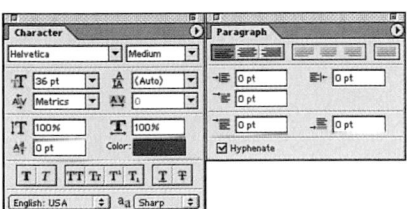

5 Set Sharpness of Text

In the **Options** bar, select the sharpness of the type. The sharpness of the image, the kind of background the text sits on, and your overall intentions will determine this setting. Use your eye to judge type for the Web. For print, try to stay with the **Strong** or **Crisp** option, unless you want a softer effect. Click the check mark in the upper-right corner of the **Options** bar to accept the current type edits and create the type layer on the image.

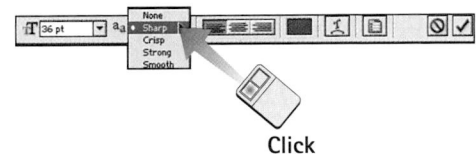

Click

6 Type Text

With the image as the active window, type the text you want to add. Highlight the text and use the **Options** bar and the palettes to change any of the characteristics of the text. When you move your cursor away from the type, the cursor changes to a gavel, indicating that a click will set the type and complete the text entry.

7 Edit the Type

The type is represented as a separate layer on the image, denoted as a type layer by the **T** icon in the **Layers** palette. Select **Window, Layers** and then select the **Type** tool and highlight the text to make further changes.

End

How to Create 3D Text

3D text refers to type that includes shading or modeling to create a three-dimensional effect on the page or image. These effects can include drop shadows, embossing, and other impressive options. This current task is specific to creating great-looking type.

Begin

1 Create the Text

Follow the instructions in Task 1 to create a text layer. When you have created the text layer, verify its existence by selecting **Window, Layers** to open the **Layers** palette.

2 Select Bevel and Emboss Effects

Choose **Layer, Layer Style, Bevel and Emboss** to launch the **Layer Style** dialog box. Make sure that the **Preview** check box is enabled.

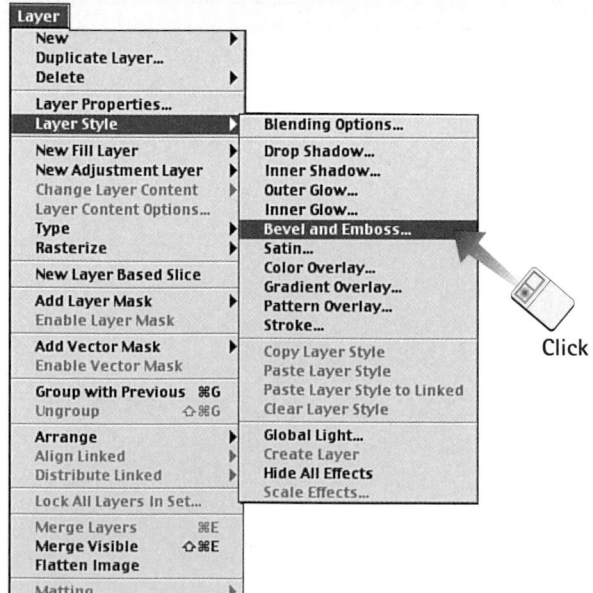

Click

3 Select the Bevel Style

From the **Style** menu in the **Structure** section of the dialog box, select the desired bevel style. Options are **Outer Bevel, Inner Bevel, Emboss, Pillow Emboss**, and **Stroke Emboss**. Because the **Preview** check box is enabled, you can select each option and see the results in the main image window.

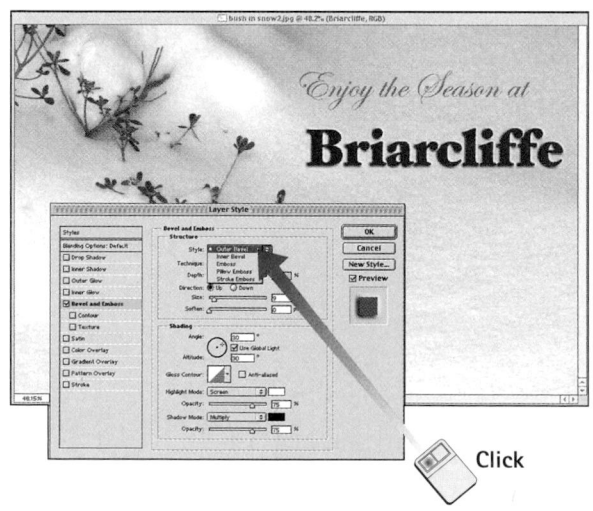

Click

4 Set the Depth

The **Depth** slider determines the thickness of the bevel. The "proper" thickness depends on the font size selected and the overall resolution of the image. The **Size** and **Soften** sliders control the spread of the effect and its sharpness. Click and drag the sliders to increase or decrease these effects.

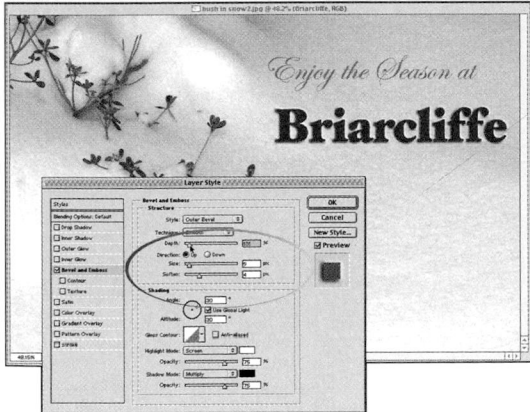

5 Set the Angle

The **Angle** option determines the angle at which the "light" falls on the text. The angle setting determines the shadows and highlights on the text. In the **Shading** section, click inside the **Angle** circle and drag to change the angle direction. You can also type a numeric angle value in the angle text box.

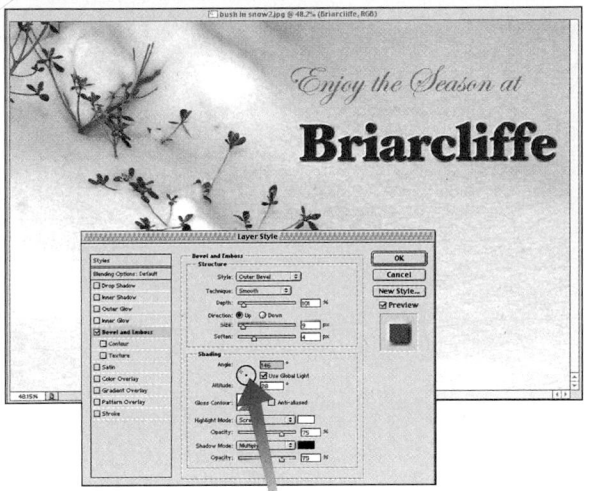

Drag

6 Tweak the Highlights and Shadows

If necessary, you can change the color for the highlight and shadow; you also can set the opacity and mode. Click the color swatch in the **Shading** section of the **Layer Style** dialog box to open the **Color Picker**, from which you can select a new color. Select the **Highlight** mode and **Shadow** mode from the pop-up menus and set the relative opacity for each mode with the slider. (Both these options act in much the same way as layer blending modes do—except that they are confined to the actual highlight and shadow areas you're creating with the effect.)

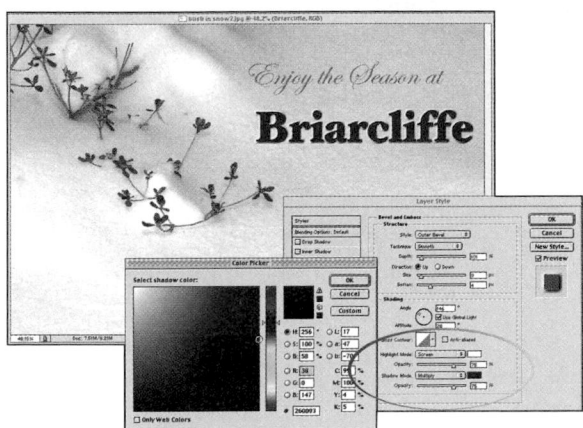

End

How to Create Typographic Style Sheets

The standard tool presets described in Part 2, Task 6, "How to Create Custom Tool Presets," are especially effective in creating text-based style sheets that help manage type treatments in image and Web design. Style sheets provide full control over all type parameters, including font, alignment, and spacing options. Photoshop even allows you to associate a specific color with a preset. Now you can easily select a specific type tool for headlines and another for captions, body text, or any other format present in the project.

Begin

1 Select the Type Tool

Select the **Type** tool from the toolbox.

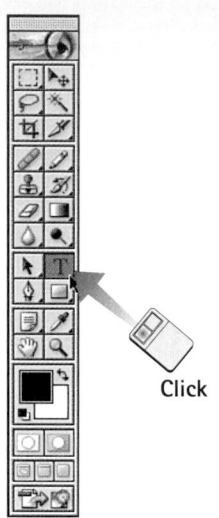

Click

2 Select the Font Parameters

Use the **Options** bar to set the basic font settings including font, size, and sharpness.

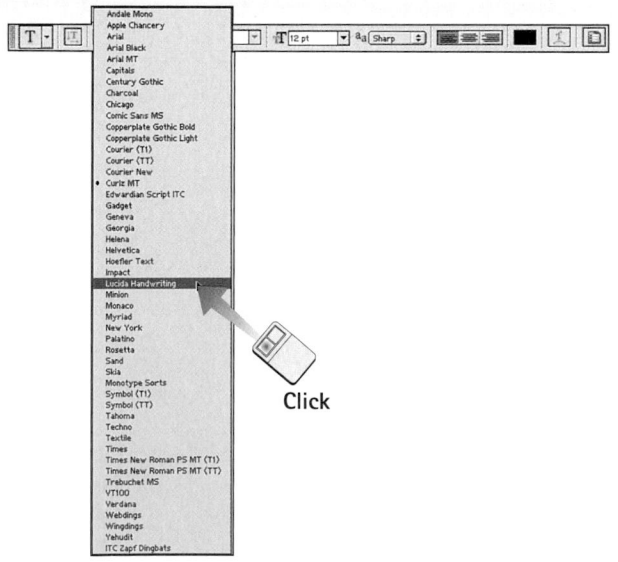

Click

3 Set Line and Character Spacing

Choose **Window, Character** to launch the **Character** palette. Set the leading, tracking, baseline shift, and vertical or horizontal shift as desired.

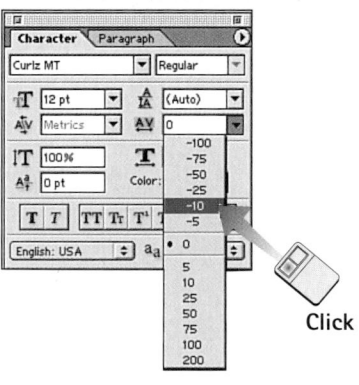

Click

4 Set Alignment

Choose **Window, Paragraph** to open the **Paragraph** palette. Set the alignment, justification, and indent settings as desired.

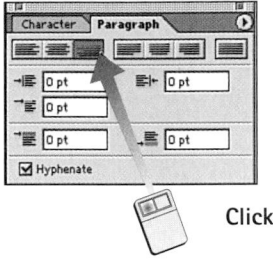

Click

5 Choose a Font Color

If you want to include a text color in the preset, click the font color swatch in the **Options** bar. When the **Color Picker** opens, select the desired color for the text.

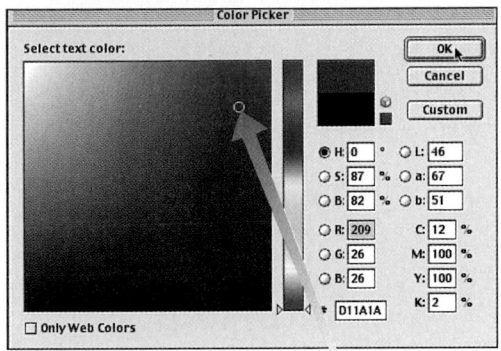

Click

6 Save the Preset

Choose **Window, Tool Presets** to open the **Tool Presets** palette. Select **New Tool Preset** from the palette menu, name the preset in the dialog box that appears, and click **OK** to save. Now you can access this text preset to load these precise text parameters whenever you need them.

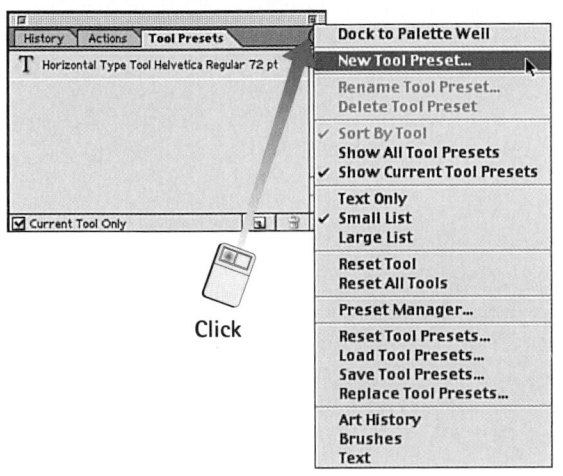

Click

How-To Hints

Don't Forget Warped Text

You can include warped text settings as part of a text preset. Select the **Warp Text** option as explained in Task 5, "How to Warp Text," before saving the text preset.

End

How to Build Filtered Text Effects

Instead of placing text as straightforward characters, you may want the text to appear as lightened or darkened areas of the image itself. You also can apply a textured effect to delineate the text characters. This task uses Photoshop filters to modify a text selection mask, creating an effect that integrates the text with the background image. In addition to filters, you can use color shifts, contrast changes, and texture effects when applying the filtering technique. Part 13, "Special Effects," introduces some of the techniques available.

Begin

1 Duplicate the Target Layer

Open the image file and determine the layer that will serve as the background for the effect. Select that layer in the **Layers** palette and choose **Duplicate Layer** from the palette menu. After the **Duplicate Layer** dialog box opens, provide a name for the layer you are creating and click **OK**.

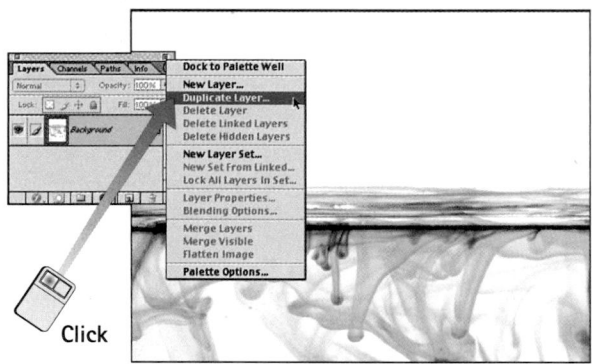

Click

2 Select the Horizontal Type Mask Tool

Select the **Horizontal Type Mask** tool from the Photoshop toolbox. In Photoshop, *masking* refers to a process of identifying a particular area for selecting or making specific modifications. In this case, we are selecting an area in the shape of the text letters.

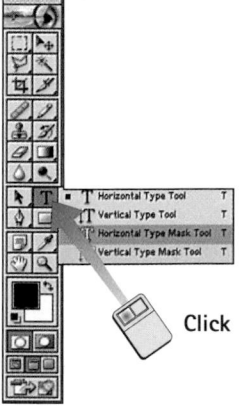

Click

3 Place the Text Starting Point

Move the cursor into the image area and click to set the text entry point. A colored type mask will appear as you do this, representing the text character selection. It's possible that the background will be masked and that the text characters will be reversed out of the masking color, based on the current Photoshop Quickmask configurations (more on that later).

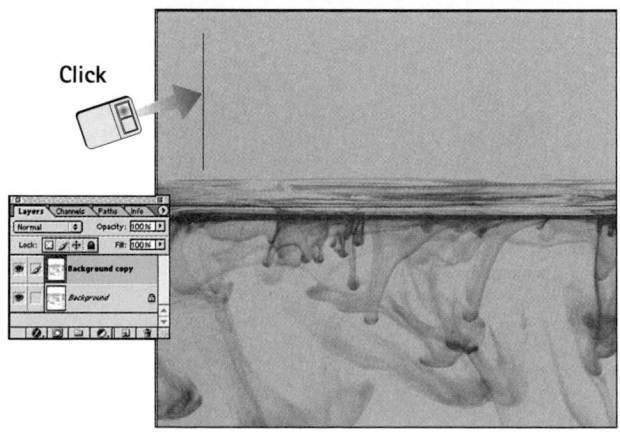

Click

4 Set Parameters

In the **Options** bar, set the font and font attributes for the text you want to add to the image. For filtered text effects, "fat" typefaces in fairly large point sizes (20 points or larger) work best.

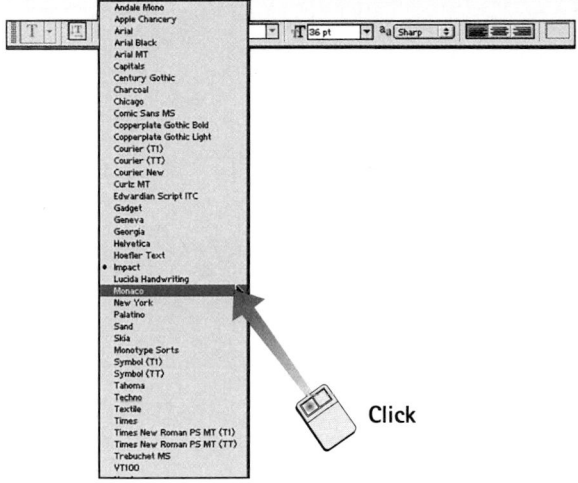

Click

5 Enter Text

Type the text in the image. As you type, the text and mask appear. Click the cursor in the image to set the type and create the selection (the "text" appears in the image in a kind of marching-ants, marquee fashion). If the size of the text is wrong, click the **Type** tool anywhere in the image to deselect the text selection and retype the text. To reposition the text, select the **Move** tool in the tool-box and drag the selection.

6 Apply a Filter

Click the **Move** tool to create the selection. From the **Filter** menu in the menu bar, select any of Photoshop's filters. This example uses the **Halftone Pattern** filter (**Filter, Sketch, Halftone Pattern**) set at Size=4, Contrast=40, Pattern Type=line. Click **OK** to apply the effect.

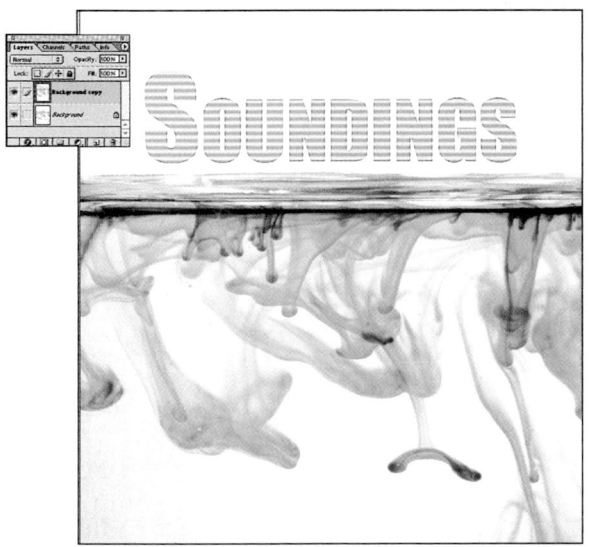

End

How to Warp Text

Warping text takes the idea of text on a path to a new level. This Photoshop feature allows you to distort the contents of an entire text layer, twisting, bloating, or stretching it into a wide range of effects. There are 15 different warping effects to choose from, and all allow bending as well as horizontal and vertical distortion.

Begin

1 Create the Text

Follow the instructions in Task 1 to create a text layer.

Ride the Wave
...and hang on for dear life

2 Select Warp Text

In the **Options** bar for the **Text** tool, click the **Warp Text** button. The **Warp Text** dialog box opens.

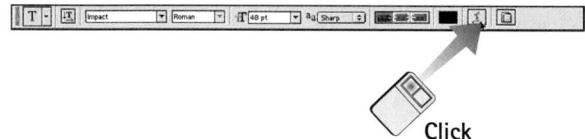

Click

3 Select Warp Text Option

From the **Style** menu in the **Warp Text** dialog box, select the desired warp variation. In addition, enable the **Horizontal** or **Vertical** radio button to determine the axis for the distortion.

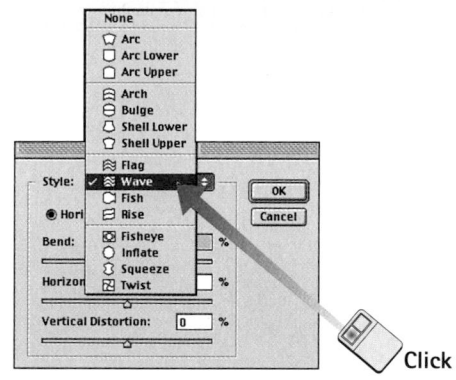

Click

4 Warp the Text

Adjust the **Bend** slider as desired to create the initial warp shape, as determined by the selection you made in Step 3. You can also experiment with the **Vertical** and **Horizontal Distortion** sliders to further pinch or stretch the effect. Click **OK** to apply the distortion.

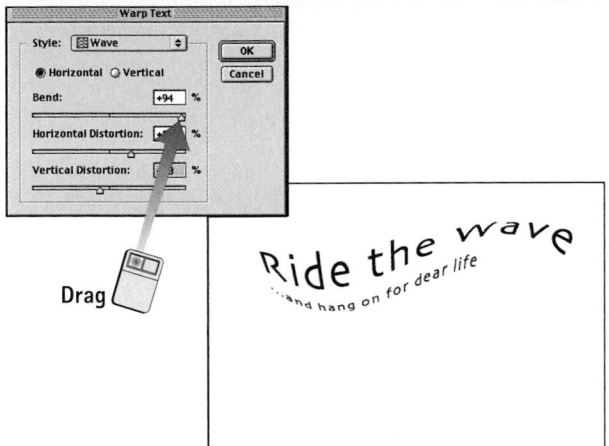

Drag

5 Edit the Text

Warped text remains editable at all times. To edit the text effect you just created, select the **Text** tool from the toolbar. Move the cursor over the warped text and click to create a blinking text insertion point. Type as you normally would to edit the text. You can also drag to select a section of text for resizing or adding color.

Click

End

How-To Hints

Circular Type

To create the effect of type in a circle, select the **Arc** option from the **Style** menu in the **Warp Text** dialog box and apply the effect as described in this task. For a true circular text effect, do not apply any of the vertical or horizontal distortions.

Cool Animation

Text warping provides a great starting point for doing GIF animations for the Web. Check out Part 12, Task 4, "How to Build Filter-Based GIF Animations" for step-by-step details.

Task

10

Using Paths

Paths offer the capability to outline shapes or areas within Photoshop files. You then can convert the paths into selections, fill the paths with color, or outline the paths as borders.

Paths offer many advantages. They add very little to the overall file size, and they use standard vector controls such as Bézier curves, points, and direction handles. If you know how to create curved segments in Adobe Illustrator or Macromedia FreeHand, you will catch on to the Photoshop path controls very quickly.

Other advantages to paths include the flexibility of being able to export them to other files and programs. If you use the **Paths** palette, you can drag paths from the palette for one image window into another open window (an easy way to move paths between Photoshop files). In addition, you can export individual paths as `.ai` files that you can open in Illustrator, FreeHand, and many other programs that support vector graphics. Doing so gives you more flexibility in illustration and layout programs when mixing vector graphics with the bitmapped images created or modified in Photoshop. ●

How to Create a Straight-Edge Path

You can use paths to define an image area that you then can select, fill, or outline. Paths are especially valuable for graphic shapes you may want to select repeatedly. You create a path using the **Pen** tool; you click points that are connected automatically with line segments. This task begins by creating a simple path with straight-line segments; later tasks show you how to create more complex path shapes.

Begin

1 Open the File

Choose **File, Open** to launch the desired file.

2 Select the Pen Tool

Select the **Pen** tool from the toolbox (you may have to select it from the pop-out menu of tools that appears after you click this button in the toolbox).

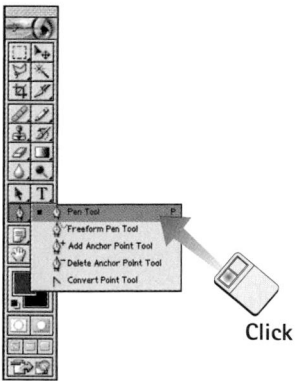

Pen Tool
Freeform Pen Tool
Add Anchor Point Tool
Delete Anchor Point Tool
Convert Point Tool

Click

3 Place the First Point

Position the pen over the image area at the spot where you want to start the path. Click once to place an anchor point.

Click

4 Place Additional Points

Click additional points as needed to complete the path. Notice that a straight line is drawn between the points you click with the **Pen** tool.

5 Close the Path

Place the last point over the starting point to close the path. A circle appears next to the **Pen** tool when the tool is positioned properly.

6 Edit the Path

To edit the path, choose the **Path Selection** tool or the **Direct Selection** tool from the toolbox (click and hold the tool in the toolbox to activate the pop-out menu and select between the two tools). Click and drag the anchor points on the image to modify the path.

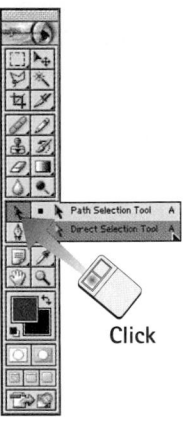

Click

7 Save the Path

Choose **Window, Paths** to launch the Paths palette. Double-click the tile for the path you just created (the tile has the title **Work Path**). The **Save Path** dialog box opens. Type a namc for the path and click **OK** to save the path.

End

How-To Hints

Deleting and Duplicating Paths

Press the **Delete** key twice to delete the path you are currently drawing. Alternatively, select **Delete Path** from the **Paths** palette menu to delete a selected path or segment.

After you have saved a path, you can duplicate it: From the **Paths** palette, select the desired path and choose **Duplicate Paths** from the **Paths** palette menu.

How to Create a Curved Path

Although the straight-line path you learned to create in Task 1 is good for basic shapes, you will no doubt want to create paths with curved lines as well. This task shows how to draw paths with curved segments, enabling you to create more complex and detailed paths.

Begin

1 Open the File

Choose **File, Open** to launch the desired file. Select the **Pen** tool from the toolbox (you may have to select it from the pop-out menu that appears after you click the tool in the toolbox).

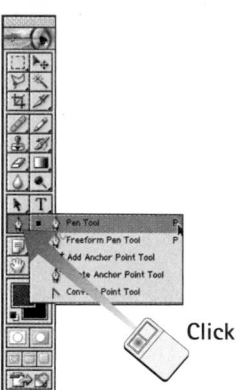

Click

2 Place the First Point

Position the pen over the image area at the spot where you want to start the path. Click once to place an anchor point.

Click

3 Create the First Curved Segment

Click and drag while placing the second point to create a curved path segment. Two handles appear out of the second point as you drag, showing the direction of the curve.

Click & Drag

4 Modify the Curve

Press and hold the ⌘ key (Mac users) or **Ctrl** key (Windows users) to change the **Pen** cursor into the **Direct Selection** tool. Click and drag either of the handles to change the shape of the curve.

Click & Drag

5 Complete the Path

Continue adding points to create additional straight or curved segments as necessary. Click the first point again to close the path, if desired.

Click

6 Save and Name the Path

Open the **Paths** palette by choosing **Window, Paths**. In the palette, double-click the tile for the path you just created (the tile has the name **Work Path**). In the **Save Path** dialog box that appears, type a name for the path and click **OK** to save the path.

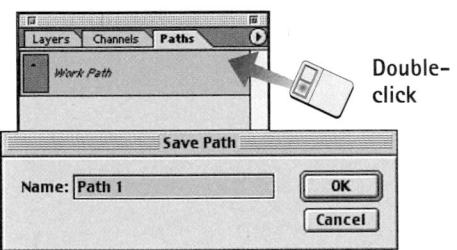

Double-click

End

How-To Hints

Editing Curved Segments

Instead of editing each curved segment as you make it, you may find it easier to approximate all the curve points and fine-tune the segments all at once. When you work this way, you can select the **Direct Selection** tool directly from the toolbox instead of pressing the ⌘ key (Mac users) or the **Ctrl** key (Windows users) as you did in Step 4.

How to Edit a Path

Photoshop offers a number of ways to edit a path; you can add, subtract, or move points with ease. You can edit a path at any time—as you're making it or later in the process. This task shows all the ways to edit a path, enabling you to pick and choose the options applicable to your project.

Begin

1 Open the File with the Path

Choose **File, Open** to launch the file containing the path you want to edit.

2 Select the Path

Choose **Window, Paths** to launch the **Paths** palette. Click the title of the desired path to select it. The path becomes visible in the image window as you highlight it.

Click

3 Move a Point

Click the **Direct Selection** tool in the toolbox. Click in the middle of a line segment to show the points on the path. Click and drag a point to move it. If the point is related to a curved segment, handles appear when you select the point, enabling you to modify the curve.

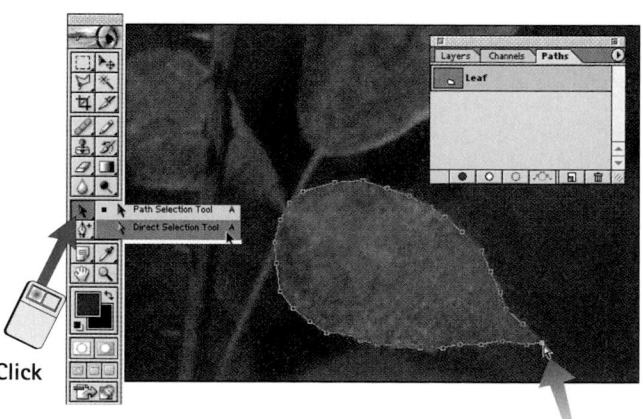

Click

Drag

4 Move Multiple Points

To move multiple points as a group, select the **Direct Selection** tool and show the points in the path, as described in Step 3. After clicking the first point, press and hold the **Shift** key and click additional points (the points darken to show that they are selected). When multiple points are selected, click and drag to move them as a group.

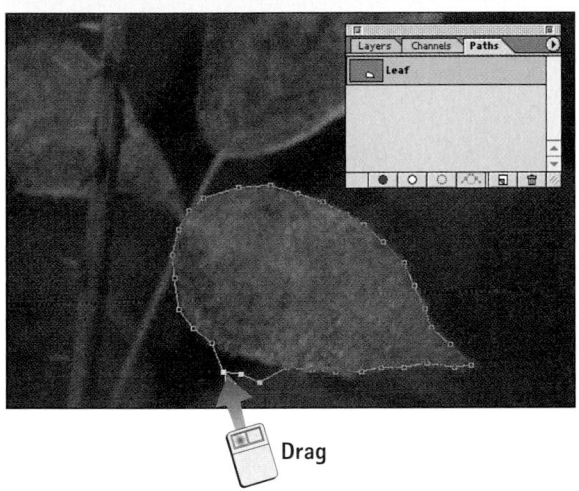

Drag

5 Add a Point

To add a point to a path, begin by selecting the **Add Anchor Point** tool from the **Pen** tool pop-out menu in the toolbox. Select the path you want to edit from the **Paths** palette, position the cursor over the path segment, and click to add a new point. Click and drag to create a point with a curved path segment.

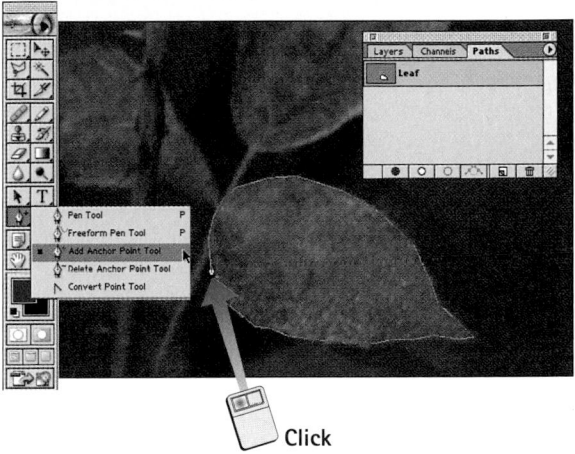

Click

6 Delete a Point

To delete a point from a path, begin by selecting the **Delete Anchor Point** tool from the **Pen** tool pop-out menu in the toolbox. Select the path you want to edit from the **Paths** palette, position the cursor over the point to be removed, and click to delete.

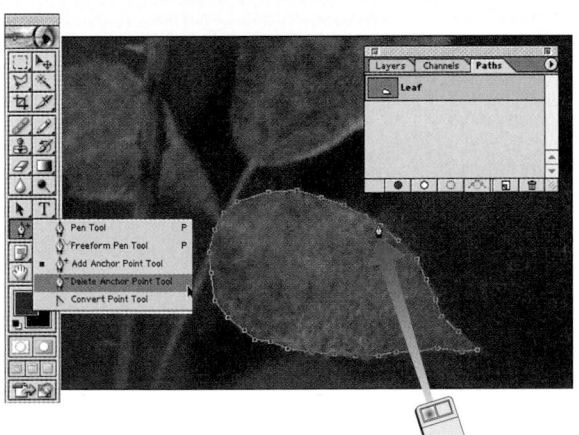

Click

7 Convert an Anchor Point

A complex path consists of both curved and straight-line segments, which are determined by smooth and corner anchor points, respectively. To convert between smooth and corner points, select the **Convert Point** tool and position it over the point to be converted. Click to convert a smooth point to a corner point; click and drag to convert a corner point to a smooth point.

Click

End

How to Convert a Path to a Selection

One of the primary reasons for creating a path is to convert it to a selection. You can convert a path to a selection as long as the path is available. Because paths take less disk space to save than do selections, you probably shouldn't save a selection when you can save the path.

Begin

1 Open the File

Choose **File, Open** to launch the desired file.

2 Create the Path

Use any of the methods described in the preceding tasks to create a path.

3 Choose Make Selection

Choose **Window, Paths** to launch the **Paths** palette. With the path tile selected, choose **Make Selection** from the palette menu. The **Make Selection** dialog box opens.

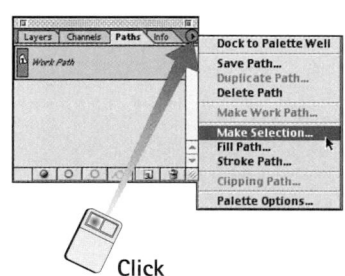

Click

4 Enter the Feather Radius

Enable the **Anti-aliased** check box and enter a feather amount if you want a selection with soft edges (or if you are making a selection around fine details, such as hair). Click **OK** to make the selection.

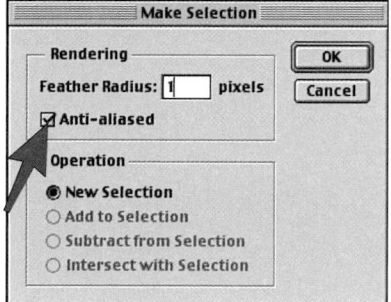

5 Deselect the Path

In the **Paths** palette, click a blank area below the path to deselect it. This action hides the displayed path and shows only the selection.

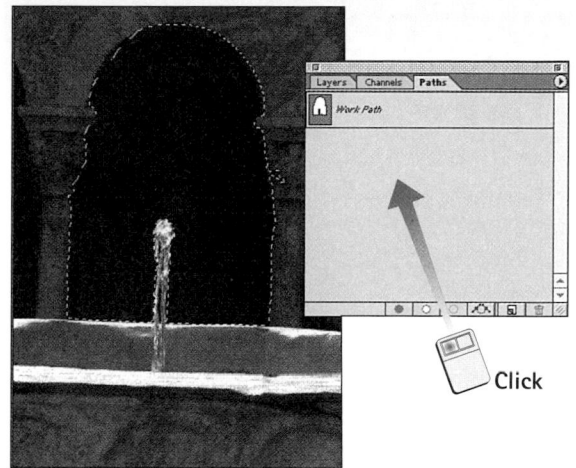

Click

End

How-To Hints

Combining Selections

You can use paths to create selections that interact with existing selections, as determined by the **Operation** section of the **Make Selection** dialog box. If no selection is active in the image area when you choose **Make Selection**, only the **New Selection** radio button is available. If another selection is active when you open this dialog box, you can choose to add to, subtract from, or intersect the path selection with the current one.

Converting a Selection to a Path

If an area already is selected, you easily can convert the selection line to a path. With a selection active, select **Make Work Path** from the **Paths** palette menu, select a tolerance level, and click **OK**. If the result is a path with too many points, undo the conversion and set a higher tolerance level. The result is a work path that you can save and name as you want.

How to Stroke Paths

Stroking a path draws an outline around a selected path. This capability is useful for outlining a rectangle for a text box, building buttons for the Web, or outlining letter forms you have saved as paths. You can create the outline by using any of Photoshop's painting or drawing tools for a wide range of effects. You can even specify the brush size, opacity, and blending mode for full control over the final result.

Begin

1 Open the File

Choose **File, Open** to launch the desired file.

2 Create or Select a Path

Use any of the methods described in the preceding tasks to create a path. In this example, I used the **Polygonal Lasso** tool to create a path around the figure in the image area.

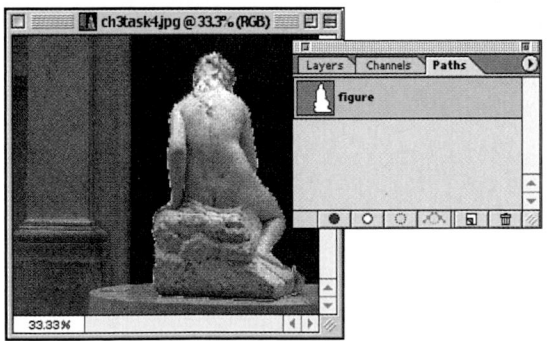

3 Configure the Stroke Tool

In the toolbox, click the tool you want to use to stroke the path. In the **Options** bar for that tool, configure the tool as desired. Choose a brush and brush size from the **Brush** menu.

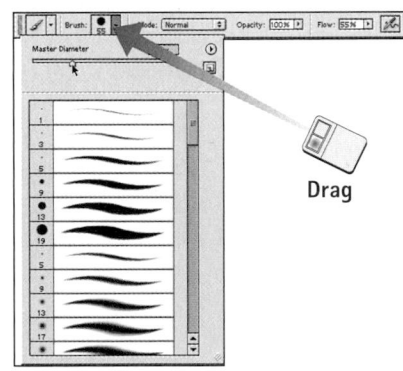

Drag

4 Select the Stroke Path

If it's not already open, choose **Window, Paths** to launch the **Paths** palette. With the desired path active, select **Stroke Path** from the palette menu. (If the path is not named, the menu option reads **Stroke Subpath**.) The **Stroke Path** dialog box opens.

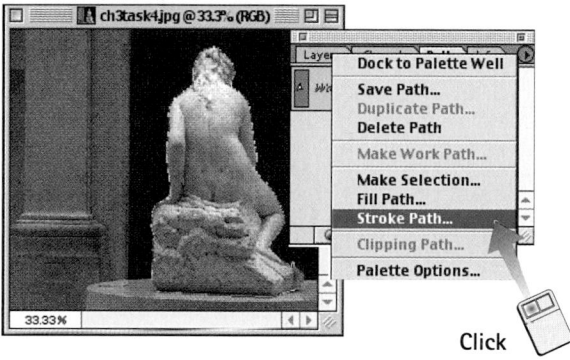

Click

5 Stroke the Path

The tool you configured in Step 3 should be selected in the **Stroke Path** dialog box when it opens. If you want to use a different tool, select it from the **Tool** drop-down list and click **OK**. A line will be drawn, in the current foreground color, along the selected path, using the tool you selected and applying the current settings for that particular tool.

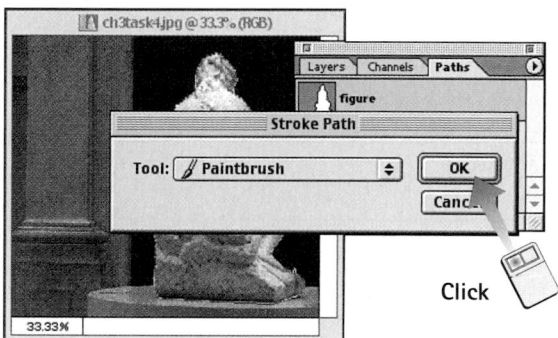

Click

6 Deselect the Path

In the **Paths** palette, click a blank area below the path to deselect it. This action hides the displayed path and shows only the final result.

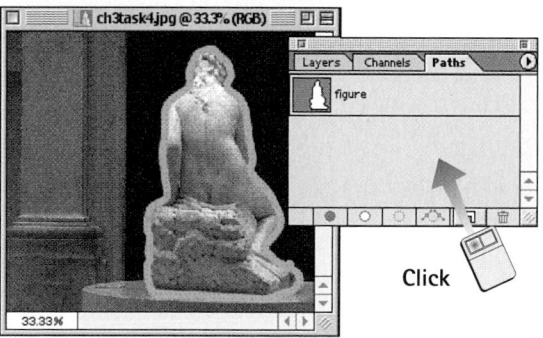

Click

End

How-To Hints

Making an Object Glow

To create an easy glow effect using the stroking method, select **Airbrush** as the stroke tool and stroke the path with a large brush at a low pressure setting. Stroke the path several more times, reducing the brush size and increasing the opacity, to build up a glowing effect.

Filling a Path

You can also fill a path with a color or pattern. Select **Fill Path** from the **Paths** palette menu and select the fill contents, blending mode, and feather details from the dialog box.

How to Create Clipping Paths

Clipping paths refer to a method of exporting a file for use in a vector or layout application in a format that masks out part of the image. The most common use is to drop out the background in a product shot so that only the product object is visible. Although the file looks normal in Photoshop, when it is placed in the new application, everything not contained in the path is masked out.

Begin

1 Open the File

Choose **File, Open** to launch the desired file.

2 Create and Name the Path

Use any of the methods described in the preceding tasks to create a path. In the **Paths** palette, double-click the **Work Path** tile and name the path you just created.

3 Select the Clipping Path

Select **Clipping Path** from the **Paths** palette menu to launch the **Clipping Path** dialog box. From the **Path** drop-down list, choose the path you want to use for the clipping path. In this example, you have only two options: **None** and the path you selected and named in Step 2.

Click

4 Set the Flatness

Set the **Flatness** level to **0.2** and click **OK** to set the clipping path. The **Flatness** setting affects how "smooth" the path will be. The pathname in the **Paths** palette appears in an outlined font to show that a clipping path has been applied using that path.

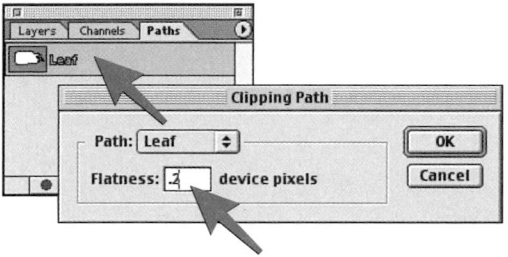

6 Set Preview and Data Options

EPS and **DSC** files bundle a preview image with the PostScript data for onscreen viewing. The **Preview** option tells Photoshop what kind of preview file should be created (1 bit, 8 bit, Mac, PC, TIFF, and so on). **Encoding** determines how the data should be bundled; leave this option set to **ASCII** if you're unsure. Unless your printer tells you otherwise, you should not select the halftone screen or transfer functions because they can interfere with your printer vendor's settings. Check the **PostScript Color Management** option if you're using a compatible system. If there are shapes or other vector info you want to attach to the file, enable the **Vector Data** check box. Finally, don't select **Image Interpolation** unless you're sure that you will not degrade image quality as you place and resize the image. Click **OK** to save the file.

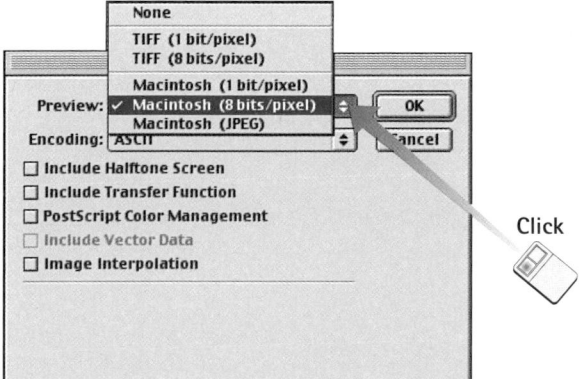

Click

5 Save the File as EPS

To preserve the clipping path along with the file so that the clipping path can be imported into a layout or illustration program, you must save the file in either the TIFF or EPS format. Choose **File, Save As** to save a copy of the file. From the **Format** drop-down list in the **Save As** dialog box, select **Photoshop EPS** or **Photoshop DCS**, type a new name for the file, and click **Save**. (Note that you can save a file in DCS format only if the color mode for the file is CMYK.)

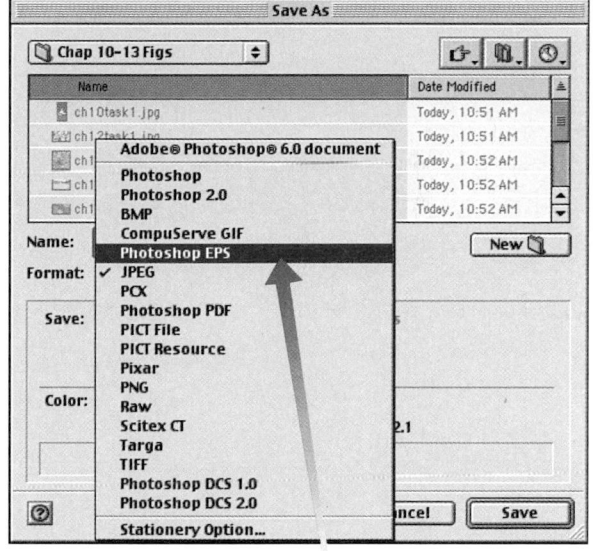

Click

How-To Hints

Watching the Flatness

If the resulting path creates printing or PostScript errors, reset the clipping path using a higher **Flatness** setting (as described in Step 4). A higher **Flatness** setting creates fewer points when the path is interpreted by the printer, which eliminates most printing errors.

End

Task

11

Working with Layers

ayers deliver flexibility, color control, and silhouetting options that factor into most intermediate to advanced image-editing tasks. It's hard to imagine doing any sort of image montage or text integration without taking advantage of layers—in some cases, it's just impossible.

Layers isolate parts of an image in a separate, *um...layer* that you can edit and modify without altering the other layers around it. Think of layered sheets of acetate stacked on top of each other. Viewed from the top, they flatten out and show an entire scene, yet they keep the elements separate from each other.

You can reposition layers in the stack to control how different components overlap with each other. You also can hide layers from view or display them with varying levels of transparency. The tasks in this part explore the essentials involved in creating and combining layers, building the foundation for professional image compositing. ●

How to Create and Move Layers

You should create a layer any time you want to isolate an element from the rest of the image. The element can be text, a second image, or an area of flat color. You can create a layer by using the **New Layer** command, by pasting an element, or by duplicating an existing layer. After you create the layer, it appears in the **Layers** palette, named in numerical sequence. To rename a layer, open the **Properties** dialog box from the **Layers** palette and type a new name there.

2 Open the Layers Palette

Choose **Window, Layers** to open the **Layers** palette.

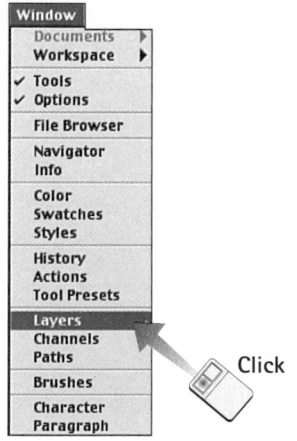

Begin

1 Open the File

Choose **File, Open** and select the image file you want to modify.

3 Create a Text Layer

To create a new layer, choose **Layer, New, Layer.** (Alternatively, select **New Layer** from the **Layers** palette menu.) In the dialog box that appears, name the layer and click **OK.** By default, the layers are given sequential numbers (**Layer 1**, **Layer 2**, and so on). For this example, create at least two layers. Make **Layer 2** a text layer by selecting the **Type** tool and clicking the cursor on the image (a layer is automatically created). Add some text and format it in a large, bold typeface.

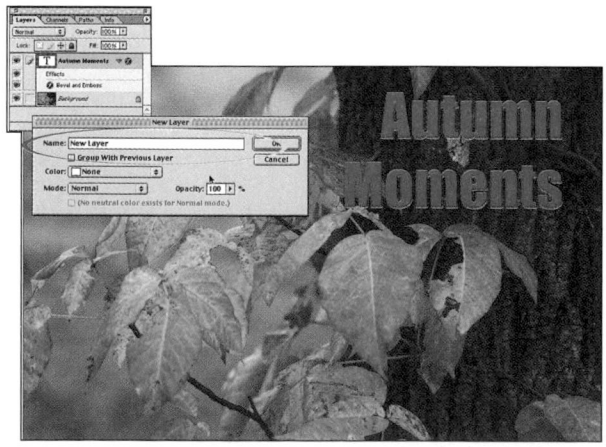

4 Control Layer Visibility

To turn a layer's visibility on and off, look at the **Layers** palette. The far-left column contains boxes with eye icons. Click the box next to the layer you want to control the visibility of to display or hide the eye icon—also called the *visibility icon*.

5 Change the Order of the Layers

You can change the order of the layers that form the image. In the **Layers** palette, click the title of the layer you want to move in the stack and drag it to its new position. Moving layers around and changing their order is a very powerful feature. For example, by changing the order of various layers, you can change the apparent order of the objects that reside on these different layers.

6 Change Layer Opacity

To make a layer transparent, select the layer in the **Layers** palette to make it the active layer. Adjust the **Opacity** slider at the top of the **Layers** palette until the active layer has the desired degree of opacity. If a layer style has been applied to a layer, you can fade the layer contents without fading the layer style. To do this, adjust the **Fill** slider. See Part 9, Task 3, "How to Create Typographic Style Sheets," for more on layer styles.

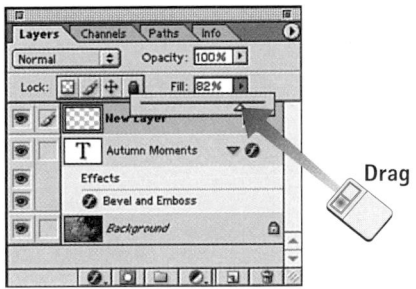

End

How-To Hints

Repositioning the Background Layer

The **Background** "layer" cannot be repositioned in the layer stack. To move the background, you first must rename it (thus "converting" it from the background/base image to a layer). Double-click the layer's name in the **Layers** palette and enter a new name in the dialog box that appears. (You may want to name it **Layer 0**.) After you rename the ex-background layer, it behaves like any other layer.

Preserving Transparency

You can preserve the transparent areas of a layer—that is, prevent them from being edited—by selecting the target layer in the **Layers** palette and placing a check mark in the **Preserve Transparent Pixels** check box. This option ensures that you "color within the lines," so to speak, and prevents any painting or editing from registering in the transparent areas.

How to Link Layers

As you accumulate multiple layers in a file, you will want to link certain layers together to preserve alignment or visibility. After you link layers, they all move as a single group as you reposition the multiple layers on the screen—even as they maintain their identities as separate layers. You also can merge linked layers together with a single command, as explained in Task 8 of this part.

Begin

1 Open the File

Choose **File, Open** and select the file you want to edit. This example starts with an image that contains several layers in addition to the basic **Background** "layer."

2 Open the Layers Palette

Choose **Window, Layers** to open the **Layers** palette.

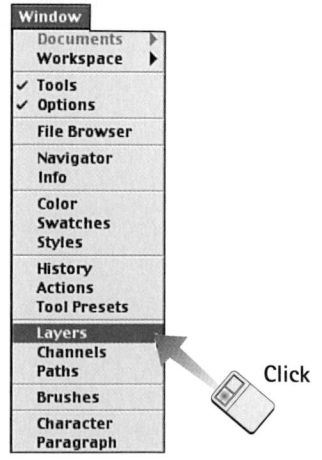

Click

3 Select the Primary Layer

In the **Layers** palette, click the name of the layer to which you want to link other layers. The layer you select here becomes the *primary* layer, or the *active* layer.

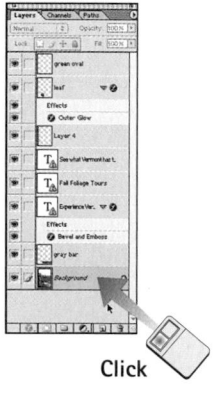

Click

4 Link Secondary Layers

Click in the column to the immediate left of any layers you want to link to the primary layer. A chain icon appears in the column, indicating that the layer is linked to the currently selected layer.

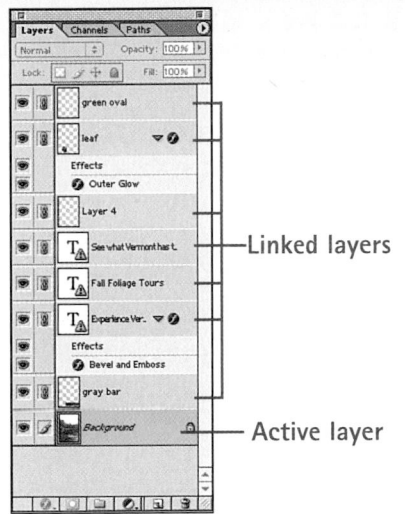

Linked layers

Active layer

5 Unlink Layers

To unlink layers, click the visible chain icons to remove them. When the chain icon is gone, the layer no longer is linked to the currently selected layer.

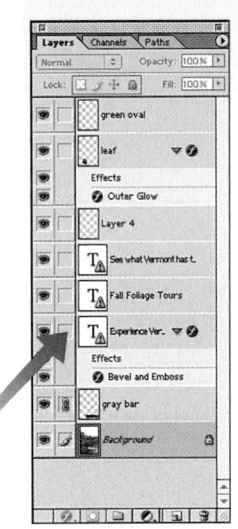

Click

End

How-To Hints

Transforming Linked Layers

Linked layers are treated as a group for more than just movement and alignment. You also can apply the **Transform** command, as outlined in Task 5, "How to Transform Layers," to modify all the linked layers at once.

How to Group Layers

Grouping layers in Photoshop involves linking multiple adjacent layers and using the transparency of the bottom layer of the group as a mask for the other layers. This means that the upper layers are visible only through the "window" created by the transparency of the bottom layer. You also can use a layer mask for the bottom layer in the group instead of actually erasing part of that layer (see Task 7, "How to Add a Layer Mask"). When layers are in a group, the thumbnails in the upper layers in the **Layers** palette are indented and shown with arrows, and the line separating the layers is dashed instead of solid.

Begin

1 Open the File

Choose **File, Open** and select the image file you want to modify.

2 Arrange Layers

Choose **Window, Layers** to display the **Layers** palette. Arrange all the layers to be grouped so that they are adjacent; make sure that the layer to serve as the mask is positioned at the bottom of the group. In this example, the **Background** layer is at the bottom of the stack, a text layer is just above it, a layer with texture is just above that, and the top layer contains lines drawn with the **Paintbrush** tool.

3 Link Layers

Link the layers of the group together, following the steps in Task 2 of this part. For this example, select the text layer and then click in the column closest to the layer name to make the chain icon appear.

Click

4 Group Layers

Make sure that no layers are linked except for those in the target group. Choose **Layer, Group Linked**. The layers that you linked are now grouped, as you can see by the arrow icons and the way the layer names are indented above the bottom, mask layer.

5 Ungroup Layers

If you want to ungroup layers in a group, select the layer to be removed from the group in the **Layers** palette. Choose **Layer, Ungroup**. This action ungroups this layer as well as any grouped layers residing above it.

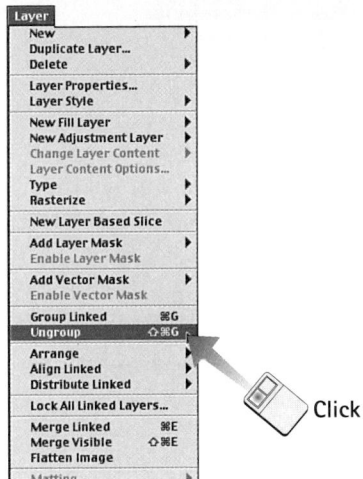

Click

End

How-To Hints

Setting Opacity and Mode

Set the opacity and mode by highlighting the base layer of the *clipping group* (a group in which the bottom layer acts as a mask for the layers above it) and modifying the **Mode** drop-down list and the **Opacity** slider at the top of the **Layers** palette.

Grouping Shortcuts

You have two methods for adding layers to a group: One is to hold down the **Option** key (Mac users) or **Alt** key (Windows users) and position the pointer over the solid line dividing two layers in the **Layers** palette. Click when the pointer changes to two overlapping circles; the two layers are now grouped. (You can also use this method to ungroup layers.) The other grouping method is to highlight a layer in the **Layers** palette and choose **Layer, Group with Previous** to group the highlighted layer with the layer above it.

How to Create Layer Sets

So far, we've seen that we can link layers to move them as one and can group layers to create a masking effect. This task explains how to create sets of layers that can be activated, hidden, or copied as a single unit. The *layer sets* feature, introduced in Photoshop 6, has been a godsend, especially for interface designers who can finally organize the dozens of layers necessary to build a Web site.

Begin

1 Open the File

Choose **File, Open** and select the image file you want to modify.

2 Display the Layers Palette

Choose **Window, Layers** to display the **Layers** palette. Using what you've learned in the preceding tasks, create the desired layers for the set.

3 Link the Layers of the Set

Link the layers of the set together by selecting each layer and clicking in the column to the immediate left of the layer name to make the chain icon appear. Follow the steps in Task 2 of this part for full details.

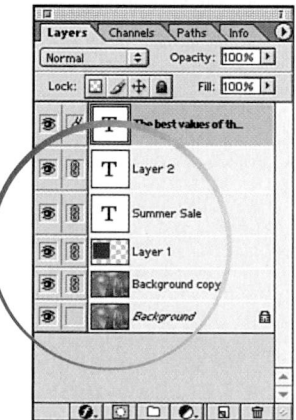

4 Create the Layer Set

Select **Layer, New, Layer Set From Linked** to create a new layer set from the linked layers. In the dialog box that appears, name the set and click **OK**. Layer sets appear in the **Layers** palette with a folder icon and an arrow that allows you to collapse or expand the list of the set's contents.

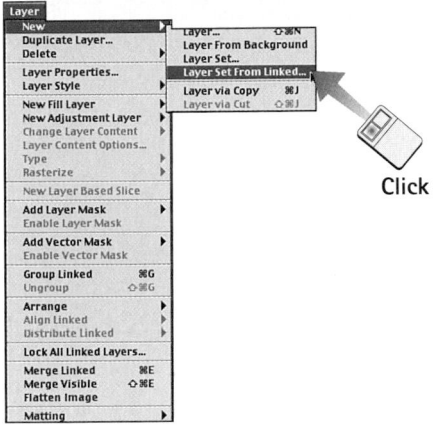

Click

5 Add Layers to the Layer Set

To add additional layers to the set, drag and drop them on the layer set. Alternatively, you can highlight the set and select **Layer, New, Layer** from the menu bar or select **New Layer** from the **Layers** palette menu.

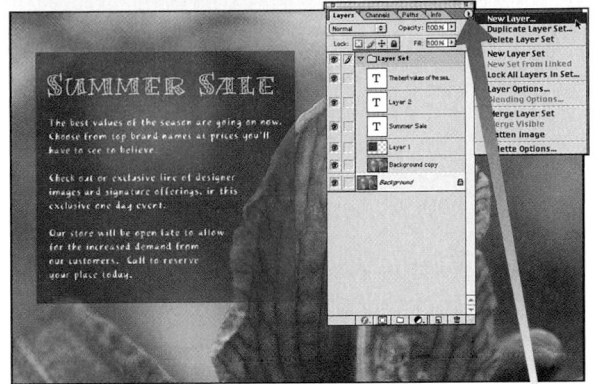

Click

6 Duplicate a Layer Set

To duplicate an entire layer set, highlight the layer set and choose **Duplicate Layer Set** from the **Layers** palette menu. You can also select **Layer, Duplicate Layer Set** from the menu bar.

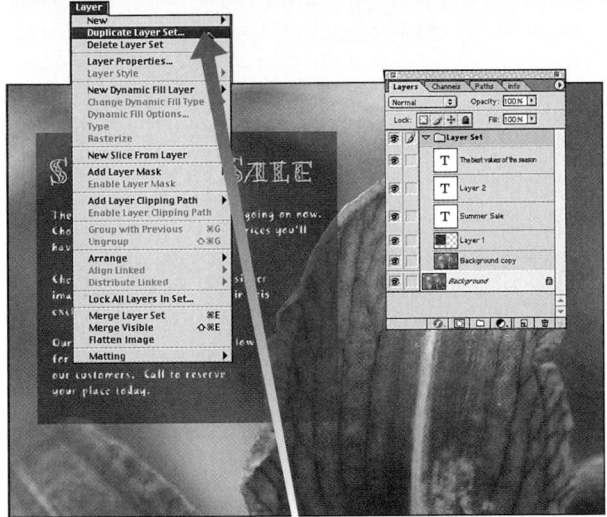

Click

End

How-To Hints

Adding the Background Layer to a Set

The **Background** layer must be converted to a standard layer before it can be added to a layer set. To convert the **Background** layer, double-click it in the **Layers** palette, name it in the dialog box that appears, and click **OK**.

Links, Groups, and Sets

The difference in layer links, layer groups, and layer sets can be classified as repositioning, masking, and unification. Linking layers allows you to reposition a series of layers as one unit. Grouping layers allows you to use the transparent areas of the lower group layer as a mask for the upper layers. Layer sets unify multiple layers as a single unit that can be activated, hidden, or duplicated as one.

How to Transform Layers

When you *transform* a layer, you modify the position, scale, or proportions of the layer. Transforming a layer is useful for changing the size or placement of a layer, as well as for adding perspective or distortion. You cannot apply the transformation process to the **Background** layer; you must convert that layer to a standard layer before you can transform it. Double-click the **Background** layer in the **Layers** palette and rename it in the dialog box that appears. Alternatively, you can duplicate the layer and transform the copy, leaving the original **Background** layer untouched.

2 Open the Layers Palette

Choose **Window, Layers** to open the **Layers** palette.

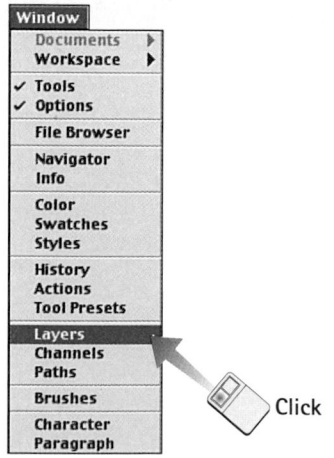

Click

Begin

1 Open the File

Choose **File, Open** and select the file you want to modify.

3 Select the Layer to Transform

In the **Layers** palette, click the name of the layer you want to transform. In this example, we select the layer that contains a graphic of a leaf.

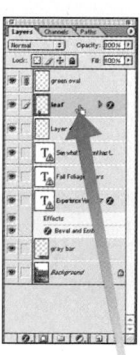

Click

4 Choose Free Transform

Choose **Edit, Free Transform** to begin the transformation process. A bounding box with handles at the sides and the corners surrounds the layer or the objects on the layer. To transform just a portion of a layer, select the area before choosing **Free Transform** so that the bounding box covers only the selected area. Background areas left by the transformation will be transparent, allowing lower layers to show through.

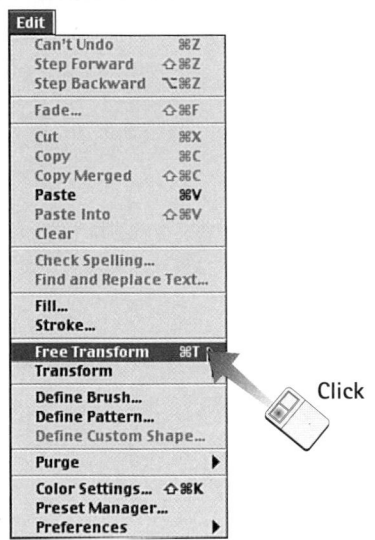

Click

5 Modify the Layer

Apply any of the following transformations to the area in the bounding box. **To move:** Place the cursor inside the bounding box and drag. **To scale:** Click and drag a handle (use the **Shift** key to keep the original proportions). **To rotate:** Position the cursor outside the bounding box until it turns into a curved, two-headed arrow and then drag. **To distort freely:** Press and hold ⌘ (Mac users) or **Ctrl** (Windows users) and drag a handle. **To skew:** Press and hold ⌘+Shift (Mac users) or **Ctrl+Shift** (Windows users) and drag a side handle. Press **Enter** or **Return** to apply the effect.

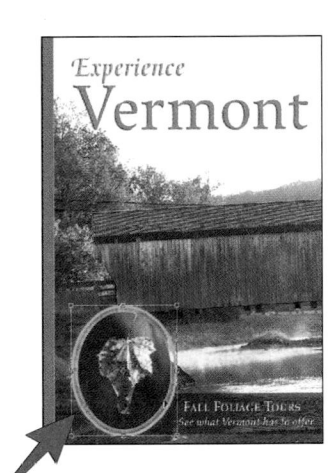
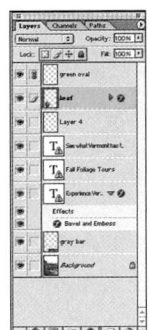

End

How-To Hints

Using the Individual Transform Commands

You also can apply individual transformation options by choosing **Edit, Transform** and then choosing the transformation option you want from the submenu that appears. This approach limits the transformation to only the selected task, such as rotating or scaling.

Transforming Numerically

You can transform a layer with numeric precision by choosing **Edit, Transform, Free Transform**. In the **Options** bar, adjust the **Position, Scale, Rotation,** and **Skew** options. This approach is especially valuable when you have to repeat the same transformation across multiple unlinked layers.

How to Create Adjustment Layers

Adjustment layers apply tone or color to all the layers that appear below them in the **Layers** palette, without altering specific layer content. With an adjustment layer, you can also apply a gradient, color, or pattern fill. An adjustment layer acts like a filter, altering the appearance of all the layers underneath it—effectively modifying multiple layers at one time. If the result is unsatisfactory, delete or turn off the layer to return to the previous state. Adjustment layers are like other layers in that you can reposition, hide, or duplicate them in the **Layers** palette.

2 Open the Layers Palette

Choose **Window, Layers** to open the **Layers** palette.

Begin

1 Open the File

Choose **File, Open** and select the file you want to modify.

3 Create an Adjustment Layer

Choose **Layer, New Adjustment Layer** and select the desired fill type. The options are **Levels, Curves, Brightness/Contrast, Color Balance, Hue/Saturation, Selective Color, Channel Mixer, Gradient Map, Invert, Threshold,** and **Posterize**.

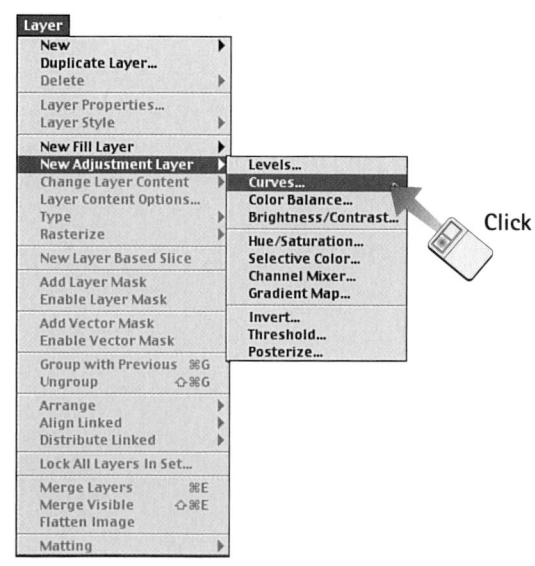

4 Create the Layer

In the **Name** box of the **New Layer** dialog box that opens, type a name for the layer that you are creating. Click **OK** to create the layer.

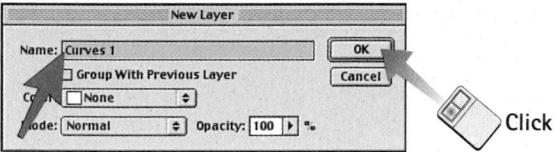

Click

5 Apply the Adjustment

An adjustment dialog box appears based on the specific layer selection you made in Step 3. Adjust the controls to your satisfaction (select colors, gradients, controls, and so on) and click **OK** to set the adjustment.

Click

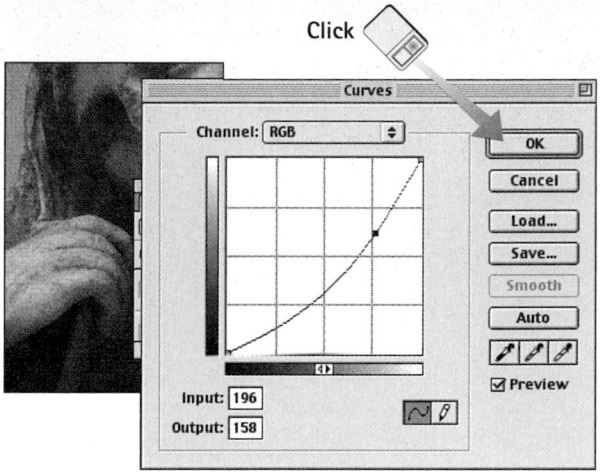

6 Edit the Adjustment

To edit the adjustment settings, double-click the icon on the left side of the adjustment layer in the **Layers** palette. The adjustment dialog box you saw in Step 5 opens so that you can make further changes.

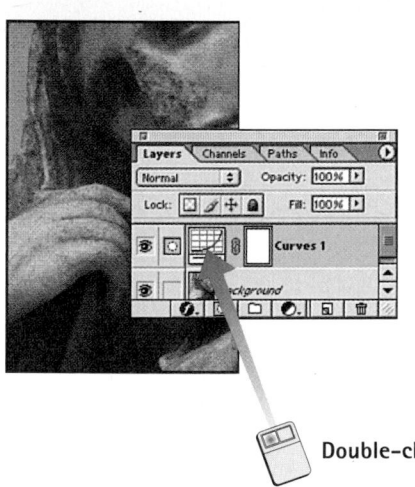

Double-click

How-To Hints

Adjustment Layers as Layer Masks

You can paint into an adjustment layer, masking how its effect is applied to the layers underneath. As with other layer masks (described in the following task), painting with black conceals the adjustment effect; painting with white reveals it. With the adjustment layer active in the **Layers** palette, select any paint tool and paint into the image. The color choices convert to grayscale while the adjustment layer is active. The line or area you paint becomes the mask through which the adjustment effect is applied to the remaining layers.

End

How to Add a Layer Mask

A *layer mask* conceals a portion of a layer without actually deleting it, allowing the lower layers to show through. Erasing the layer mask restores the layer's original appearance so that nothing is lost. The general approach to applying a layer mask is to brush it on using any of the paint tools, controlling the visibility and transparency with grayscale values. As you saw Part 3, Task 4, "How to Use Quick Mask," a black value conceals the layer image, white reveals it, and a grayscale value dictates the transparency.

Begin

1 Open the File

Choose **File, Open** and select the image file you want to modify. For this task, I've opened an image with two layers. The lower layer is of an arrangement of foliage, and the top layer is of a museum statue. By "painting" in a mask, I'll make it appear as if the statue is surrounded by the foliage and not sitting in the corridor of a museum.

2 Open the Layers Palette

Choose **Window, Layers** to open the **Layers** palette.

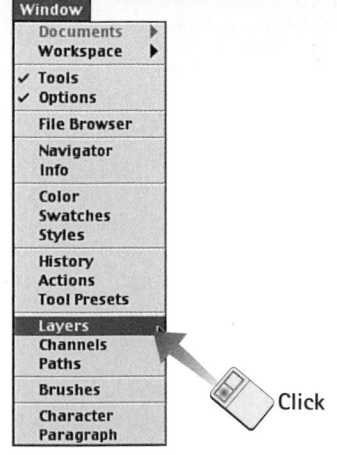

Click

3 Select the Mask Layer

Select the layer to be masked by clicking its name in the **Layers** palette. In this example, select the layer containing the statue image.

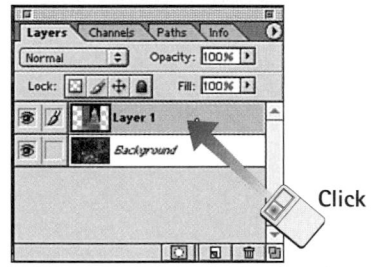

Click

4 Add the Layer Mask

Click the **Add A Mask** button at the bottom of the **Layers** palette to add a layer mask to the current layer. The layer mask is indicated in the image tile by a white thumbnail next to the image thumbnail. The border of the new thumbnail is bold, indicating that it is selected.

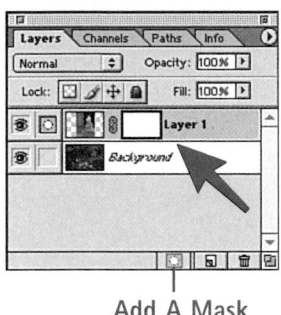

Add A Mask

5 Paint the Mask

Select the **Paintbrush** tool from the toolbox. Move the cursor into the image area and paint the mask. As you do so, you'll see the current layer disappearing and the lower layer showing through; the thumbnail mask icon is updated to show the current mask. In this example, notice that the museum area behind the statue is being "erased" and the woodsy **Background** layer is showing through.

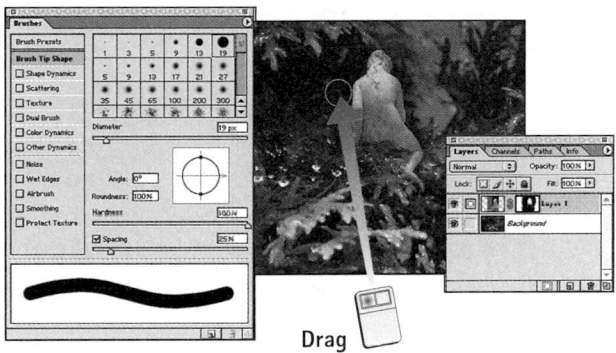

Drag

6 Delete the Mask

To erase or fade part of the mask, change the foreground color to white and repaint the mask. The image layer reappears as you work. To paint in transparency, select a gray foreground color or reduce the **Opacity** setting in the **Options** bar for the paint tool you are using. Note that pressing the **X** key enables you to quickly toggle between the foreground and background colors. This is helpful while adjusting the edges of the mask.

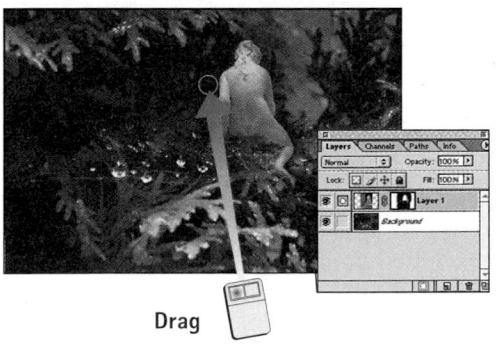

Drag

7 Apply the Mask

Because layer masks add significantly to file size, you should consider applying them to the layer when you're confident that you will not be making any further changes. To apply the mask to the layer, choose **Layer, Remove Layer Mask, Apply**.

End

How-To Hints

Make Sure That You Paint the Mask

When applying a layer mask, make sure that the mask thumbnail is highlighted in the **Layers** palette before you make any changes. As you're working, it's easy to forget that the image thumbnail should be selected; if it's not selected, you'll be painting directly into the image.

How to Merge and Flatten Layers

In a complex design, it's not hard to accumulate dozens of layers, which can bloat file size and make it hard to find what you're looking for. Whenever possible, you should look for opportunities to merge and flatten layers to keep the design clean and well ordered. *Merging* layers refers to combining some of the layers in a design while keeping other layers separate. *Flattening* the image involves compressing all the layers into one flat background layer.

2 Launch the Layers Palette

Choose **Window, Layers** to open the **Layers** palette and show all existing layers.

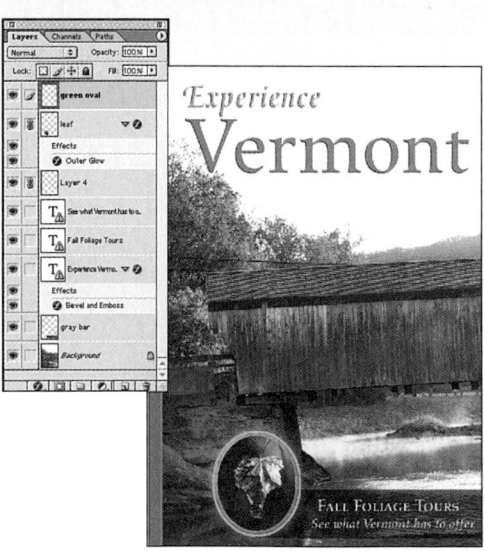

Begin

1 Open the File

Choose **File, Open** and select the file you want to modify.

3 Merge Multiple Layers into One

To merge two layers into one, drag them one above the other in the **Layers** palette and select the layer at the top of the two. Choose **Layer, Merge Down** to combine the selected layer with the layer below it in the list. The name of the lower layer is used when you combine layers with the **Merge Down** command.

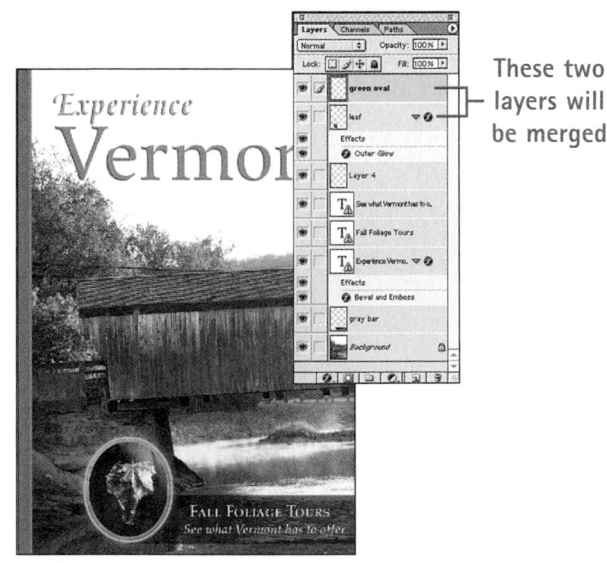

These two layers will be merged

4 Merge the Linked Layers

To merge more than one layer at a time, first link the layers as described in Task 2 in this part. Then choose **Layer, Merge Linked** to combine all the linked layers.

These linked layers will be merged

5 Merge All Visible Layers

An alternative to merging linked layers is to first turn off the visibility of all layers that you do not want to merge. Choose **Layer, Merge Visible** to combine all visible layers. Then go back to the **Layers** palette and turn the hidden layers back on. The current, or active, layer name is used when you combine layers using the **Merge Visible** command.

These visible layers will be merged

6 Flatten the Image

To reduce all the layers in a document to one, choose **Layer, Flatten Image**. If any layers are hidden as you do this, a dialog box appears, asking whether you want to discard the layer or cancel the operation. Click **Discard** to flatten the image and delete the hidden layers.

All layers are combined

How-To Hints

Watching the Layer Order When Merging

If linked layers are not adjacent to each other, the image could be altered when you merge the layers. This is especially true when opacity or blending modes have been used.

End

Task

PART 12

Building Web Files

*A*dobe has done an excellent job transforming Photoshop from an advanced image-editing tool into an advanced Web-production tool—without losing the image-editing features along the way. Using the ImageReady feature set, users now can build tables, create JavaScript rollovers, and slice an image into multiple images with custom optimization for each piece.

Note: Much of the work in the tasks in this part will be done in ImageReady and not in Photoshop itself. It is extremely easy to move back and forth between the two programs, calling on the strengths of each as necessary. In fact, the two programs are closely linked, and you can open one from the other and move files back and forth between the applications.

Photoshop and ImageReady automatically optimize, rename, and generate solid HTML code on-the-fly, supporting a wide variety of Web tasks. The code is saved as a separate HTML file that can dovetail with an existing page or, in the case of tables, be used on its own.

Be sure to set the HTML settings in both Photoshop and ImageReady to make sure that the code being created is optimized for the platforms and browsers for which you're developing. In addition, you should check out the file-naming conventions in the ImageReady and Photoshop **Preferences** boxes to make sure that the autonaming schemes are compatible with your overall process. See Part 1, "Getting Started with Photoshop," for details on setting these preferences. ●

How to Preview Files in Browsers and Platforms

Image files look different on Macs than they do on PCs and from browser to browser. PC monitors have a higher gamma setting than Mac monitors, so images are darker when displayed on PCs. Differences in browser types tend to show themselves when you're building tables or working with other layout issues. When preparing files for the Web, it is imperative that you check each file on all platforms and in as many browsers as possible. This task covers most of your preview options and looks at file-format previews.

1 Open the File in ImageReady

Open the image file in ImageReady. Although you can do this in Photoshop, ImageReady offers a few general advantages for Web optimization such as GIF animation and Java rollovers.

2 Preview for Windows

If you're on a Mac and you want to see what the file will look like on a Windows machine, choose **View, Preview, Standard Windows Color**. This command adjusts the monitor's appearance to reflect the 2.2 gamma setting typical for most PCs. In Photoshop, you would select **View, Proof Setup, Windows RGB**.

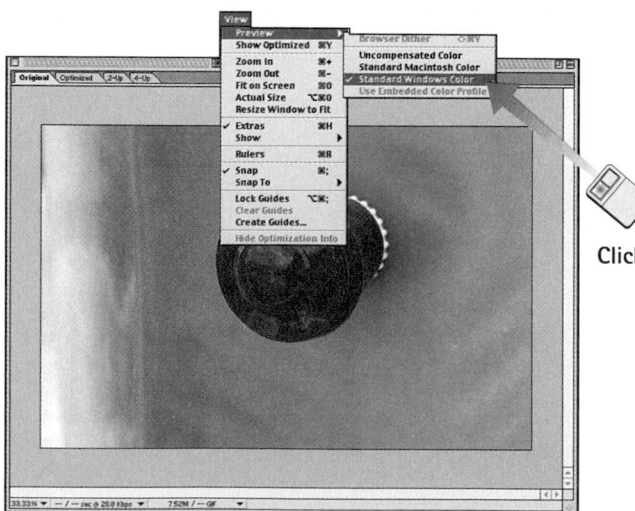

Click

3 Preview for Mac

If you're on a PC and you want to see what the file will look like on a Macintosh, choose **View, Preview, Standard Macintosh Color**. This command adjusts the monitor's appearance to reflect the 1.8 gamma setting typical for most Macs. In Photoshop you would select **View, Proof Setup, Macintosh RGB**.

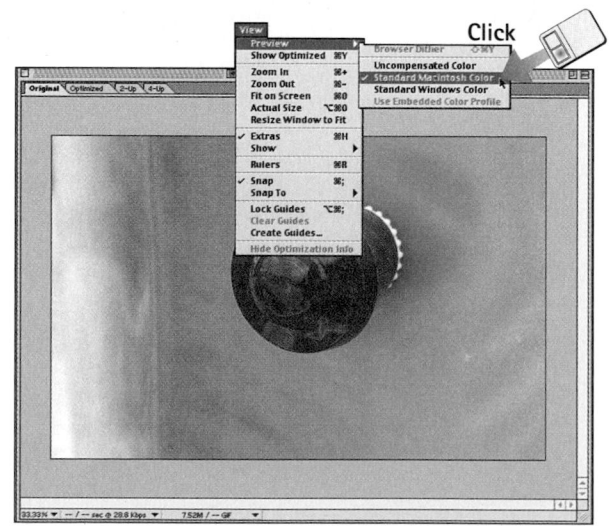

Click

4 Preview as JPEG

After you set the preview to Mac or PC, you should determine the best compression format for your image. To test the results of JPEG compression, choose **Window, Optimize** to open the **Optimize** palette. Select **JPEG** from the **Optimized File Format** drop-down list and click the **Optimized** tab.

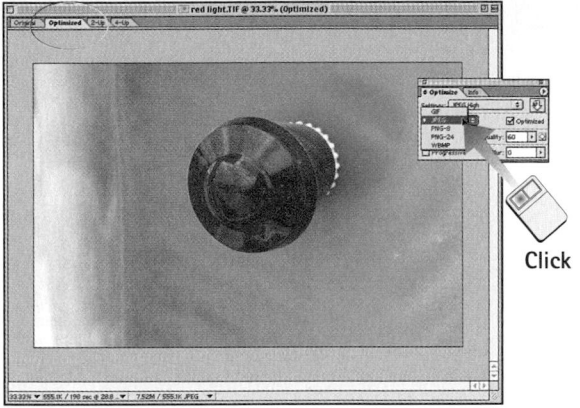

Click

5 Preview as GIF

To test the results of GIF compression, choose **Window, Optimize** to open the **Optimize** palette. Select **GIF** from the **Optimize File Format** drop-down list. Look at the status line at the bottom of the image area: The file's original size appears, followed by the size the file will be if saved as a GIF. For details on GIF optimization, see Part 4, Task 4, "How to Build GIF Files for the Web."

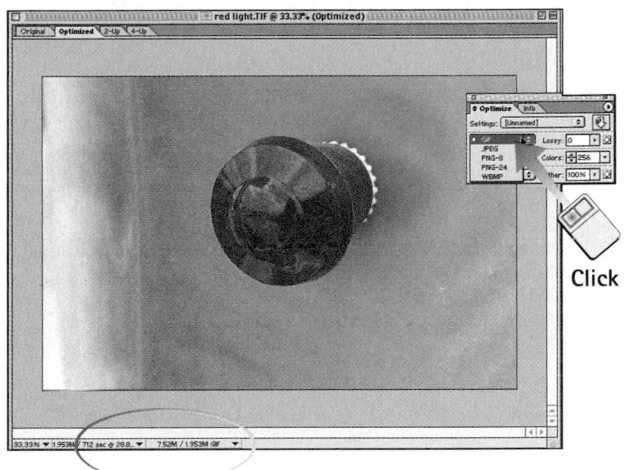

Click

6 Preview in Browsers

To preview a file or table in a browser, click the **Browser Preview** button in the toolbox. This command launches the specified browser and loads the current file. Here the image is shown in the Netscape Navigator browser. To select an alternative browser, click and hold the tool button and select from other browser options as available on your system. You can also select **File, Preview In, <Browser Name>** and select the desired browser.

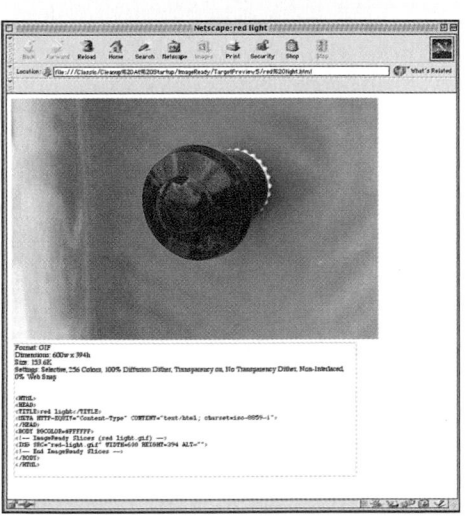

How-To Hints

Setting Browser Preferences

To load a browser so that it appears in the toolbox pop-put menu or the **File, Preview In** submenu, you first must specify the available options. Select **File, Preview In, Other**; in the dialog box that opens, navigate to the desired browser application. Click **OK**, and that browser will appear as a browser option in these menus.

End

How to Slice Images for the Web

Slicing an image for the Web involves dividing a larger image into smaller tiles that are assembled in a table as the page is loaded. These smaller tiles often load faster than one large image and are necessary if you want a portion of a large image to act as a *rollover* or an *animation*. ImageReady lets you divide a graphic with a grid of horizontal and vertical lines and then creates individual files on the fly—including the necessary HTML code to build the table.

Begin

1 Open the File in ImageReady

In ImageReady, choose **File, Open** and select the image file you want to modify.

2 Show Rulers

If the rulers are not already visible, choose **View, Rulers** to display rulers along the top and left sides of the image window.

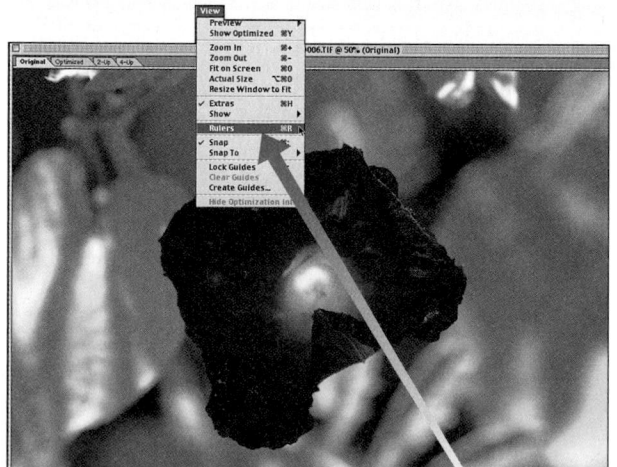

Click

3 Drag Guides

Position the mouse pointer over one of the rulers and hold down the mouse button until the pointer changes to a double-headed arrow. Drag into the image to create a horizontal or vertical guide. Position guides to correspond to the slices you want to create.

Drag

4 Slice Along Guides

Choose **Slices, Create Slices from Guides** to slice the image along the current guidelines. The slices show up on the image area as rectangular sections outlined in a highlight color. The currently selected slice appears in gold.

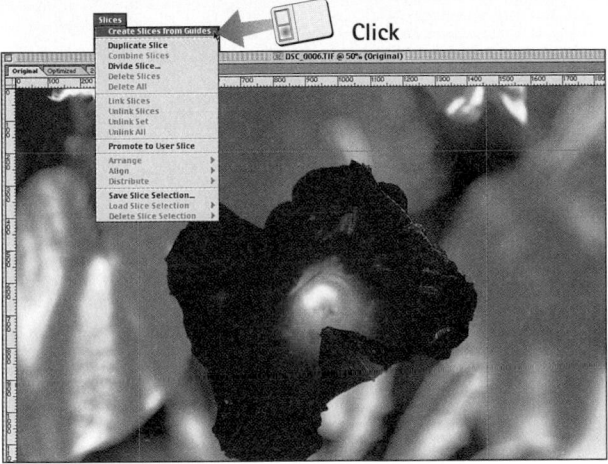

Click

6 Save Files

Choose **File, Save Optimized** to open the **Save Optimized** dialog box. Select **HTML and Images** from the **Format** pop-up menu if you want ImageReady to create the HTML file for the associated table. If you are saving a large number of slices, you might want to click the **New Folder** button and name the new folder to keep all the associated files in one place. Click **Save** to save and optimize each slice. Multiple files will be created, each file containing a single slice. The files have the original filename and a sequentially assigned number appended to the filename.

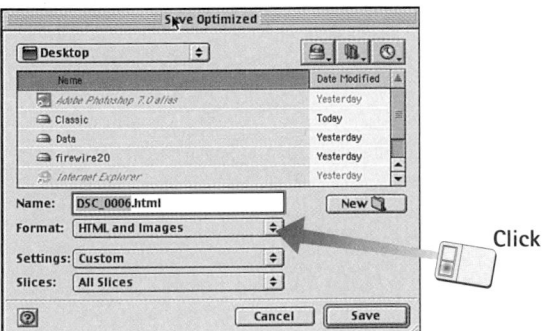

Click

5 Optimize Slices

Click the **Slice Select** tool from the toolbox and click the first slice in the image area to select it. Then open the **Optimize** palette (choose **Window, Optimize**) and set the optimization for that section, just as you would for an entire file. Repeat this step for each slice in the image area. See Part 4, "Converting Files," for more information on using the **Optimize** palette. *Note:* Don't choose **View, Show Optimized**, which shows the results of the current **Optimize** palette settings rather than simply launching the palette.

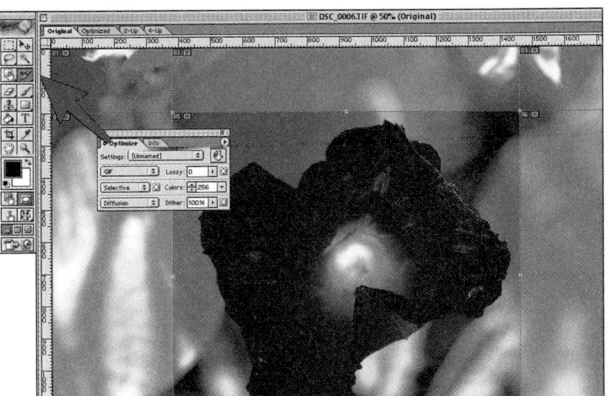

How-To Hints

Moving Guides

To reposition a slice guide after you have placed it, click the **Move** tool in the toolbox, position the mouse pointer over the guide, and drag the guide as needed.

Setting Slice Preferences

Select **File, Output Settings, Slices** to specify the exact naming conventions of slices as they are displayed in ImageReady. In addition, you can also select **Edit, Preferences, Slices** to control slice color and highlight attributes.

End

How to Build Imagemaps

Imagemaps allow you to create *hot spots* in Web images that link to other pages, actions, or information. You could create a graphic with buttons, elaborate text treatments, or image-based information, designating the exact areas within the image for the links. ImageReady makes it easy to designate areas for imagemaps, allowing you to specify the link information and even to save the necessary HTML code to finish the effect.

Begin

1 Open the File in ImageReady

In ImageReady, choose **File, Open** and select the desired image file. In this image, I will draw imagemap areas around each line of text, which will link to the respective pages in a Web site.

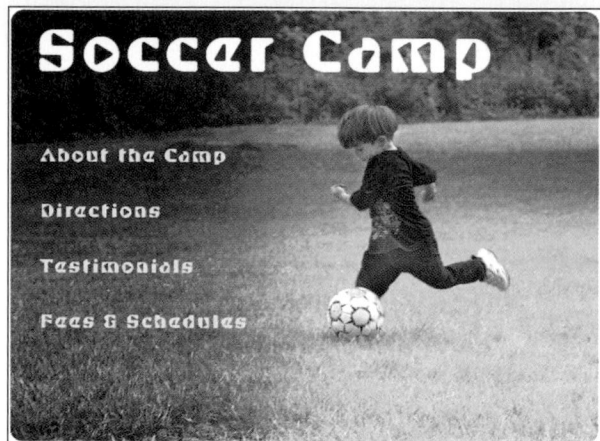

2 Select the Image Map Tool

Click and hold the **Image Map** tool in the toolbox to display all the Image Map tools in a pop-out menu. The tool options allow you to draw rectangles, circles, and polygonal shapes. There is also a tool for selecting the imagemap shapes after they're drawn. Select the desired shape tool from the menu.

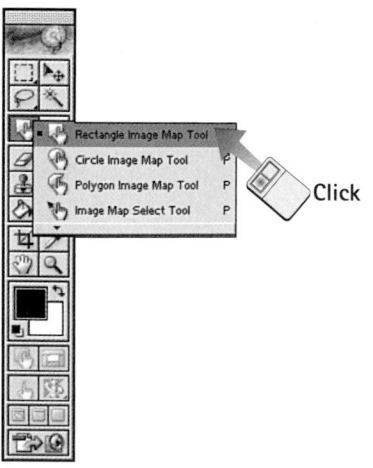

3 Draw the Imagemap Shapes

Move the mouse pointer over the image and click and drag to draw the shape. It will appear outlined with handles on each side. To edit the shape after it is drawn, select the **Image Map Select** tool, select the imagemap shape, and move the handles as desired to resize.

4 Open the Image Map Palette

If it's not open already, select **Window, Image Map** to open the **Image Map** palette. Adjust the **X** and **Y** settings in the **Dimensions** section to control the exact placement of the shape. Adjust the **Width**, **Height**, or **Radius** controls (depending on the shape type you selected in Step 2) to resize the shape.

5 Set HTML Information

Enter a unique name for the imagemap shape you just drew, as well as the target URL for the link. After entering a URL, you may choose a target value to control the kind of window in which the link will open. Select **_blank** for a new window or **_self** for the current window (the **_parent** and **_top** options are used primarily for framset targeting). If desired, enter an **Alt** value, which appears if someone views the page with the graphics off.

6 Save the Files

To save the image and the HTML parameters, it is necessary to save a graphic file *and* an HTML file. To do this, optimize the file as explained in Part 4, Task 4, "How to Build GIF Files for the Web," and then select **File, Save Optimized**. In the **Format** pop-up menu, make sure that **HTML and Images** is selected and that the files are in the desired directory. Click **OK** to save the image and HTML files.

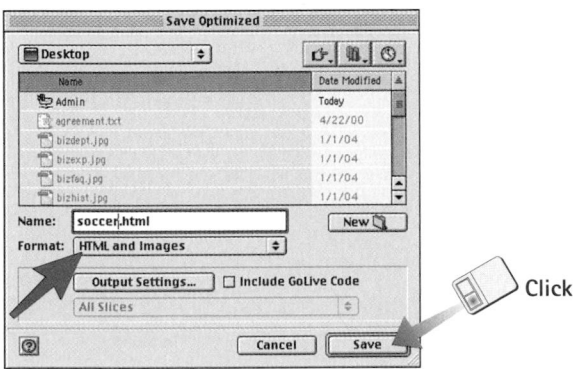

Click

End

How-To Hints

Aligning Shapes

When working with multiple imagemap shapes, use ImageReady's precision alignment tools to center the shapes or align them along an edge. Select the **Image Map Select** tool and hold down the **Shift** key to select multiple shapes. You can then select from any of the align or distribute tools that appear in the **Options** bar.

Imagemaps from Layers

If you have a shape that is isolated on its own layer (such as a graphic button), select **Layer, New Layer Based Image Map Area**. This option creates a new imagemap shape based on the currently active layer.

How to Build Filter-Based GIF Animations

Photoshop and ImageReady enable you to create impressive animation sequences using progressive applications of various texture filters or distortion filters. (You can create the frames in Photoshop—as layers—but only ImageReady can create the animation.) By creating duplicate layers of the same file and then applying a filter with increasing intensity, it is easy to animate the filter application. In this task, we take a close-up image of a flower and apply the **Twirl** filter in successive layers to create a nifty animation. Although you can start with any type of file, animations must be saved in the GIF format.

Begin

1 Open the File in ImageReady

In ImageReady, choose **File, Open** and select the file you want to animate with a filter.

2 Duplicate Layers

Choose **Window, Layers** to open the **Layers** palette. Choose **Duplicate Layer** from the palette menu multiple times to create several individual states for the animation. In this example, I created three more layers.

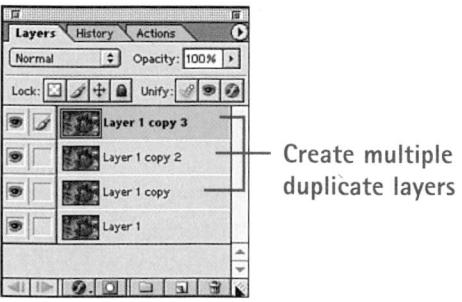

Create multiple duplicate layers

3 Filter the Layers

Select the first layer in the **Layers** palette and open the desired filter (for this example, I chose **Filter, Distort, Twirl**). Apply a modest filter amount and click **OK**. Select the other layers in sequence, applying the filter to each layer with increasing intensity.

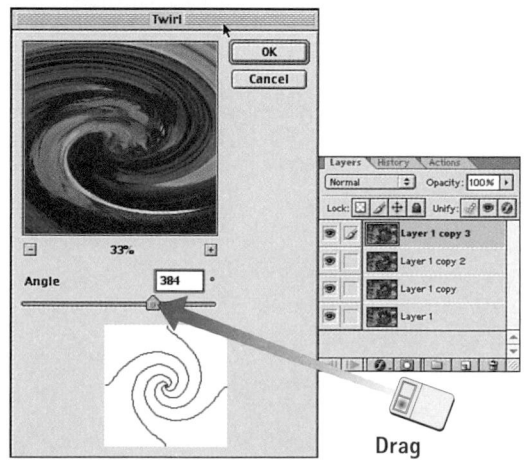

Drag

4 Open the Animation Palette

Choose **Window, Animation** to open the **Animation** palette.

5 Create Frames

Choose **New Frame** from the **Animation** palette menu to create a new animation frame. Repeat this step to create a corresponding frame for each filtered layer you created in Step 3. For example, if you have the original layer and created three filtered copies in Step 3, create four animation frames now.

Make as many frames as you have layers

6 Assign Layers to Frames

With both the **Layers** and **Animation** palettes visible, click the first animation frame and select the corresponding first layer of the filter progression. Click the visibility icons (the eye icons) for all the other layers so that only the selected layer is visible. Then click the next animation frame and select the next filtered layer in the **Layers** palette, making sure that only the selected layer is visible. Continue until each frame is assigned to a layer.

Click

How-To Hints

Begin in Photoshop if Necessary

Because Photoshop offers many more filter options than does ImageReady, you might want to perform Steps 1 through 3 of this task in Photoshop. After you have filtered all the layers, click the **Jump To** button at the bottom of the toolbox to open the file in ImageReady and continue with Step 4.

Continues

7 Play Back in ImageReady

Click the **Play** button at the bottom of the **Animation** palette to play the animation. Check for smoothness, alignment, and timing between frames. The animation will replay continuously; click the **Stop** button to stop the playback.

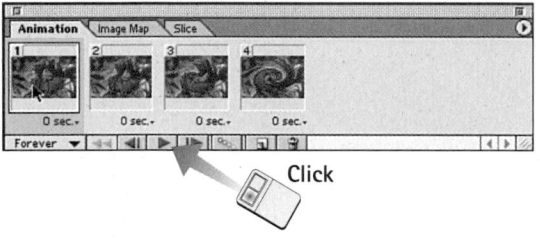

Click

8 Set the Loop Count

The **Loop Count** option controls whether an animation plays once, forever, or a specific number of times. Select **Once** or **Forever** from the pop-up menu; alternatively, select **Other** and enter the number of repetitions in the dialog box that appears.

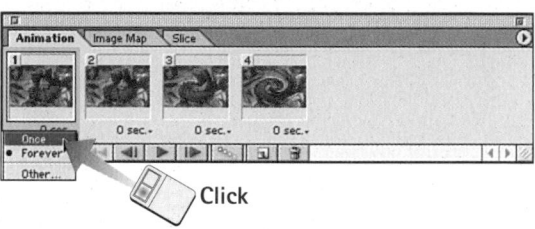

Click

9 Set the Frame Timing

To add a timing delay for a single frame, click the timing pop-up menu underneath the frame you want to modify and select the desired time delay. For example, you might want to add a longer delay to the first frame to emphasize the original state of the image.

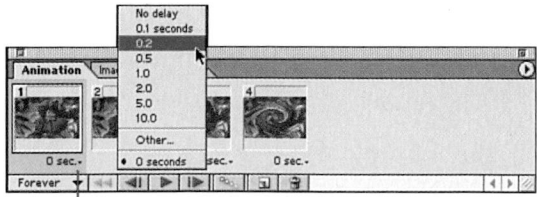

Click here to change timing

10 Set GIF Optimization

Choose **Window, Optimize** to open the **Optimize** palette. Optimize the animation as a GIF file as explained in Part 4, Task 4, "How to Build GIF Files for the Web."

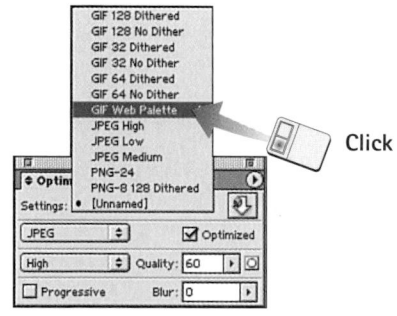

Click

11 Preview in a Browser

Choose **File, Preview In** and select the target browser from the **Preview In** submenu. The animation file opens in the specified browser with information about the file size, file type, and compression type displayed at the bottom of the window.

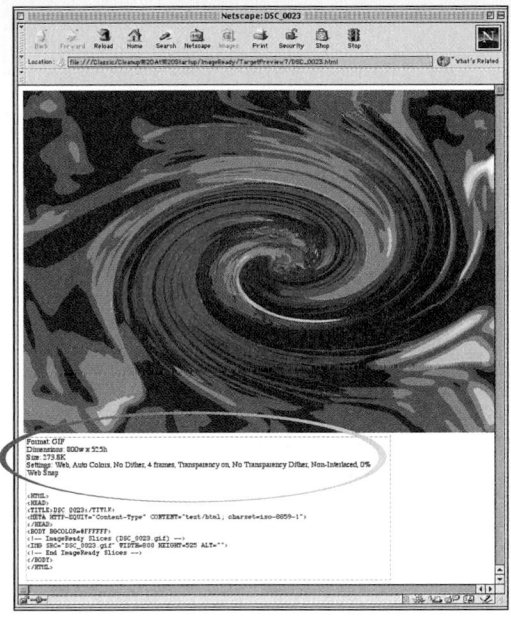

12 Save as GIF

Configure the GIF format settings in the **Optimize** palette and select **File, Save Optimize** to save the GIF file. For details on how to save GIF files, refer to Part 4, Task 4.

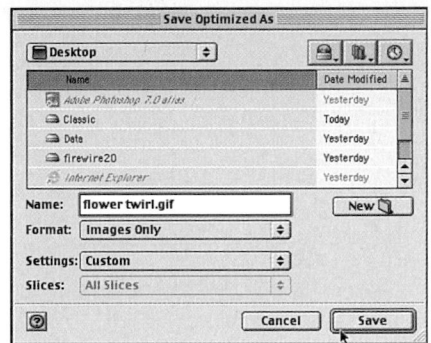

End

How-To Hints

Optimizing and Saving

Although you optimized the image file as a GIF in Step 10 of this task, you must also save the file as a GIF in Step 12. Optimizing the file as a GIF sets the number of colors and so on; it does not save the file. You must save the file using the GIF89a format, or the file will not animate.

Keeping the Number of Animation Frames to as Few as Possible

Animation frames dramatically increase file size and, consequently, download times. Keep the number of frames to a minimum to ensure fast download times and to guarantee fast-loading pages.

Animating Text with Warp Text

Consider using the **Warp Text** tool for sophisticated text animation. Create the text with the **Type** tool, build animation frames, and apply **Warp Text** effects gradually to each frame. **Warp Text** is an icon in the upper-right corner of the **Options** bar for the **Text** tool.

How to Build JavaScript Rollovers

Rollover animations are graphics that change as you pass your mouse over a specific spot onscreen. These animations are useful for emphasizing links, especially in graphics that may not be clearly marked. Rollovers consist of a normal state, a mouse-over state, and a click state, so this task creates a separate image variation for each state. To explain the rollover effect, this task creates a basic button and then changes the state of the button. After you create the button and its three states, you must save the HTML code as well as the graphics and then paste the code into the target Web page.

Begin

1 Create a New ImageReady File

In ImageReady, choose **File, New** to open the **New Document** dialog box so that you can create a new file. For this task, give the document the filename **RolloverTest,** specify a height and width of **100** pixels for the image size, and select the **White** radio button. Click **OK.**

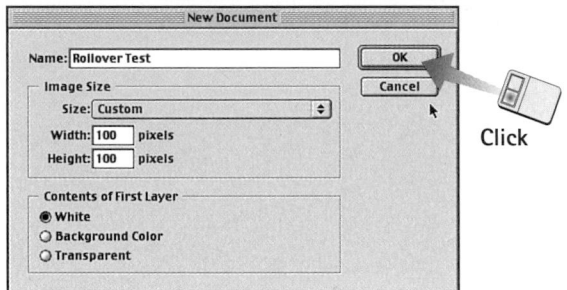

Click

2 Create the Button

Set the foreground color to the color you want to use for the button you'll be drawing. Select the **Elliptical Marquee** tool and Shift-drag within the image to draw a circle the size of the final button. Use the **Paint Bucket** tool to fill the button shape with the foreground color.

3 Add the Layer Effect

To give the button a 3D effect, choose **Layer, Layer Style, Bevel and Emboss.** Set the desired parameters in the **Bevel and Emboss** palette that appears. If you want, you can also add an **Outer Glow Layer** effect to create a realistic shape, as I did here.

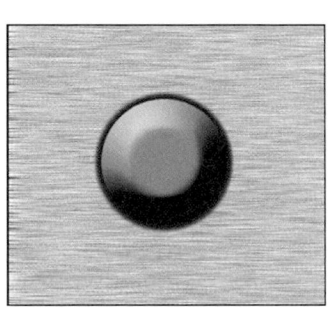

4 Make Layer Duplicates

From the **Layers** palette menu, choose **Duplicate Layer** to copy the button and its effects. Choose **Duplicate Layer** again to create a total of three layers, each of which shows the same button and bevel.

5 Color the Layers

In the **Layers** palette, select the first duplicate layer and open the **Inner Glow Layer Effect** dialog box. Add the light green glow color and click **OK.** Go back to the **Layers** palette and select the second duplicate layer. Open the **Hue/Saturation** dialog box and adjust the **Hue** slider to change the color of the button to red. Change the glow color to orange and click **OK.**

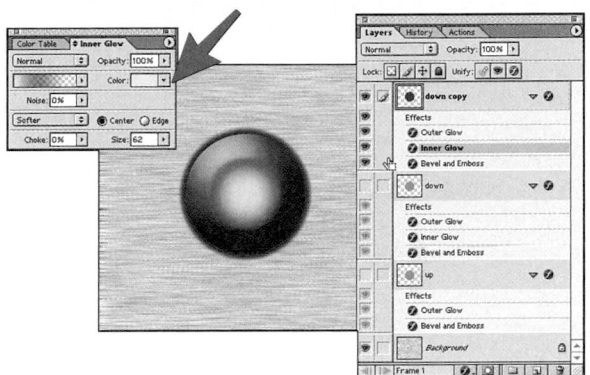

6 Create Rollover States

Choose **Window, Rollovers** to open the **Rollovers** palette. Select **New State** from the palette menu to create a new state caller **Over State.** Select **New State** again to create another new state called **Down State.** You now should have a total of three states: **Normal, Over,** and **Down.** (And, unbeknownst to you, ImageReady is creating the JavaScript code to make all this work!)

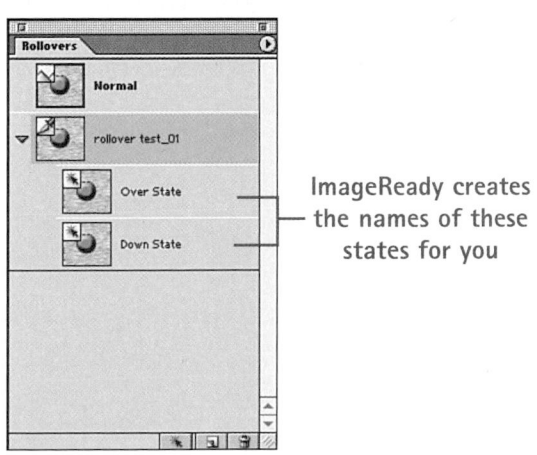

ImageReady creates the names of these states for you

7 Assign Layers to States

In the **Rollovers** palette, select the **Normal** state; in the **Layers** palette, select the layer that shows the color you want the button to be in its normal state. Repeat for the **Over** state and **Down** state. Choose **File, Save Optimized** to save the file, making sure that **Format, HTML and Images** is selected.

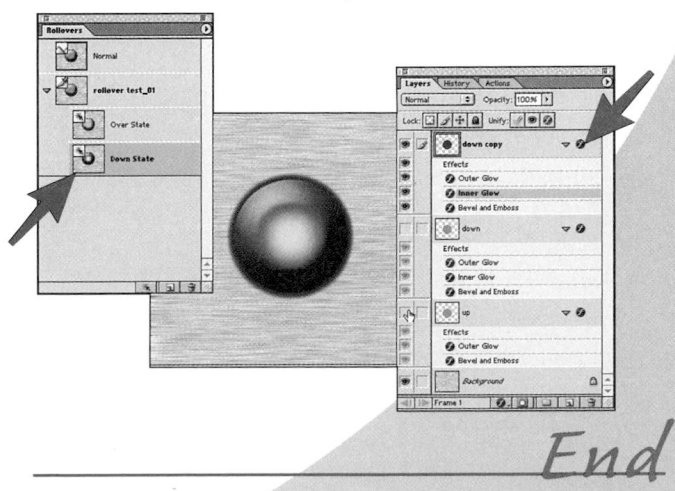

End

How to Build a Web Gallery

The **Web Photo Gallery** feature in Photoshop is a great way to quickly post to the Web a thumbnail directory of images that includes links to full-sized images, filenames, and the photographer's name. Anyone who wants to post a directory of images should take advantage of this feature, which is built around Photoshop's **Actions** technology. Users place images into a single folder, set the parameters, and step back. The script runs everything right before your eyes, building the code, optimizing the images and thumbnails, and creating all the links.

Begin

1 Select Web Photo Gallery

In Photoshop, choose **File, Automate, Web Photo Gallery** to open the **Web Photo Gallery** dialog box. Select a page layout from the **Styles** pop-up menu, observing the thumbnail on the right side of the dialog box to evaluate the results.

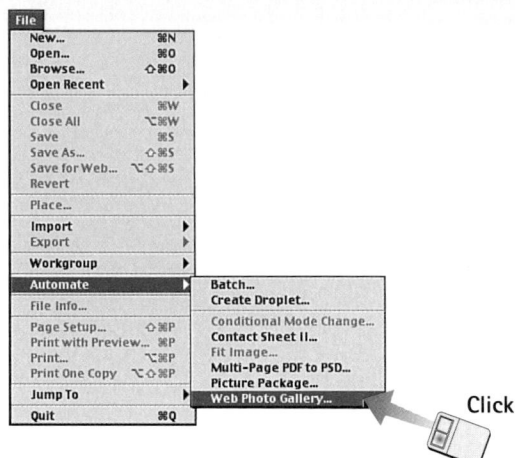

Click

2 Set File Source and Destination

In the **Folders** section, click the **Choose** button and navigate to the source folder (the folder that contains all the images). Click **Choose** to close the **Select Image Directory** dialog box. Now click the **Destination** button and navigate to the destination folder (where the final files and HTML documents will be stored). Click **Choose** to make your selection.

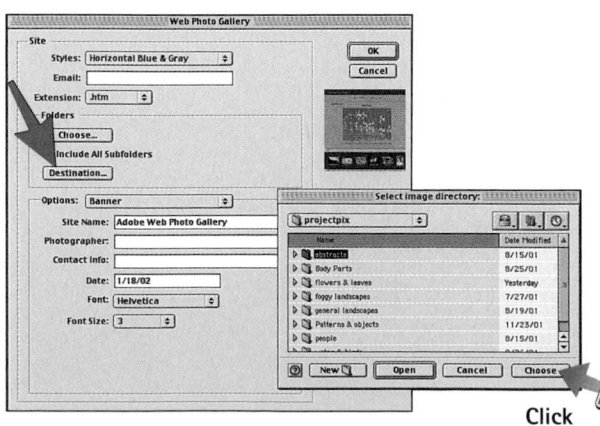

Click

3 Name and Date the Site

From the **Options** menu, select **Banner**. In the bottom section of the dialog box, fill in all appropriate fields, listing the site name, date, and photographer information. You can also select the date, font, and font size if you want.

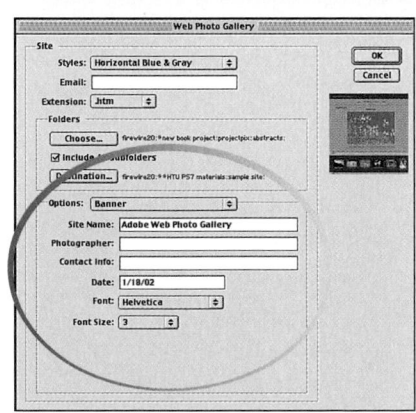

4 Resize Images

From the **Options** menu, select **Large Images** to see more options. Enable the **Resize Images** check box if you want to resize the main images that open from the thumbnails. With this box enabled, choose the image size from the adjacent pop-up menu and the JPEG compression rate from the **JPEG Quality** pop-up menu. To enter a specific JPEG compression value, select the quality setting from the **JPEG Quality** menu.

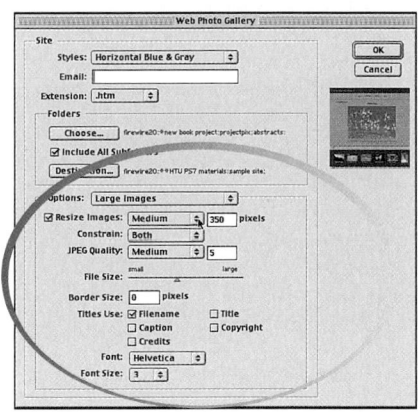

5 Set the Page Layout

Select **Thumbnails** from the **Options** pop-up menu. To use the filename or the text stored in the **File Info** section as a caption, check the appropriate box. Set the font parameters and the column and row parameters as desired.

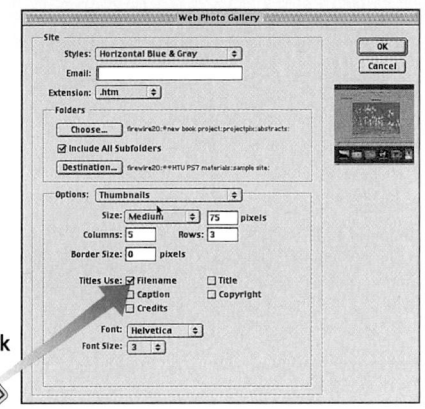

Click

6 Build and Test the Site

Click **OK** to build the Web Photo Gallery site. Photoshop runs the script on its own, opening files, compressing, and saving everything to the source folder you specified in Step 2. When the script is complete, Photoshop launches the **Web Photo Gallery** in a browser window for you to test. Click the thumbnails to test the links and make sure that everything is listed properly.

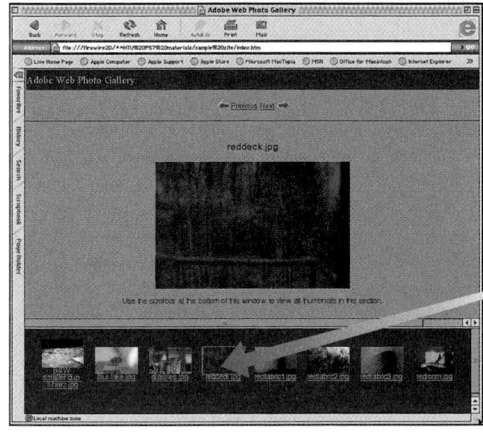

Click

How-To Hints

File Structure

Photoshop creates several files and folders within the source folder you designated to support the Web Photo Gallery. All the images are stored in an **images** folder; thumbnails go into a **thumbnails** folder. A separate HTML page also is created for each image and is stored in a folder called **pages**. The main gallery page is called **index.htm**. When posting your gallery page online, be sure to include all these elements on your server.

Custom Colors

Select **Custom Colors** from the **Options** menu to specify the text, link, background, and banner text colors. Click each color swatch to launch the **Color Picker** and select the desired color. Enable the **Only Web Colors** check box in the **Color Picker** to restrict the choices to Web-safe colors.

End

Task

13

Special Effects

Y ou can perform two kinds of tasks with Photoshop. One is the basic, utilitarian task of image processing, and the other is the dynamic, eye-catching effects you can create by using filters and special Photoshop commands.

Until this point, you've only looked at the image-processing side of things—exploring how to crop, rotate, and paint images. Although you almost always will need these skills more than you will need creative special effects, the reality is that special effects are just more fun. To that end, the tasks in this part of the book look at a variety of special effects you can apply fairly easily in Photoshop.

A good special effect is often the result of a careful selection so that the effect applies to only a portion of the image. A good special effect might also combine a filter or effect with surrounding layers or the previous image state. By creating effects in combination or by applying them to specific areas, you can create effects that are professional and distinctive.

The tasks in this part spend a fair amount of time looking at various filter options; with more than 100 native Photoshop filters built into version 7, we won't scratch the surface of all that's available. I've selected certain filters you can combine with other effects, such as blur or lighting effects. The filters I've selected also let me explain the general approach to working with filters, emphasizing the use of the **Fade** command and the filter color selection.

Of the filters not covered here, be sure to check out the **Artistic** and **Brush Strokes** filters, which create a staggering variety of strokes, textures, and abstractions. ●

How to Use Blending Modes

Blending modes are one of the fastest ways to experiment with imaging effects in your Photoshop files. Think of them as preset functions that apply a range of imaging effects that standard Photoshop commands can't touch. The basic function of a blending mode is to compare two sets of pixel data and combine them in different ways. Although I could write an entire chapter on exactly how these options work, 99 percent of Photoshop users simply experiment until they get an effect they like.

Begin

1 Blending Modes in Layers Palette

Select **Window, Layers** to open the **Layers** palette. The **Blending Mode** drop-down menu is at the top of the palette. Highlight a layer tile in the list and click and hold the menu to select one of the modes. The contents of the selected layer are compared with all the layers below it to achieve the result. Keep in mind that you cannot apply a blending mode to the **Background** layer.

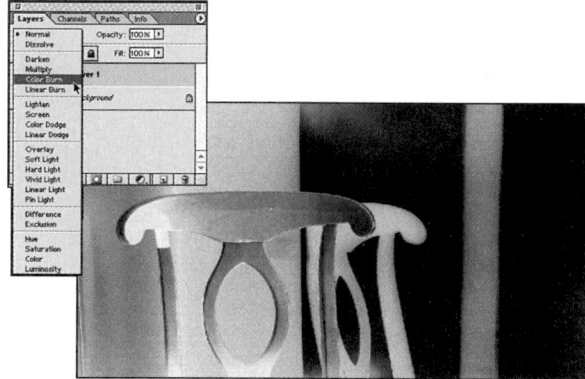

2 Blending Modes in Paint Tools

You can select any of the paint or shape tools and apply them using the blending modes. With the tool selected, select an option from the **Mode** menu in the **Options** bar. This approach to modes compares the values from the paint color or source data (if you're using the **Clone Stamp** or **History Brush** tool) with the underlying image. Blending modes are available with the following tools: **Airbrush, Paintbrush, Clone Stamp, History Brush, Gradient,** and **Shape.**

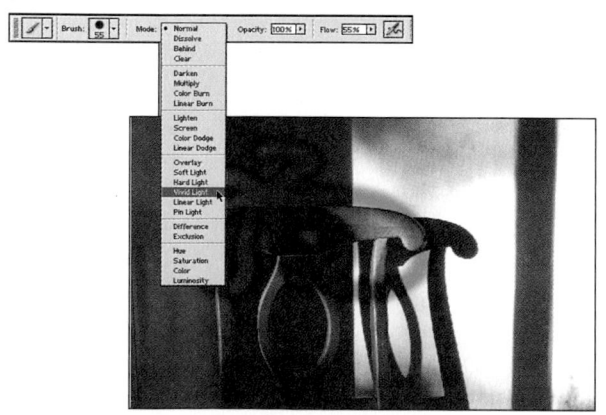

3 Blending Modes with Filters

After applying a filter, select **Edit, Fade <filter name>.** The **Fade** dialog box opens with an **Opacity** slider and a **Mode** menu. Select the desired mode from the menu and click **OK** to apply the effect. This approach to modes compares the original image data with the results of the filter effect.

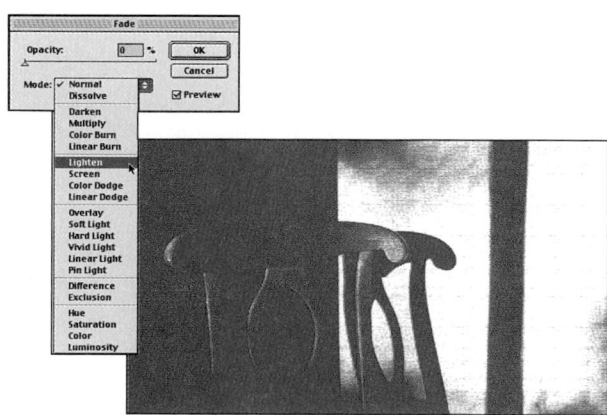

4 Blending Modes with Fills

Select **Edit, Fill** to launch the **Fill** dialog box. Select **Foreground Color** or **Background Color** from the **Use** menu and then select the desired blending mode from the **Mode** menu. If you want, you can enter a percentage value in the **Opacity** text box to apply the mode with a degree of transparency. This approach to modes compares the current foreground or background color with the image.

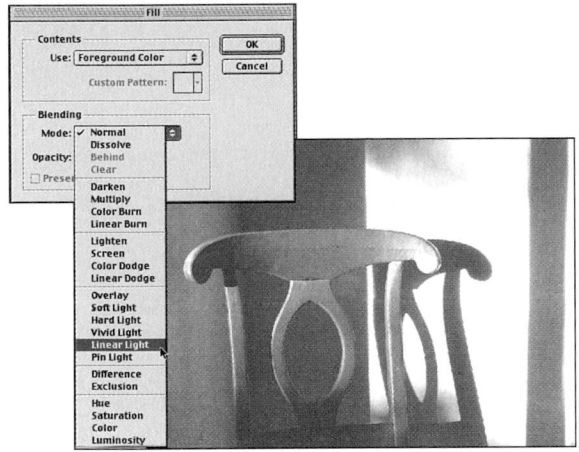

5 Blending Modes with Pattern Fills

Select **Edit, Fill** to launch the **Fill** dialog box. Select **Pattern** from the **Use** menu and select a pattern preset from the **Custom Pattern** list. Choose the desired blending mode from the **Mode** menu. If you want, enter a percentage value in the **Opacity** text box to apply the mode with a degree of transparency. This approach to modes compares the pattern values with the image.

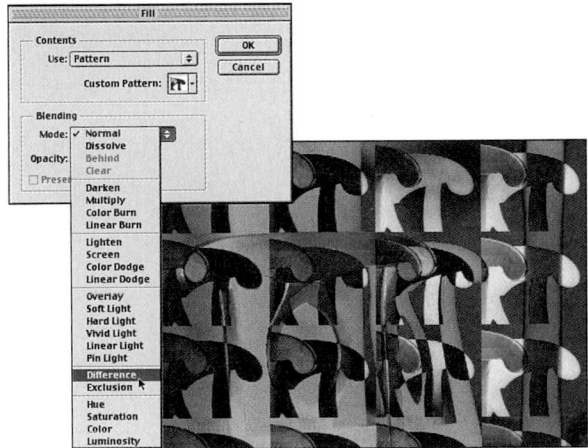

6 Blending Modes with History

Follow the steps in Part 8, Task 4, "How to Use the History Brush," to set the History source in the **History** palette. Then select **Edit, Fill** to launch the **Fill** dialog box. Select **History** from the **Use** menu and select the blending mode from the **Mode** menu. If you want, enter a percentage value in the **Opacity** text box to apply the mode with a degree of transparency. This approach to modes compares the selected history state with the image.

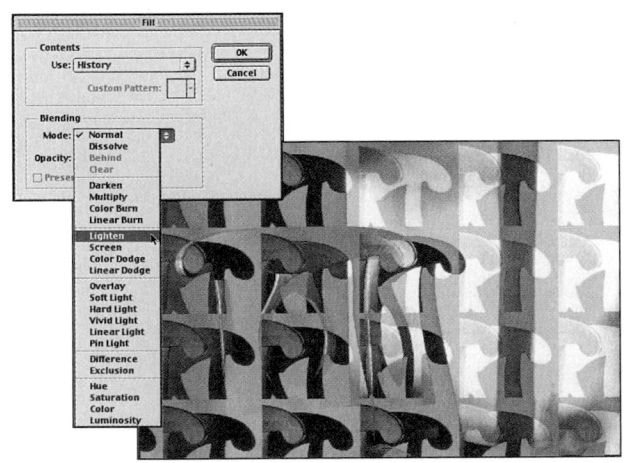

End

How-To Hints

Blending Modes with Tone and Color Adjustments

Because a blending mode requires the comparison of two sets of data, it's not possible to apply modes when using the color and tone adjustments found in the **Image, Adjustments** menu. However, you can create an adjustment layer and apply a blending mode to *that* layer as described in Step 1. This achieves the same result and also provides the flexibility of being able to hide or move the layer.

Blending with the Liquify Command

You can also fade and blend the **Liquify** command. After applying the **Liquify** command (**Filter, Liquify**), select **Edit, Fade Liquify** to launch the **Fade** dialog box. Select the desired mode and opacity and click **OK**.

How to Build a Glow Effect with Stroke Path

You can add an effect around a featured object that looks like a glowing halo that softly fades into the background. In addition to having aesthetic appeal, the effect described in this task works well when you're silhouetting an object against a white or dark background. It also works to separate the object from its background.

Begin

1 Open the File and Draw a Path

Choose **File, Open** and select the file you want to modify. Select the **Pen** tool from the toolbox. Use the techniques described in Part 3, "Selection Techniques," to draw a path around the desired object.

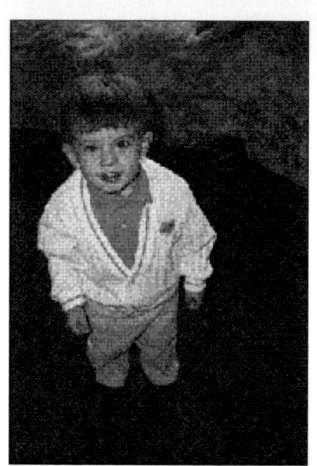

2 Select the Outside of the Object

Choose **Window, Paths** to open the **Paths** palette. With the path tile selected, choose **Make Selection** from the palette menu and click **OK** in the **Make Selection** dialog box that appears. Then choose **Select, Inverse** to deselect the object and select only the background.

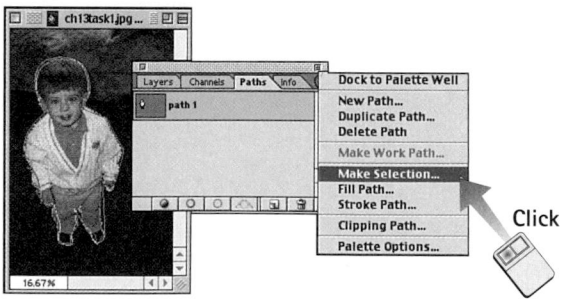

Click

3 Select the Glow Color

Double-click the **Foreground** color swatch in the toolbox; after the **Color Picker** opens, select a color for the glow. Click **OK** to close the **Color Picker.**

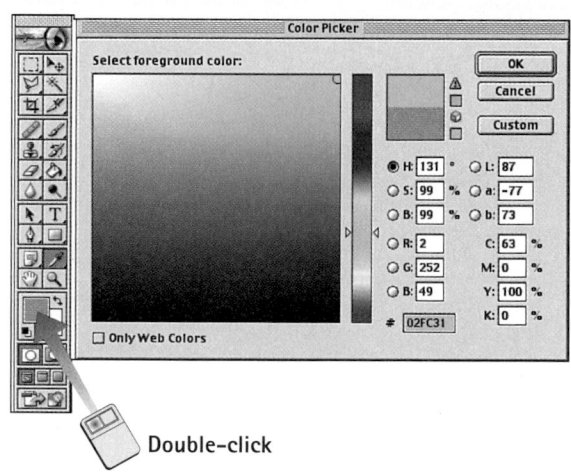

Double-click

4 Configure Settings

Select the **Paintbrush** tool in the toolbox. In the **Options** bar, drag the **Pressure** slider to about 8% or 10% percent and select a very large feathered brush. Click the **Brush** icon and set the **Master Diameter** slider for the brush size. Select the **Airbrush** icon in the **Options** bar and set the **Flow** and **Opacity** as desired.

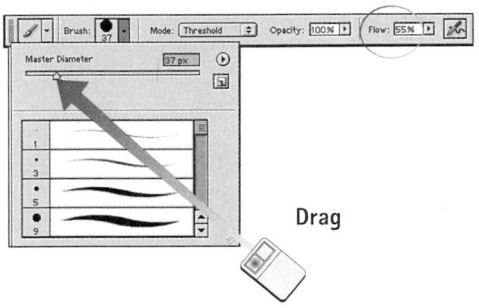

Drag

5 Stroke the Path

With the new path selected in the **Paths** palette, select **Stroke Path** from the palette menu. In the **Stroke Path** dialog box that appears, click **OK** to apply the stroke using the brush settings specified in Step 4.

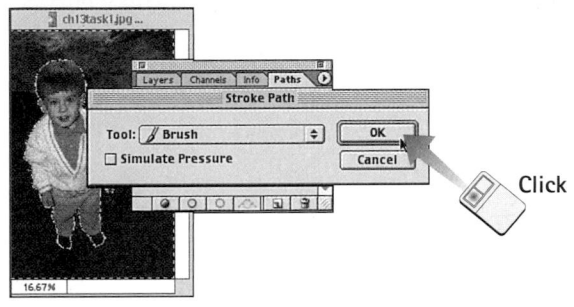

Click

6 Modify Brush Settings

Restroke the path several times by repeating Steps 4 and 5. Each time you reapply the stroke, select a smaller brush size and increase the pressure. This intensifies the stroke as it gets close to the object, simulating the glow effect. Deselect the path in the **Paths** palette to view the effect unobscured by the path.

How-To Hints

Hiding the Path

It can be hard to evaluate the effect of the stroke while the path is selected because the outline of the path obscures the image edge. After you apply each stroke, you may want to deselect the path in the **Paths** palette. After evaluating the stroke results, reselect the path (by clicking with one of the **Pen** tools) and continue building the effect.

Other Path-Creation Methods

You can also use any other method described in this book to create a selection. For example, you can use Quick Mask to paint a selection, or you can use the **Magnetic Lasso** tool. After you create the selection, you can easily transform it into a path by clicking the **Make Work Path** icon at the bottom of the **Paths** palette. You can then edit the path using any of the **Pen** tools from the toolbox.

End

How to Create Lighting Effects

The **Lighting Effects** filter casts multiple spotlights of different colors, falling across the image as though it were a flat surface. The filter gives you full control over the focus and direction of the light, as well as the color, exposure, surface texture, and ambient light characteristics. Use this filter to add depth and drama to an image, as well as to build interest into a composition by highlighting a focal point.

Begin

1 Open the File

Choose **File, Open** and select the file you want to modify.

2 Select Lighting Effects

Choose **Filter, Render, Lighting Effects** to open the **Lighting Effects** dialog box. You will see a thumbnail of the image on the left side of the dialog box, with one spotlight already placed over the image.

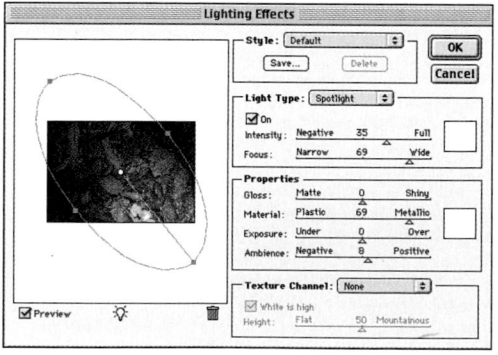

3 Reposition the Light

Click and drag the center of the light to reposition the light circle in relation to the thumbnail image. Then click the point where the light-source line meets the light circle and drag to move the light source. Finally, drag the handles on the light circle to widen or narrow the light beam as it is cast on the image.

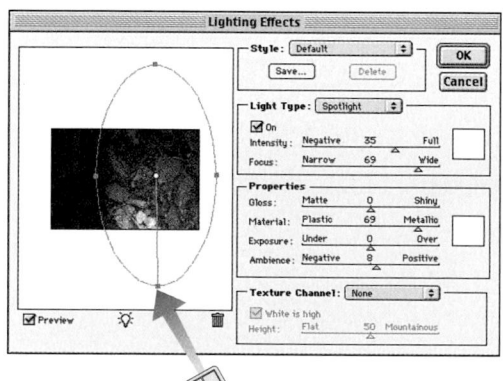

Drag

4 Configure the Light Type

Modify the **Intensity** and **Focus** sliders as desired to brighten the image and focus the light beam. Click the color swatch to display the **Color Picker** so that you can select a color for the light itself.

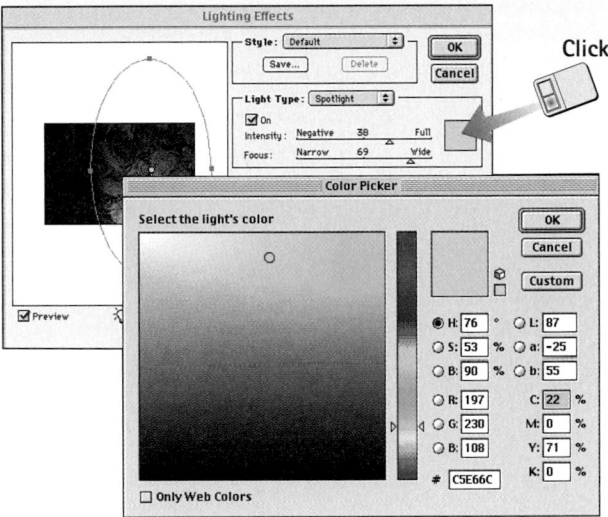

Click

5 Configure Properties

The four **Properties** sliders control the appearance of the surface of the image as well as the overall brightness of the exposure. Adjust the **Gloss** and **Material** sliders to modify the surface brightness. The **Exposure** slider controls image brightness, and the **Ambience** slider controls the amount of secondary ambient light. You can click the color swatch in this area of the dialog box to modify the color of the ambient light.

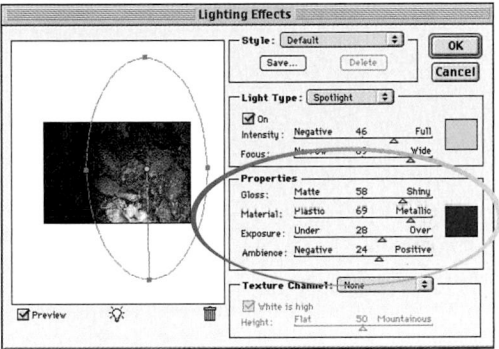

6 Add Other Lights As Needed

To add other light sources, click and drag the light bulb icon into the thumbnail image. Reposition and reset the parameters as described in Steps 3 through 5. The **Style** drop-down list at the top of the **Lighting Effects** dialog box contains many more fun options with which you can experiment. If you want to remove a light, drag it to the trash can icon at the bottom of the dialog box. Keep in mind that you need at least one light source.

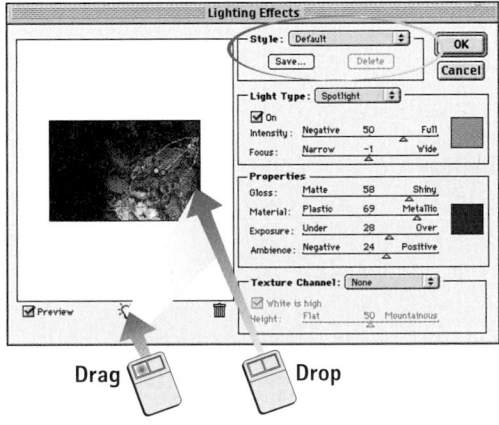

Drag   Drop

End

How-To Hints

Other Kinds of Light

In addition to spotlights, you can use omni-directional lights and directional lights. *Omni lights* radiate light equally in all directions from the center point; *directional lights* cast an even blanket of light across the entire image. Select **Directional** and **Omni** lights from the **Light Type** drop-down list in the **Lighting Effects** dialog box.

Using Presets

The **Style** drop-down list in the **Lighting Effects** dialog box offers 16 lighting presets. In addition to exploring these options, you can save your own combinations by clicking the **Save** button and naming the effect in the **Save As** dialog box that appears. This option saves the current configuration of Lighting Effects settings as a preset, which then appears in the **Style** list.

How to Apply a Radial Blur

A *radial blur* is an interesting effect that blurs an image in toward a center point or rotates it around a center point. The effect is similar to the photography technique of making a zoom lens time exposure that creates a tunnel effect in toward the subject. This is a good way to create emphasis on a central subject or image area and to control the composition as a whole.

Begin

1 Open the File and Select the Filter

Choose **File, Open** and select the file you want to modify. Choose **Filter, Blur, Radial Blur** to open the **Radial Blur** dialog box.

Click

2 Set the Amount Slider

Drag the **Amount** slider to control the degree of blur being applied to the image.

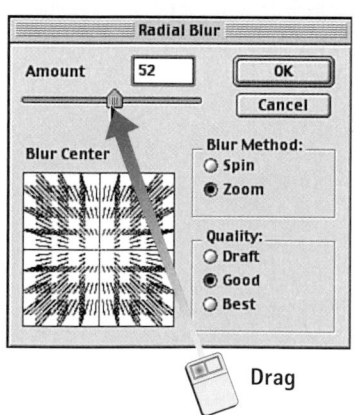

Drag

3 Set the Blur Method

Select either **Spin** or **Zoom** to determine whether the blur rotates around a center point in the image or zooms straight into the image.

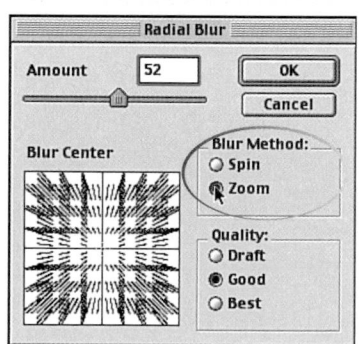

4 Set the Quality Setting

Select **Draft, Good,** or **Best** as the **Quality** mode, keeping in mind that the higher the quality, the longer it takes to apply the effect. Note that higher quality does not affect the file size, just the amount of time it takes to display the image.

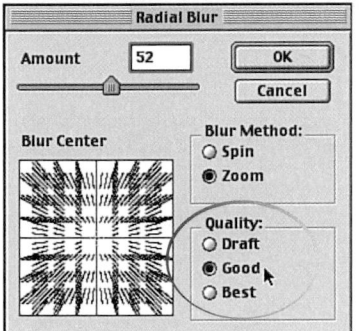

5 Apply the Filter

Click **OK** to apply the **Radial Blur** filter.

End

How-To Hints

Moving the Center Point

While working in the **Radial Blur** dialog box, click and drag in the grid preview section to move the center point of the effect. Try to position the center point of the grid over the corresponding focal point of the image.

Fading the Effect

Because the blur effect often obscures much of the image, consider restoring some of the image by choosing **Edit, Fade Radial Blur** immediately after you apply the **Radial Blur** filter and reducing the opacity or using a blending mode.

TASK **5**

How to Add Texture

Texture emphasizes the surface of an image, even as it creates a global graphic effect. Photoshop offers built-in texture maps that simulate sandstone, burlap, canvas, and other surfaces. To apply the **Texture** filter, you select a surface and then control the light direction and the size of the texture as it is mapped onto the surface of the image.

Begin

1 Open the File and Select the Filter

Choose **File, Open** and select the file you want to modify. Choose **Filter, Texture, Texturizer** to open the **Texturizer** dialog box.

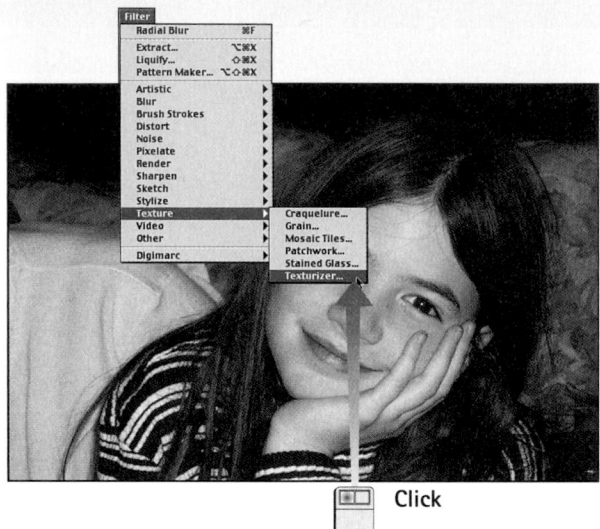

Click

2 Set the Texture Type

From the **Texture** drop-down list box, choose **Brick, Burlap, Canvas,** or **Sandstone.** Notice the results as they appear in the preview window.

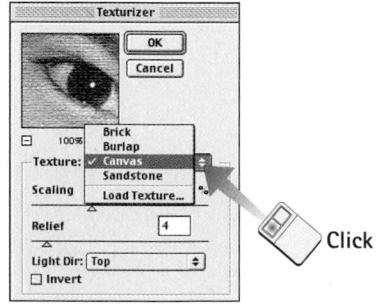

Click

3 Set the Scaling

Scaling refers to the size of the texture effect in relation to the image. In this example, the **Scaling** setting affects how coarse the weave of the canvas looks. Adjust the **Scaling** slider to the desired setting, watching the results in the preview window.

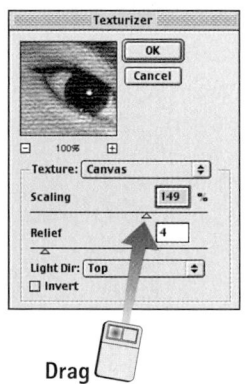

Drag

4 Set the Relief

Relief determines the strength of the texture as it is applied to the image. In this example, the **Relief** setting affects just how "thick" the canvas pattern looks. Adjust the **Relief** slider to achieve the desired effect.

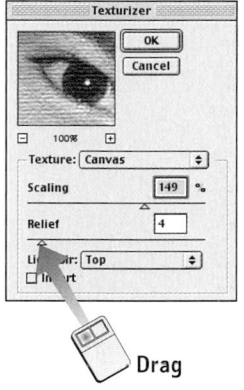

Drag

5 Set the Light Direction

Select a light direction from the **Light Dir** drop-down list. Experiment with selections and observe the effect produced in the preview window.

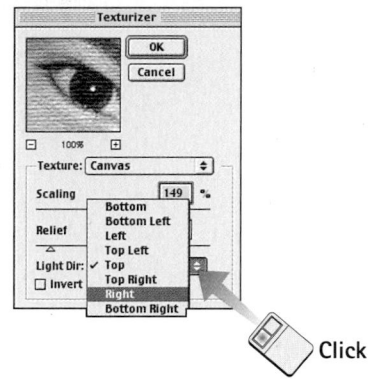

Click

6 Apply the Effect

Click **OK** to close the **Texturizer** dialog box and apply the effect.

End

How-To Hints

Using Other Texture Filters

In addition to the **Texturizer** filter, five other texture filters are offered on the same **Texture** submenu: **Craquelure, Grain, Mosaic Tiles, Patchwork,** and **Stained Glass.** Experiment with all of them to see how they differ and how you can use them to enhance an image.

Clicking Thumbnail for Before and After Comparison

As you work in the **Texturizer** dialog box, the results of the current settings are displayed in real-time in the preview thumbnail. To compare the current state of the image with the original state, click and hold the mouse button while the cursor is over the preview thumbnail; the thumbnail reverts to the original, unaltered image.

How to Add a Lens Flare

Adding a *lens flare* to an image creates a bright spot of light that simulates the lens flare created when a photographer points a camera lens into the sun. Although this is a bad thing for photographers, the lens flare effect often works as a design element, adding a specular accent (a white highlight) to a digital composite.

1 Open the File

Choose **File, Open** and select the file you want to modify.

2 Select the Lens Flare Filter

Choose **Filter, Render, Lens Flare** to open the **Lens Flare** dialog box.

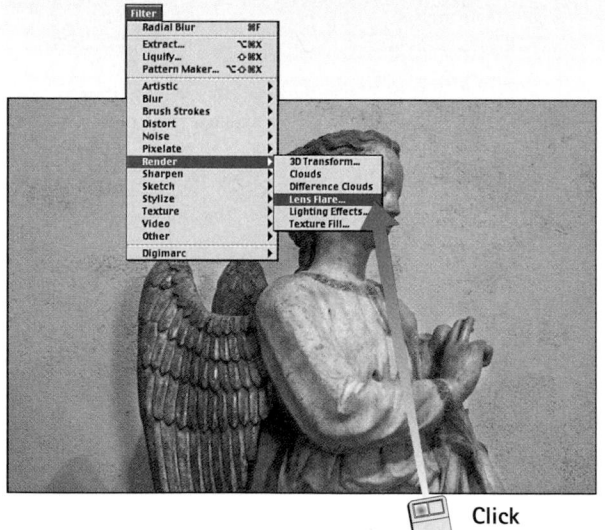

Click

3 Move the Flare Center

A small lens flare preview appears in the **Flare Center** thumbnail of the dialog box. Click and drag the cross at the center of the flare to reposition it in relation to the image.

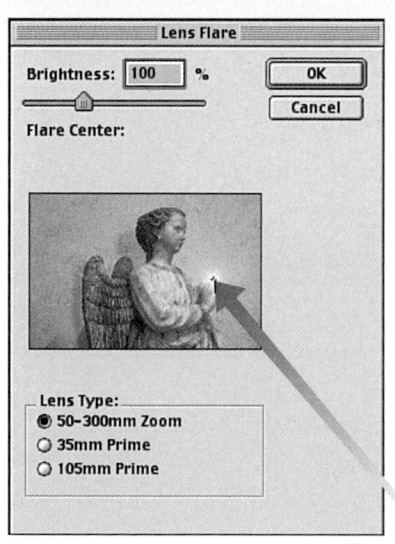

Drag

4 Set the Brightness

Adjust the **Brightness** slider to control the intensity of the flare. Observe the effect in the preview window.

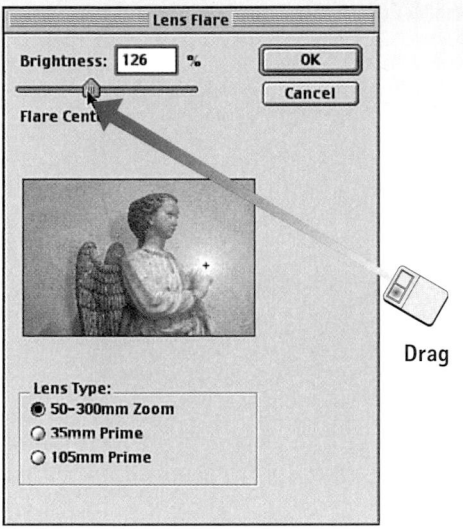

Drag

5 Choose the Lens Type

Select one of the three options at the bottom of the dialog box to specify the type of lens simulated in the effect. Each lens effect mimics the effect of a different focal-length camera lens.

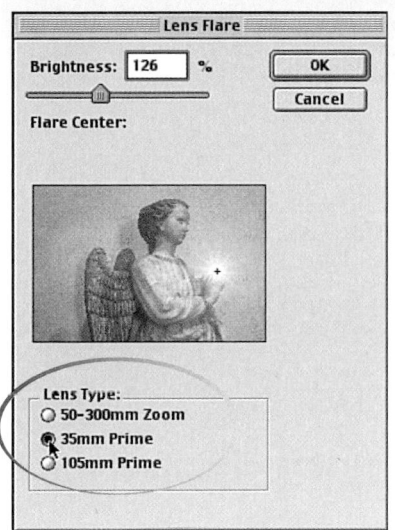

6 Apply the Effect

Click **OK** to close the **Lens Flare** dialog box and apply the filter.

End

How-To Hints

Building Lens Flare Animations

The **Lens Flare** is a perfect filter to use when building a progressive GIF animation, as described in Part 12, Task 4, "How to Build Filter-Based GIF Animations." Increase the brightness progressively in the animation to create the effect of a starburst.

How to Add Noise Texture

In digital imaging, *noise* refers to a coarse, pointillist pattern that is applied to create a graphic feel in an image. Noise is often used when an image is blurry to start with and resists sharpening with Photoshop's standard filters. In this case, you may like the effect created when you add noise and create a graphic look for the image, masking the lack of sharpness.

Begin

1 Open the File

Choose **File, Open** and select the file you want to modify.

2 Select the Noise Filter

Choose **Filter, Noise, Add Noise** to open the **Add Noise** dialog box.

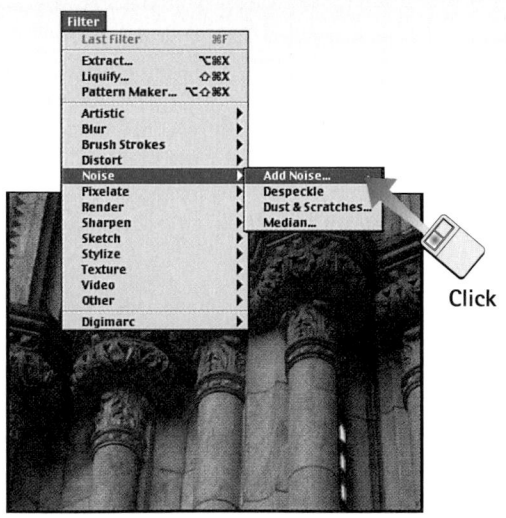

Click

3 Set the Amount

Move the **Amount** slider to control the amount of noise in the image. Observe the effect in both the preview window in the dialog box and in the original image area.

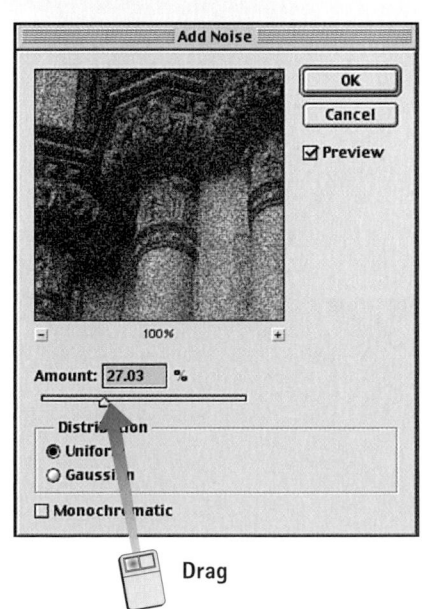

Drag

4 Set the Distribution

Select either the **Uniform** or **Gaussian** option to control how the effect is applied. The **Gaussian** option tends to mimic more closely the noise that appears on the emulsion of photographic film.

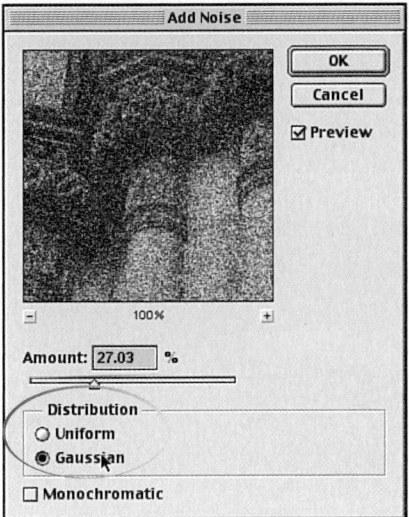

5 Select the Monochromatic Effect

Enable or disable the **Monochromatic** check box and observe the effect this option has on the image. By default, noise is added to an image using randomly colored pixels. These colors can be distracting in some images; the **Monochromatic** option adds noise using grayscale pixels.

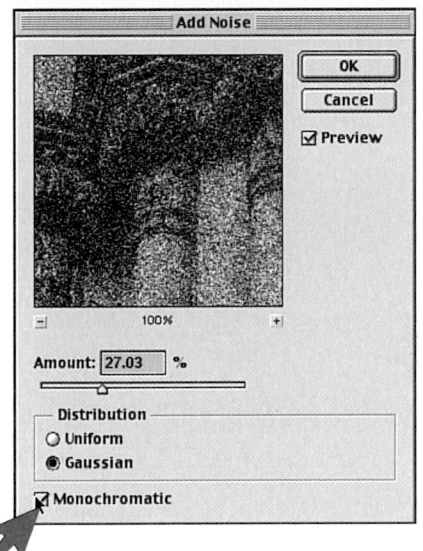

6 Apply the Effect

Click **OK** to close the **Add Noise** dialog box and apply the effect.

End

How-To Hints

Noise on a Layer

Instead of applying the **Noise** filter directly to the image, create a new layer filled with a color. Apply the **Noise** filter to the new layer and then adjust the opacity or blending modes to combine the color layer with the image layer. This approach lets you turn the effect on and off and apply it selectively using layer masks (see Part 11, Task 7, "How to Add a Layer Mask").

How to Simulate Photo Grain

Photoshop enables you to simulate the softer grain effects found in photography. This effect works well when you need to emphasize the photographic aspects of an image while adding a uniform graphic feel. The only problem with the Photoshop **Grain** filter is that the grain is rendered in a spectrum of bright colors—which is nothing like the grain found in photography. To create more natural colors, this task converts the image to Lab color and isolates the effect to the **Lightness** channel to maintain natural color.

Begin

1 Open the File and Convert to Lab Color

Choose **File, Open** and select the file you want to modify. Choose **Image, Mode, Lab Color** to convert the image into Lab color mode. In this example, we are using Lab color so that we can add a special effect to the **Lightness** channel without affecting the other color channels.

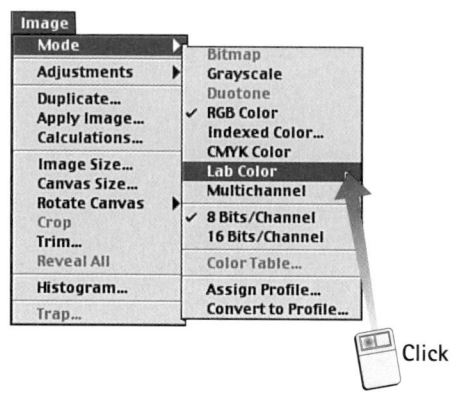

Click

2 Select the Lightness Channel

Choose **Window, Channels** to open the **Channels** palette. Highlight the **Lightness** channel to select it and click the visibility icon (the eye) for the Lab composite image. This action makes only the **Lightness** channel visible and also previews the full composite image.

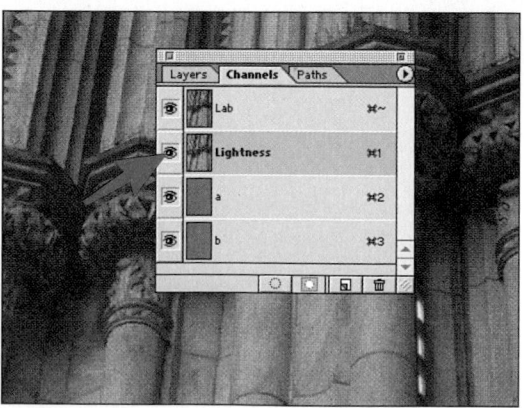

3 Select the Grain Filter

Choose **Filter, Texture, Grain** to open the **Grain** dialog box.

Click

4 Set the Grain Type

Choose the overall grain pattern from the **Grain Type** drop-down list at the bottom of the dialog box. Notice the effect your selection has on the preview window at the top of the dialog box.

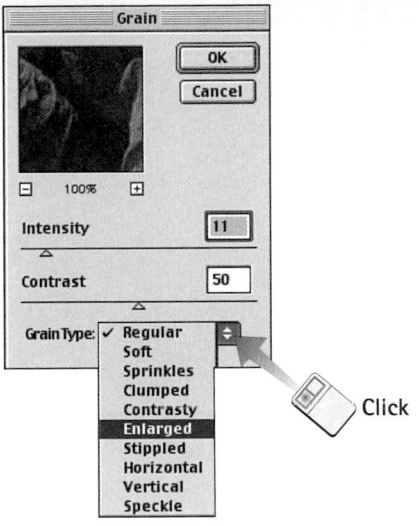

Click

5 Set Intensity and Contrast

Adjust the **Intensity** slider to control the amount of grain applied to the image. Adjust the **Contrast** slider to make the grain pattern more or less pronounced.

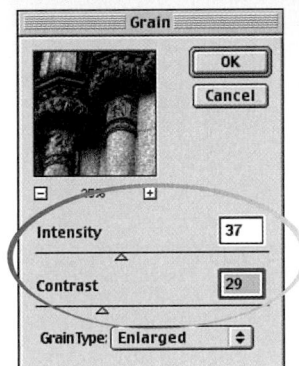

6 Apply the Effect

Click **OK** to close the **Grain** dialog box and apply the effect. Depending on the file format you want to save the file in, you may want to convert the color mode back to RGB or CMYK.

End

How-To Hints

Experimenting with Grain Type

You can select one of 10 effects from the **Grain Type** list in the **Grain** dialog box; these effects offer a wide range of styles. Take some time to experiment with the options, choosing the right effect for your image.

How to Distort an Image with Liquify

Liquify is a fun, interactive technique that allows you to push and smudge the pixels around in an image, creating a brushed-in, fluid distortion. The entire process feels something like finger painting, and you can vary the brush size and pressure as you work.

Begin

1 Open the File

Choose **File, Open** and select the file you want to modify.

2 Choose Liquify

Choose **Image, Liquify** to launch the **Liquify** interface window.

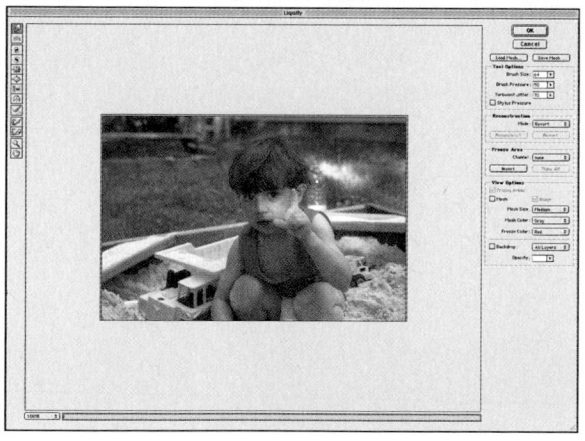

3 Protect Image Areas

Select the **Freeze** tool from the toolbar on the left of the window, specify the brush size and pressure in the **Tool Options** section, and brush a mask over the areas you want to protect. The distortion effect will not be applied to the areas you freeze.

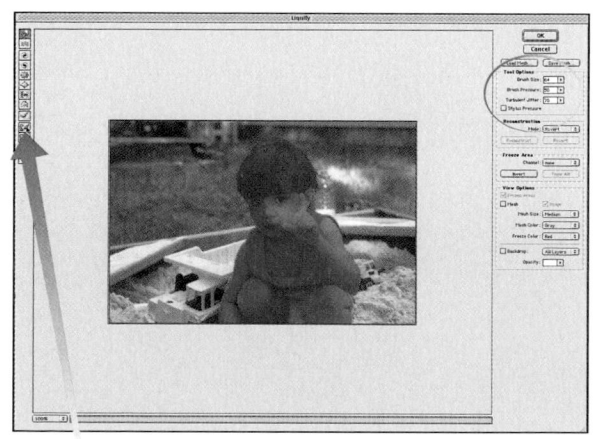

 Click

4 Distort the Image

Select any of the distortion brushes from the toolbar. From the **Tool Options** section, select a brush size and pressure and then paint the effect into the image. Drag the brush with a circular motion and let the effect build to the desired intensity. The distortion tool options include the **Warp, Turbulence, Twirl Clockwise, Twirl Counterclockwise, Pucker, Bloat, Shift Pixels,** and **Reflection.**

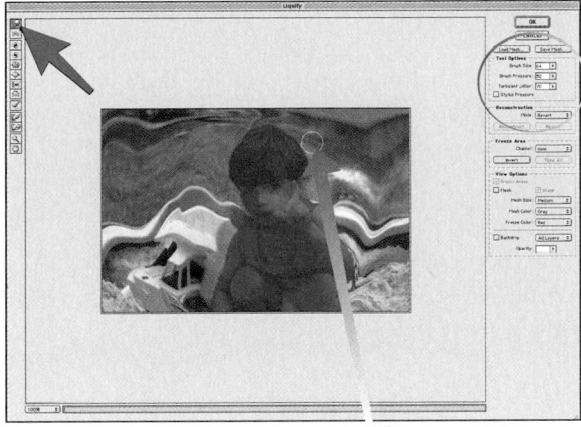

Drag

5 Reconstruct the Original Image

To diminish or erase the effect from Step 4, select the **Reconstruct** tool, and select the desired mode from the **Reconstruction** section. Brush over the distorted area until the effect is reduced or eliminated.

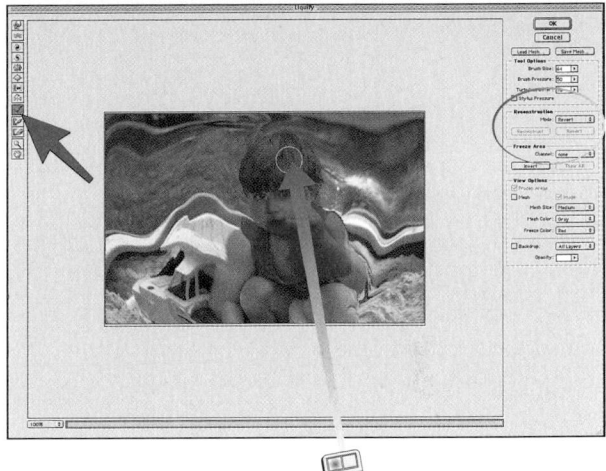

Drag

6 Modify the Protected Area

To modify the mask created in Step 3 so that you can make further modifications, select the **Thaw** tool from the toolbar and brush over the mask to erase or lighten it. You can continue to apply distortions, erase them, and adjust the mask until you achieve the desired effect. Click **OK** to close the **Liquify** window.

How-To Hints

When All Else Fails, Revert!

If the distortion gets out of hand and you want to go back to where you started, click the **Revert** button in the **Reconstruction** section of the **Liquify** window. Similarly, you can click the **Thaw All** button in the **Freeze Area** section to completely erase an existing mask.

Viewing Options

To control how effects and masks are presented in the **Liquify** window, make modifications in the **View Options** section. You can control the presentation of the mask, image, and the underlying mesh grid that controls the actual distortion.

End

How to Create a Halftone Pattern

The **Halftone Pattern** filter creates a graphic effect that simulates a halftone screen being applied to an image. This effect reduces the image to two colors and creates a stylized graphic feel that is distinctive and unique. The colors used for the filter are taken from the foreground and background colors, so be sure to select these colors before applying the filter, as explained in Step 2.

Begin

1 Open the File

Choose **File, Open** and select the file you want to modify.

2 Select Colors

Because the halftone effect uses the foreground and background colors, you must set these colors before applying the filter. Click the **Foreground** color swatch in the toolbox and choose the desired color from the **Color Picker.** Click the **Background** color swatch and select the second color.

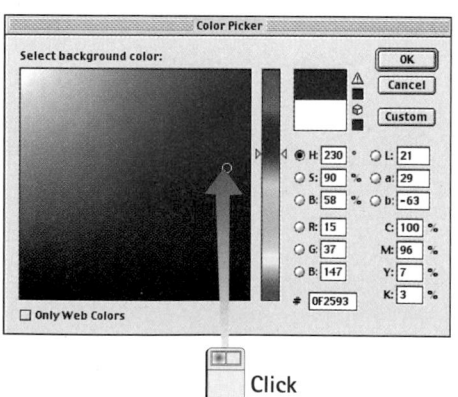

Click

3 Choose the Halftone Pattern Filter

Choose **Filter, Sketch, Halftone Pattern** to open the **Halftone Pattern** dialog box.

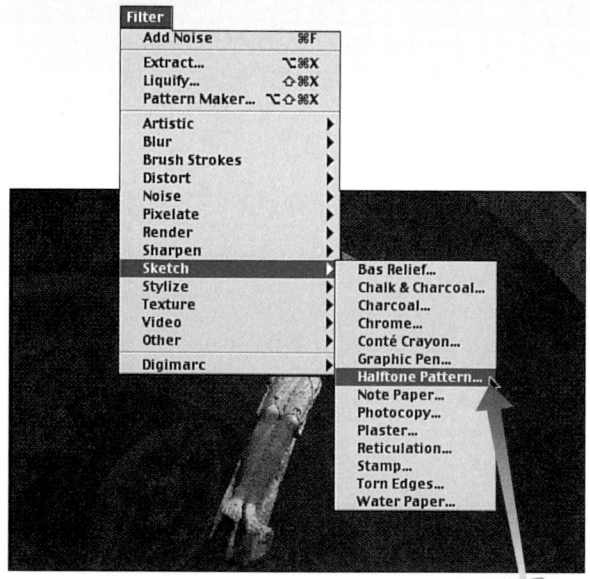

Click

4 Select the Pattern Type

From the **Pattern** drop-down list box, choose **Dot, Circle,** or **Line** to determine the actual halftone pattern to be used. Observe the effect your selection has on the preview window at the top of the dialog box.

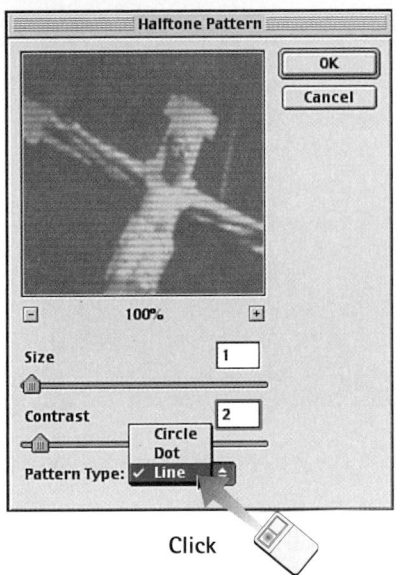

Click

5 Select the Size and Contrast

Adjust the **Size** slider to control the size of the halftone pattern relative to the image. Adjust the **Contrast** slider to control how prominently the effect is applied to the image.

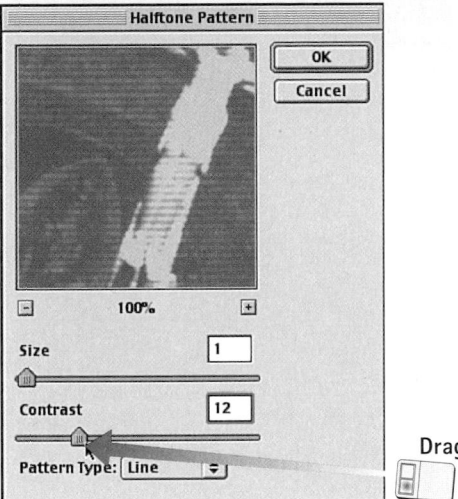

Drag

6 Apply the Effect

Click **OK** to close the **Halftone Pattern** dialog box and apply the effect to the image.

End

How-To Hints

Fading with Blending Modes to Combine Effects

Halftone pattern effects work very well with blending modes because of their graphic feel and flat areas of color. When combined with the original image, interesting hybrid effects can be achieved. Choose **Edit, Fade Halftone Pattern** directly after applying the filter to use the blending modes and to change the opacity of the filter.

Switching the Color Order

The **Halftone Pattern** filter applies the foreground color to the shadows and the background color to the highlights. If you don't like the color distribution as initially applied, undo the filter and click the **Switch Colors** icon in the toolbox to reverse foreground and background colors. Reapply the filter and compare the results.

How to Apply a Ripple Effect

Photoshop is full of filter effects that can create wavy, distorted lines within an image. In fact, an entire filter submenu, called **Distort,** is full of these effects. The ripple effect described in this task uses the **ZigZag** filter to create the look of rippling concentric circles across the image surface.

Begin

1 Open the File

Choose **File, Open** and select the file you want to modify.

2 Open the ZigZag Filter

Choose **Filter, Distort, ZigZag** to open the **ZigZag** dialog box.

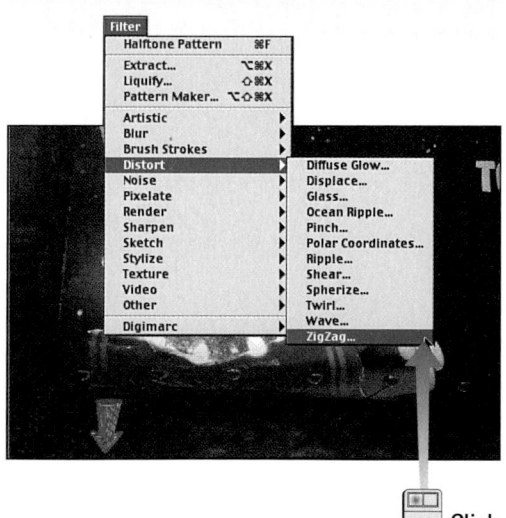

Click

3 Set the Style

From the **Style** drop-down list, choose a distortion pattern. The pattern you choose is reflected in the wireframe preview window at the bottom of the dialog box and in the preview window at the top of the dialog box.

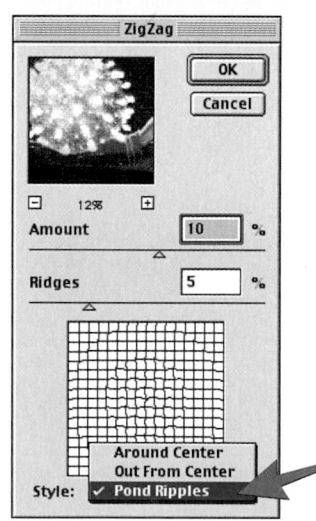

4 Set the Amount

Adjust the **Amount** slider to control the percentage of distortion. Watch the effect of your changes in the preview windows.

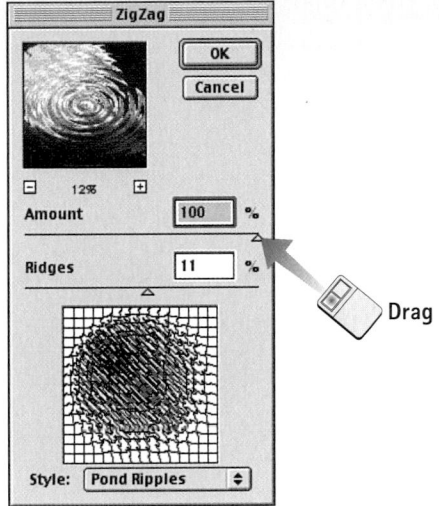

Drag

5 Set the Ridges

Adjust the **Ridges** slider to control how many circular ridges are applied in the pattern.

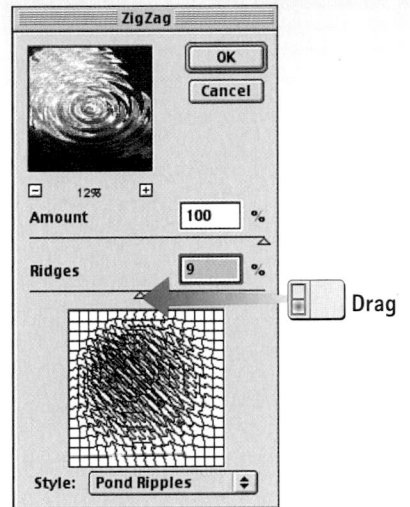

Drag

6 Apply the Filter

Click **OK** to close the **ZigZag** dialog box and apply the filter.

End

How-To Hints

Negative Amounts Implode

Use negative percentages with the **Amount** slider in Step 4 to create an imploding effect that draws into the center rather than emanates out from the center.

How to Brush In a Filter Effect

Instead of applying an effect to an entire image or to a selected area, you can opt to "brush in" an effect using the **History** brush. You have absolute control with respect to the brush size and the opacity of the effect and can create great effects using any of the built-in and plug-in filters available with Photoshop.

Begin

1 Open the File

Choose **File, Open** and select the file you want to modify.

2 Apply a Filter

Apply any of Photoshop's filters to create a desired effect. In this example, we applied the **Graphic Pen** filter to the image.

3 Open the History Palette

Choose **Window, History** to open the **History** palette. Click the snapshot at the top of the palette to revert the image to its previous state. The state reflecting the filter application is still in the **History** palette but is grayed out. When you start with the History "snapshot," you have something (an effect) to brush back into the photograph.

Click

4 Set the History Source

Click in the column to the left of the filter state you applied in Step 2 to set the History brush source for the filter effect. In this example, we are setting the History brush so that it will paint in the Graphic Pen filter.

Click

5 Set History Brush Options

In the **Options** bar, set the **Opacity** as desired and choose a brush size from the **Brushes** section.

6 Paint the Effect

Move the cursor into the image and paint with the History brush to selectively brush in the filter effect. In this example, we paint the Graphic Pen filter over the background to give it a more textured appearance.

Drag

How-To Hints

Applying More Than One Filter

To paint from more than one filter source, apply multiple filters and save a snapshot of each one in the **History** palette. To save a snapshot, choose **New Snapshot** from the **History** palette menu when the filter effect is active. Set the History brush source to the desired snapshot to paint with a specific filter effect.

End

Glossary

A

actions   Preset scripts that automate repetitive tasks. With just a single mouse click, you can create special effects without having a clue as to how they are done.

adjustment layer   A color-correction layer that allows you to adjust the tone or color in an image without altering the content of the layers beneath it.

alias   The name for the jagged edges ("jaggies") that are seen when an image doesn't contain enough information to make a smooth transition on angled or rounded edges. Also called *stair-stepping* because the edge may look like a series of steps.

alpha channel   The "layer" in which you can save a selection.

anti-aliasing   The method of reducing jagged edges in an image or text by slightly blurring the edges of shapes and text to make them appear smooth.

B

baseline shift   The process of raising or lowering text characters to control positioning or alignment in a design. A positive baseline shift value raises the text, while a negative value lowers it, as calculated from the initial baseline positioning.

bicubic   An interpolation method that delivers the highest quality results when enlarging an image. Other interpolation methods are bilinear and Nearest Neighbor.

blending modes   Preset functions that compare a source image with new data such as a separate layer or paint tool. Blending modes compare and combine these two sets of pixel data to create unique imaging effects.

border   The outlined edge of a path or selection. Borders can be selected independently and can be filled and stroked.

C

caching levels   A Photoshop method for speeding screen redraws by storing commonly used elements for rapid access. You can set the number of levels you want to use on the Image Cache page of the Preferences box.

clipping paths   A method of exporting a file for use in a vector or layout application. The clipping path format masks out part of the image (for example, you can use this method to drop out the background in a product shot so that only the product object is visible).

CLUT (Color LookUp Table)   *See* GIF file.

CMYK color model   A color process using cyan, magenta, yellow, and black color variables. Used primarily in offset printing, CMYK color sports a smaller color range than its RGB counterpart. The conversion process between RGB and CYMK must be managed to ensure consistent and high-quality results.

CMYK image   A color image that uses the CMYK color model, featuring cyan, magenta, yellow, and black channels.

color model A way of quantifying color. There are several color models in which you can identify a particular color; CMYK, RGB, HSB, Web, and Lab colors are all supported in Photoshop. In the RGB color model, for example, a particular color is identified as having a particular quantity of red, a particular amount of blue, and a particular amount of green. The range of available color varies between color models, so it is important to use a model that is suited to the specific image, as well as the overall Web or printing process being used.

Color Picker A dialog box from which you can select the foreground or background color. The Color Picker displays a window with a range of color in a particular hue; move the Hue slider to see a different range of color. Click in the color window to select a color. The selected color is quantified in terms of Hue/Saturation/Brightness, Red/Green/Blue, Lab, CMYK, and hexadecimal (if you need to specify your colors to that degree).

color space The range of unique colors that can be created for a given color model such as RGB or CMYK.

contact sheet A Photoshop file that contains thumbnail references for all the images in a given folder. You can use contact sheets to send your client a list of images for approval, to archive, or just to help organize your graphics visually rather than with archaic filenames.

crop To cut an image down to a specific square or rectangular section, excluding all other unwanted areas.

D

dithering The process used to fool the human eye into seeing more colors in an image than are really there. The process works by combining two or more existing colors into patterns. When viewed by the human eye, these patterns appear as solid colors.

dot gain A measurement that describes and anticipates the way ink spreads and is absorbed on different kinds of paper. For example, ink spreads a lot more on newsprint than it does on glossy card stock, so you have to compensate to keep the dots from filling in completely.

duotone A grayscale image that is tinted with one color for a graphic effect. Although duotones were originally designed to extend the tonal range of standard grayscale images, designers have embraced them for their graphic look and feel.

E

EPS format Stands for Encapsulated PostScript file. The process of converting an image into postscript data while bundling a lower-resolution preview so that the image can be viewed and proofed onscreen.

exposure The degree of effect applied to the image. You can also think of it as *intensity* or *pressure*.

F

feather To dissipate the hard-line edge of an area, creating a vignette effect. You can feather a border, for example, so that it fades off into the surrounding area. You can also feather a selection line. When you choose a brush style, you can choose a brush that has a feathered tip.

File Browser A floating content window that allows the review, selection, and launch of image files from within Photoshop. The File Browser also shows file information and the global directory structure.

file extension The three (or more) letters after the dot in a filename (for example, in **filename.ext**, **.ext** is the extension). The file extension frequently identifies the format of the file. For example, the extension **.txt** tells you that the file is an unformatted text file; the extension **.jpg** tells you the file is a JPEG graphics file.

flatten In the context of layers, flattening the image involves compressing all the layers into one flat background layer.

flip To change the presentation of an image as if by turning a print of the image over on the desktop—any text is now mirrored (reversed) and left hands look like right hands. When you flip an image, make sure that you are not misrepresenting anything.

frameset targeting The Web design process of directing links to load contents into a specific frame within an Internet site's frameset.

G

gamma A term used to measure relative monitor brightness. Standard gamma settings are 1.8 for Macintosh and 2.2 for Windows.

gamut The range of unique colors that can be created for a given color model such as RGB or CMYK. Also referred to as *color space*.

GIF file An efficient, compact file, perfect for use on the Web. GIF files create a color lookup table (CLUT) for each image; each color (up to 256 colors) in the image is categorized and stored in the CLUT. Because of this table (as well as algorithms that track repeating pixels), GIF files compress very well.

gradient A fill that gradually blends two or more colors together.

grayscale The method for creating a continuous-tone monochrome image using a tonal palette consisting of 256 shades of gray.

grid An underlying matrix of lines that can be used for general alignment of all items on the page.

guide A user-defined alignment line that is drawn from the rulers. Guides can also be used in ImageReady to slice an image for use on the Web.

H

halftone A filter effect that reduces an image to two colors and creates a stylized graphic feel.

Heal Brush A modified version of the Clone tool that uses color, tone, and texture data to smooth blemishes and unwanted areas within an image.

histogram A profile that charts and quantifies the distribution of image pixels across the entire tonal spectrum.

hot spots Active areas within Web site imagemaps that include links to other pages or actions. These hot spots change the cursor icon as the mouse passes over them; the change in cursor shape identifies the area's additional functionality.

I

image caching A buffering process that speeds screen redraws and scrolling.

image prep tasks *See* pre-processing tasks.

imagemap A Web image that includes hot spots with links to other pages, or triggers for other actions.

J

jitter Variations in brush strokes that can be controlled by the Shape Dynamics options in the Brushes palette.

JPEG file A file format that works very well for photographic images because the compression algorithm tends to create artifacts that pixelate the image. Although these effects can degrade the quality of hard-edged graphics, they are easier to hide in photographs.

K

kerning   The spacing between individual pairs of letters.

L

layer   A Photoshop method for separating image components for easy access and editing. Layers follow the metaphor of clear acetate overlays that can be stacked and rearranged.

layer mask   A mask that conceals a portion of a layer without actually deleting it, allowing the lower layers to show through those areas of the mask.

layer set   A complete group of layers that can be moved deleted, or copied within the Layers palette as a single unit. Layer sets can be viewed in the Layers palette and can be expanded or compressed as needed to view details of the set's contents.

layer tile   In the Layers palette, each layer is represented as a horizontal tile. These tiles can be hidden or revealed, linked, grouped, or combined into working layer sets.

leading   The spacing between lines of text. Leading values are usually expressed in points and are compared to the font's point size.

lens flare   A bright spot of light on an image that simulates the lens flare created when a photographer points a camera lens into the sun.

lossy   A term normally used to describe the nature of the compression method used by the JPEG format. The compression format is referred to as *lossy* because some information is discarded, or lost. It is because of this technique that JPEG images can be compressed to a much smaller file size than images compressed with other formats. In the Save For Web dialog box, the Lossy option removes colors to create a smaller file size.

M

mask   The process of defining an area of an image or layer for selection, modification, or transparency.

merge   In the context of layers, merging refers to combining some of the layers in a design while keeping other layers separate.

mode   A way to apply editing and painting techniques. Palettes have Mode drop-down lists. *See also* palette.

multiple views   More than one window opened for a single image file. You can open two separate windows of the same file, specify a high rate of magnification for editing in one window, and leave the other at full screen size to check your progress as you work.

N

naming format   A process that controls the automatic naming of files when new files are created, as used in ImageReady image slicing. When selected from the File, Output Settings, Slices menu, names can be automatically generated using a wide range of criteria, such as alphanumeric sequences, date stamping, and file format.

noise   A coarse, pointillist pattern that is frequently applied to an already blurry image to create a graphic feel.

O–P

Options bar   The horizontal bar at the top of the Photoshop and ImageReady interface windows that contains all available options for the currently selected tool.

palette One of many control elements you can use to fine-tune your use of Photoshop and ImageReady tools. A palette is associated with a single element of the image (for example, the Brushes palette controls the size and shape of the cursor when you are using a painting tool). Each palette has a drop-down menu of options associated with the element it controls.

palette menu When any palette is open, a menu of options specific to that palette is available. Click the right-facing arrow at the top of the palette to display the palette menu of options.

palette well The darker gray box at the end of the Options bar that collapses and stores palettes for easy access. To add a palette to the well, drag a palette over the dark gray box; the palette collapses so that only the palette's title tab is visible.

path A linear outline of an image area or shape.

Pattern Maker A Photoshop filter module that generates complex, random patterns from user-defined image selections.

Photoshop EPS format *See* EPS format.

Photoshop PDF format Stands for Portable Document File. A format used by Adobe for compressing and viewing images and documents, based on the Adobe Acrobat family of compression and viewing software.

pixels Dots that serve as the individual building blocks of an image.

plug-in Third-party filters and utilities that extend the basic functionality of Photoshop.

posterize To reduce all areas of an image to flat color, eliminating shading and fine detail.

pre-processing tasks Preliminary tasks that typically clean up an image and get it ready for layout placement or more in-depth editing. These tasks include cropping, rotating, and using the Unsharp Mask filter.

Preset Manager In Photoshop, a single, multi-tabbed palette that allows you to preset the settings for features such as brushes, paths, and patterns.

Q

quadtone A grayscale image to which are added three colors for a total of four colors (called *plates*).

R

radial blur An interesting effect that blurs an image in toward a center point or rotates it around a center point. The effect is similar to the photographic technique of making a zoom lens time exposure that creates a tunnel effect in toward the subject.

rasterize The process of creating pixel data from vector elements.

relief The strength of a textured filter effect as it is applied to the image. In a burlap filter, for example, the relief affects the perceived depth of the weave.

render layer To convert a type layer from the scalable, PostScript-based character format to a static, pixel-based format. The conversion is often necessary before other Photoshop effects can be applied.

resolution The detail within a digital image, as determined by the number of dots (or pixels) per inch.

RGB color model A color process using red, green, and blue color variables. This is the native format for digital files, as created from scanners and digital cameras. There are multiple RGB color models to choose from, including Adobe, sRGB, and Apple RGB. Each offers a specific color range, and care should be taken when deciding which model to use.

rollover A graphic that changes as you pass your mouse over a specific spot on the screen.

rotate To change the presentation of an image, as if by placing a print of the image on the desktop and spinning it—nothing about the image changes except the presentation.

S

sample point   The reference point that provides pixel data to determine how certain Photoshop tools operate. For example, the Clone Stamp tool uses a sample reference point to determine what pixel values it should paint into the image. The Background eraser also uses a sample point to determine which part of the image to erase.

scaling   The act of enlarging or reducing an image, layer, or effect. Although an entire image can be resized, scaling can also modify the size of a textured filter effect in relation to the image. In a burlap filter, for example, the scaling affects the coarseness of the weave.

scatter   The way the brush stroke spreads out from the line drawn by the mouse or pen. Scatter can be controlled with the Scattering options in the Brushes palette.

scratch disk   A Photoshop term referring to the system hard drive(s) that are used as a buffer for storing interim versions of images.

sharpening   A method that brings out additional detail in virtually all images except those created on the highest quality scanners. To sharpen an image in Photoshop, you use the Unsharp Mask filter.

slice   To divide a large image intended for the Web into smaller tiles that are assembled in a table as the page is loaded. These smaller tiles often load faster that one large image and are necessary if you want a portion of a large image to act as a rollover or an animation.

snapshot   An image state that resides in the History palette that was captured to represent a particular stage of image development. These history states are not effected by the History State value listed in Photoshop's General Preferences box, and they remain available for the current editing session until the image is closed and saved.

stroke   To draw an outline around a selected path. Stroking a path is useful for outlining a rectangle you want to use as a text box, for building buttons for the Web, or for outlining letterforms you may have saved as paths.

T

thumbnail   A small graphic that represents a larger image. Thumbnails are often used in palettes to give a visual history of the states in the image.

tonality   The grayscale values from 0 to 255 that differentiate an image's pixels. Tonality is black and white and shades of gray; tonality is one of the most expressive elements in an image. If you want to create a strong feeling in an image, consider exaggerating the tonality in some way.

tool preset   A user-defined set of tool parameters accessible through the Tools Preset palette. Options bar information, foreground color, and external palette information (where applicable) can be saved as part of a tool preset.

tracking   The spacing between entire lines of letters.

transform   To modify the position, scale, or proportions of a layer. Transforming a layer is useful for changing the size or placement of a layer, as well as for adding perspective or distortion.

transparency checkerboard grid   The checkerboard background that appears "through" an image when you have made some part of an image transparent. You can control the size and color of the checkerboard grid using the **Preferences** dialog boxes.

tritone   A grayscale image to which are added two colors for a total of three colors (or plates).

U-Z

variable compression   A feature that allows you to alter image compression and quality in different areas of the same image. You can focus more detail around a central character or image while allowing details to erode in unimportant areas such as the background or flat areas of color. The result is an optimized image that delivers higher quality and lower bandwidth.

vertical type   Text arranged in a descending vertical column down the image.

video alpha capability   A special-effect transparency technique available with certain video boards.

warp   A text effect that takes the idea of text on a path to a new level. This Photoshop feature allows you to distort the contents of an entire text layer, twisting, bloating, or stretching it into a wide range of effects. There are 15 different warping effects to choose from, and all allow bending as well as horizontal and vertical distortion.

work path   The "line" created whenever the Path tool begins drawing a path. The work path represents the "working" path that is in progress or under construction. After the path is saved, the new, named path replaces the work path.

Index

C

Rotate Canvas, 142-143
Save As, 86-89
Save For Web, 94-95
Save Optimized, 225
Save path, 191-193
Smooth Selection, 79
Stroke Path, 199
Texturizer, 246-247
TIFF Options, 87
Type Tool, 178-179
Unsharp Mask, 114-115
Variations, 122-123
Warp Text, 186-187
Web Photo Gallery, 234-235
ZigZag, 258-259

Direct Selection tool, 191

directional lighting effects, 243

disks, scratch disk preferences, 36, 45

display preferences, 32

distorting images
Liquify effect, 254-255
ripple effects, 258-259

dividing images, 224-225

Dodge tool, 112-113

dots per inch (dpi), 136

drawing shapes, 162-163

Duotone command (Mode menu), 133

Duotone Curve dialog box, 133

Duotone Options dialog box, 133

Duplicate Layer Set command (Layer menu), 211

duplicating. See copying

E

Edge Highlighter tool, silhouette effects, 144-145

Edit menu commands, 10
Color Settings, 22, 90
Define Custom Shape, 163
Fade, 238
Fade Halftone Pattern, 257
Fill, 239
Free Transform, 213
Transform, 213
Undo Paint Bucket, 169

editing paths, 194-195
curved paths, 193
straight-edge paths, 191

electric color effects, 131

Elliptical Marquee tool, 68-69

enabling. See activating

Engine pop-up menu (Color Settings dialog box), 26

enlarging images, 137

Eraser tool, 152-153

erasing
backgrounds, 154-157
images, 152-153

error handling, batch processing, 65

Expand Selection dialog box, 79

expanding
palettes, 14
selections, 79

exposure, 112-113

Extract command (Image menu), 144

Extract dialog box, 144-145

Eyedropper tool, 18, 106-107

F

faces, blemish corrections (Heal Brush tool), 147

Fade command (Edit menu), 238

Fade dialog box, 115

Fade Halftone Pattern command (Edit menu), 257

Feather Selection dialog box, 80

feathering, 80, 117

File Browser
content areas, 50
image folders, accessing, 50
images
rotating, 51
selecting, 51
opening, 50
repositioning, 51
thumbnail previews, 51

File menu commands, 10
Jump To, 9
Print Options, 90
Save As, 86
Save For Web, 94-95
Save Optimized, 225

files
annotating, 54-55
contact sheets, creating, 48-49
copying, 87
GIF
building for Web, 94-95
optimizing color sets, 96-97
transparencies, 98-99
JPEG
building for Web, 100-101
saving files as, 87
monitoring size of, 83

global color corrections, 124-125

glow effects
brush strokes, intensity of, 241
colors, selecting, 240
object selection, 199, 240

Gradient Editor, opening, 130, 174-175

Gradient tool, 172-175

gradients
applying, 172-173
creating, 174-175
reapplying, 173

Grain dialog box, 252-253

grain effects, simulating, 252-253

graphics. See images

Gray pop-up menu (Color Settings dialog box), 23-25

grayed-out commands, 13

Grayscale command (Mode menu), 132

grayscale images. See also tonality
converting to, 118-119
duotones
creating for print, 132-133
creating for Web, 130-131
mapping, 25
preferences, 23
quadtones
creating for print, 132-133
creating for Web, 131
tritones, creating for Web, 131-133

grid preferences, 35

Group Linked command (Layer menu), 208-209

Group with Previous command (Layer menu), 208-209

grouping
layers, 208-209
palettes, 15, 151
shortcuts, 208-209

guides
activating, 21
locking, 21
preferences, 20, 35
snap-to parameters, 21

H

Halftone Pattern dialog box, 256-257

halftone patterns, 256
blending modes, 257
color order, switching, 257
type selection, 257

Heal Brush tool
blemish corrections, 147
blending modes, 147
function of, 146
sample point settings, 146
selecting, 146
similarity to Clone tool, 146

help
Adobe.com Web site, 9
tool tips, 15

Help menu commands, 11
Adobe Online, 9
Top Issues, 13

hexadecimal colors, 17

hiding
icons, 55
paths, brush strokes, 241

History brush, 57, 158-159

History command (Window menu), 56

History palette
blending modes, 239
brushing in filter effects, 260-261
copying files, 57
opening, 56
preferences, 56
reverting to previous state, 57
taking snapshots, 56

horizontal text distortion, 187

Horizontal Type Mask tool, 184-185

Hue slider (Color Picker), 16

Hue/Saturation command (Adjust menu), 127

Hue/Saturation dialog box, 127

I

icons, hiding, 55

Image Map Select tool, 226

Image Map tool, 226

image maps
creating, 226-227
preferences, 41

Image menu commands
Adjustments, 239
Canvas Size, 138
Extract, 144
Image Size, 90, 136
Liquify, 254
Rotate Canvas, 142

Image Size command (Image menu), 90, 136

reapplying gradients, 173

Reconstruct tool, 255

Rectangular Marquee tool, 68-69

relief setting (texture), 247

renaming files, 86

repositioning
File Browser, 51
lighting effects, 242

Resize button, 14

resizing
canvas, 138-139
images, 136-137
palettes, 14

resolution
dots per inch (dpi), 136
reducing, 137

reverting
back to original images, 255
to black and white, 19
to previous state, 57

RGB pop-up menu (Color Settings dialog box), 23-24

ripple effects
implosion settings, 259
ZigZag filter, 258-259

rollover animations
creating (JavaScript), 232-233
layer states, 233

Rotate Canvas command (Image menu), 142

Rotate Canvas dialog box, 142-143

rotating images, 51, 142-143

Rubber Stamp tool (Clone Stamp), 160-161

rulers
activating, 20
displaying, 224
preferences, 20, 34

Rulers command (View menu), 20, 224

S

sampling colors, 18

sampling options (Background Eraser), 155

saturating color intensity, 112-113

Save As command (File menu), 86

Save As dialog box, 86-89

Save For Web command (File menu), 94-95

Save For Web dialog box, 94-95

Save Optimized command (File menu), 225

Save Optimized dialog box, 225

Save Path dialog box, 191-193

Save Selection command (Select menu), 82

saving
color tables, 97
files
in other formats, 86-89
preferences, 30-31
luminosity, 129
paths, 191-193
selections, 82-83
transparency, 205

scaling texture effects, 246

scatter effect, brush behavior, 165

scratch disk preferences
ImageReady, 45
Photoshop, 36

Select menu commands, 11
Color Range, 72, 126
Inverse, 79, 240
Load Selection, 83
Save Selection, 82
Similar, 80
Transform Selection, 81

selecting
colors
background colors, 18
Color palette, 19
foreground colors, 18
Swatches palette, 19
Heal Brush tool, 146
image areas
color ranges, 72-73
Elliptical Marquee tool, 68-69
Lasso tool, 71
loading selections, 82-83
Magnetic Lasso tool, 71
modifying selections, 78-81
paths, 76-77
Polygonal Lasso tool, 70-71
previewing selections, 73
Quick Mask tool, 74-75
Rectangular Marquee tool, 68-69
saving selections, 82-83
Type Mask tool, 75
Pantone-type colors, 17
paths, 194
tools
ImageReady, 9
Photoshop, 8

**subtle color changes,
128-129**

subtracting from selections, 78

**Swatches command
(Window menu), 19**

Swatches palette, 19

switching

foreground and background colors, 19

between Photoshop and ImageReady, 7-9

T

tables

2-up comparison tables, 95

4-up comparison tables, 95, 100

color tables, saving, 97

target resolution, 136-137

tech notes, viewing, 13

text

3D text, 181

bevel effect, 180

depth settings, 181

emboss effect, 180

shadow effect, 181

adding to images, 178-179

annotations, 54-55

circular effect, 187

circular type, 187

filtered text effects, 184-185

warping, 186-187

texture

adding, 246-247

light direction, 247

noise texture, 250-251

photo grain, 252-253

relief settings, 247

scaling, 246

types, selecting, 246-247

**Texture command (Filter
menu), 246**

**Texturizer dialog box,
246-247**

**three-dimensional text (3D),
181**

bevel effect, 180

depth settings, 181

emboss effect, 180

shadow effect, 181

TIFF, saving files as, 87-89

TIFF Options dialog box, 87

**tile sizes, modifying (Pattern
Maker), 171**

tolerance settings

Background Eraser, 155-157

Magic Wand, 81

Paint Bucket tool, 169

**tonal ranges, optimizing,
108-109**

tonality

converting to grayscale, 118-119

increasing contrast, 110-111

lightening and darkening images, 112-113

optimizing tonal range, 108-109

pixel values, 106-107

saturating and desaturating intensity, 112-113

**Tool Presets command
(Window menu), 58-59**

toolbox, 6-9

tools

Add Anchor Point, 195

Audio Annotation, 55

Background Eraser, 154-157

Burn, 112-113

Clone Stamp, 160-161

Color Sampler, 107

Convert Point, 195

Crop, 140-141

Custom Shape, 163

Delete Anchor Point, 195

Direct Selection, 191

Dodge, 112-113

Elliptical Marquee, 68-69

Eraser, 152-153

Eyedropper, 18, 106-107

Gradient, 172-175

History Brush, 158-159

Image Map, 226

Image Map Select, 226

Lasso, 71

Magic Erase, 154-157

Magic Wand, 156

Magnetic Lasso, 71

Notes, 54-55

Paint Bucket, 168-169

Paintbrush, 150-151

Path Component Selection, 191

Pattern Stamp, 161

Pen, creating paths, 190-193

Polygonal Lasso, 70-71

presets

creating, 58-59

saving, 59

Quick Mask, 74-75

Rectangular Marquee, 68-69

selecting

ImageReady, 9

Photoshop, 8

Sponge, 112-113

Type, 178-179

Zoom, 52